Financial Statements for Smaller Companies

A guide to practice and the FRSSE

Mark A Lennon MSC, ACA

Isobel N Sharp BSC, CA, ACIS

Arthur Andersen

The Institute of Chartered Accountants
in England and Wales
Gloucester House
399 Silbury Boulevard
Central Milton Keynes
MK9 2HL
Tel: 01908 248000

This book is based on legislation and regulation extant at 28 February 1997. Whilst considerable care has been taken in the preparation of this book, no responsibility for loss occasioned to any person acting or refraining from action as a result of any material in this publication can be accepted by the authors or publishers.

British Library Cataloguing-in-Publication Data
A catalogue record for this book is available from the British Library

ISBN 1 85355 728 5

Typeset by York House Typographic Ltd
Printed in Great Britain by Biddles Ltd, Guildford and King's Lynn

Financial Statements for Smaller Companies

A guide to practice and the FRSSE

Contents

Contents

Chapter Four
The FRSSE

Chapter Five
Policies and Profit and Loss Account Matters

Chapter Six
Balance Sheet and Notes Matters

Chapter Seven
Modified and Abbreviated Accounts

Chapter Eight
Implications for Auditors and Accountants

Appendices

Preface

If ever invited to write some guidance on preparing financial statements for smaller companies, first reactions might be to say yes, that should be relatively straightforward. Our advice, based on our recent experience, is don't do it.

In seeking to set out the current regime for smaller companies' financial statements and how that might change in the immediate future, we have been struck by the complexity of the task. Preparers of such accounts are faced with questions such as which rules to follow, which filing options to take and whether an audit is necessary. The matrix of the various options produces a landscape for smaller companies which is much more complex than that for the larger public companies in the land, who simply follow the, albeit lengthy, list of rules.

Yet small companies' financial statements are at a threshold. Small companies now have a bespoke schedule in company law and within, it is hoped, a few months a new Financial Reporting Standard for Smaller Entities. With the Accounting Standards Board set to establish a permanent advisory committee to review that Financial Reporting Standard, there will be a focus for small company matters. These are developments to be welcomed. But, as with most change there is some pain before we reach the border of the promised land. Our purpose in writing this book is to assist preparers, auditors and others to understand the present regime, how it is likely to change and the consequences for financial statements for smaller companies.

Finally, as they say in all the best text books, the following are not responsible for any errors or omissions. We are extremely grateful to our secretarial team of Kay Champ and Jayne Payne for their hard work and infinite patience in dealing with the various drafts. We are also very grateful to our colleague, Nick Crockford, for his assistance in checking the content.

Mark A Lennon
Isobel N Sharp
February 1997

Chapter One

Introduction

One size fits all?

1.1 Small companies are a relatively new creation in company law. Introduced in the Companies Act 1981, which implemented the EU Fourth Company Law Directive, a small company was then defined as one in which for the financial year and the one immediately preceding it at least two of the following three conditions applied:

- its turnover did not exceed £1.4 million;
- its balance sheet total did not exceed £0.7 million; and
- its average weekly number of employees did not exceed 50.

But the debate over differential reporting has raged for at least 100 years. Over this time, people have argued that there should be different rules to reflect the different nature or size of companies.

1.2 The first great divide came in 1907 when the Companies Act of that year introduced private companies. The reason for doing so was to allow such private companies not to file their balance sheets with their annual returns because, using the words in the Committee's Report at that time, 'as they do not appeal to the public for subscriptions, there is no need for publishing their private affairs, and . . . the disclosure involved in the filing of the documents would, or might, seriously prejudice their interests'.

1.3 By the time of the 1948 Companies Act, that exemption was considered too sweeping and so that Act introduced the 'exempt private company'. A company qualified as such, and was thus exempt from filing its balance sheet, if it met three conditions:

1 principally that no body corporate was a holder of any shares or debentures in the putative exempt private company. Detailed rules on shareholdings were set out in Schedule 7 to the Act, the principal thrust of which was to stop private companies whose shares were held by public companies being exempt from disclosure;
2 the number of persons holding debentures were not more than 50; and
3 no body corporate was a director of the company and neither the

company nor any of its directors were party or privy to any arrangement 'whereby the policy of the company is capable of being determined by persons other than the directors, members and debenture holders or trustees for debenture holders'.

1.4   The next major step was the publication of the Jenkins Report in 1962. It recommended the abolition of the distinction between exempt and non-exempt private companies. So disclosure of financial information became identified with the comment that 'disclosure is the price to be paid for limited liability'. When the 1967 Companies Act implemented this element of the Jenkins Report, it required all limited companies to file full accounts, while allowing certain limited companies to reregister as unlimited ones to avoid this requirement. However, the 1967 Act permitted non-disclosure of certain items in the accounts for shareholders, which were also the accounts to be filed with the Registrar of Companies, for certain companies. For example, a company which was neither a holding company nor a subsidiary and whose turnover did not exceed £50,000 was exempt from disclosing its turnover for the financial year. So began differential reporting in earnest.

The early accounting standards

1.5   In 1970, the UK's first accounting standard setting body began work. Established as a Committee of the Institute of Chartered Accountants in England and Wales, which had hitherto issued non-mandatory 'Recommendations on accounting principles', this Accounting Standards Steering Committee, on which members of other accountancy bodies participated, issued its first Statement of Standard Accounting Practice (SSAP 1) *Accounting for the results of associated companies* in January 1971. The general rule which the Committee adopted was that standards were to be applied to all financial statements intended to give a true and fair view of the financial position and profit or loss. But, exceptions to that general rule were given in future standards. SSAP 3 *Earnings per share* issued in February 1972 was applicable only to listed companies. When a Statement of Source and Application of Funds was introduced into financial statements in August 1975, the relevant accounting standard, SSAP 10, provided an exemption for companies with turnover or gross income of less than £25,000 per annum.

1.6   The next controversial accounting standard, in which application to smaller companies was an issue, was SSAP 16 *Current cost accounting* issued in April 1980. By this time, the Accounting Standards Steering Committee had been transformed into the Accounting Standards Committee, which was constituted as a creature of the six principal accountancy bodies in the UK and Ireland. In SSAP 16, exemption was given from the need to prepare current cost accounts for companies which did not have any class of share or loan capital listed on the Stock Exchange and which satisfied at least two of the following three criteria:

1 a turnover of less than £5 million per annum;
2 a balance sheet total at the commencement of the relevant accounting period of less than £2.5 million as shown in the historical cost accounts; and
3 the average number of employees in the UK or Ireland of less than 250.

Exemptions were also given for certain classes of company, including most wholly-owned subsidiaries and charities, building societies, friendly societies, trade unions and pension funds.

The small company in law

1.7 As previously noted, it was the 1981 Companies Act which divided private companies amongst those which were small, medium-sized and the rest. Prior to that Act, the government had published a Green Paper *Company accounting and disclosure* in September 1979. It had two major proposals for small companies. The first was to reduce significantly the amount of information to be disclosed by what it then termed the 'proprietary company'. The second major question was the possibility of an independent review of the accounts for small companies, instead of an audit. As history now shows, it took a further 15 years for some exemption from audit to be given to active companies. But the 1981 Act gave statutory effect to reducing the disclosure requirements for the accounts filed with the Registrar of Companies for small and medium-sized companies and limited the information to be disclosed in the accounts of companies for certain specific items.

1.8 With the clear classification of companies according to size in company law and the increasing number and complexity of accounting standards in the 1980s and 1990s, so the debate over establishing a clear set of rules for larger companies, popularly referred to as big GAAP, and a set of accounting rules for smaller companies, little GAAP, continued in earnest. The development of the debate on the application of accounting standards to smaller entities is discussed in Chapter 3, while Chapter 2 sets out the present legal requirements affecting small companies' financial statements.

Chapter Two

Company Law and Smaller Companies

Introduction

2.1 The Companies Act 1985 (the 'Act') requires the directors of all companies to prepare financial statements for each financial year. These should contain a balance sheet and profit and loss account which respectively give a true and fair view of the company's state of affairs as at the end of the financial year and of its profit or loss for the year.

2.2 The financial statements are produced for the shareholders, or members, of the company. The directors are responsible for sending financial statements to the members who will, in accordance with custom, formally approve them at an Annual General Meeting (unless the members have elected to dispense with such meetings). Certain other parties, such as debenture holders, may be entitled to receive the financial statements and attend the meeting at which they are due to be approved. The directors are also required to send a set of financial statements to be filed by the Registrar of Companies. These financial statements are then on public record and copies can be obtained, for a fee, by any interested party. As explained below such accounts for filing may be the same as those prepared and sent to shareholders but in certain circumstances, which are explained in Chapter 7, the directors may take advantage of certain exemptions in the Act and omit some accounting information from the public record.

2.3 The accounting provisions in the Act have developed over many years from sources as diverse as the recommendations of UK company law committees, attempts to deal with specific problems or perceived abuses and the implementation of EU Company Law Directives. The proliferation of accounting standards has also impacted, both directly and indirectly, on the volume of disclosure required under the Act. Indirectly, the requirement for accounts to be true and fair requires adherence to accounting standards which in recent years have become more detailed and complex. Directly, many requirements of accounting standards have been introduced into the Act's schedules detailing the requirements for financial statements as follows:

Schedule

4   Form and content of company accounts
4A   Form and content of group accounts
5   Disclosure of information: related undertakings
6   Disclosure of information: emoluments and other benefits of directors
     and others
7   Matters to be dealt with the directors' report
8   Form and content of accounts prepared by small companies
8A   Form and content of abbreviated accounts of small companies
     delivered to registrar.

2.4   A major consequence of the evolution of company law has therefore
been an inexorable increase in the required extent of disclosures and greater
uniformity in the financial statements of companies, irrespective of their
size.

2.5   Not surprisingly this has led to something of a backlash, with the result
that as part of the Deregulation Initiative, the Department of Trade and
Industry (DTI) began a review of the impact of statutory accounting requirements, with an overall aim of minimising the burdens imposed on
companies, while at the same time ensuring that the information provided
met the reasonable needs of users of accounts.

2.6   Unfortunately the end product is confused and confusing. The following sections on recent changes in company law affecting small companies
seek to explain the present hotchpotch of requirements.

Modified and abbreviated accounts

2.7   Both small and medium-sized companies are permitted to omit from
the accounts prepared for filing with the Registrar of Companies certain
aspects of the statutory accounts drawn up and sent to members. Such
financial statements are usually termed 'abbreviated accounts'. In addition
small and medium-sized companies meeting certain conditions may be able
to take advantage of disclosure exemptions in the financial statements drawn
up for the shareholders. Such financial statements are usually termed 'modified accounts'. As explained more fully in Chapter 7, the concessions
available are confusing; they are also subject to periodic changes.

2.8   Significant revisions to the requirements for the financial statements to
be drawn up by small and medium-sized companies were introduced by SI
1992 No 2452, The Companies Act 1985 (Accounts of Small and Medium-
sized Enterprises and Publication of Accounts in ECUs) Regulations 1992.
These regulations revised Schedule 8 to the 1985 Companies Act dealing
with the content of accounts which could be prepared for filing, (which

rather confusingly were then generally termed 'modified accounts' although as noted above this phrase now denotes accounts taking advantage of disclosure exemptions prepared for shareholders). The principal changes introduced by SI 1992 No 2452, which entailed the restructuring of Schedule 8 and the introduction of certain disclosure exemptions, for small companies' accounts for members are set out in Annex 1 to this chapter.

2.9 In July 1996 the DTI published further proposed amendments to Schedule 8 which were enacted in March 1997. The revised requirements of Schedules 8 and 8A and the modified and abbreviated accounts drawn up taking advantage of the regime therein are discussed in more depth in Chapter 7.

Audit of accounts

2.10 One of the more far reaching changes affecting small companies was introduced by SI 1994 No 1935, The Companies Act 1985 (Audit Exemption) Regulations 1994. This abolished the statutory requirement for the audit of accounts of those small companies which meet the conditions within sections 249A to E of the Companies Act 1985. By this one measure some 500,000 smaller companies were no longer required to have their financial statements audited. Two subsets of company were established, being:

- those with a balance sheet total of no more than £1.4m and an annual turnover of no more than £350,000 (£250,000 for charities) which no longer require an audit but are required to obtain a report on their financial statements from a qualified independent accountant; whereas
- those with a balance sheet total of no more than £1.4m and a turnover of no more than £90,000 are exempt from either an audit or the report from an independent accountant.

2.11 The exemption from audit is not available to a company where members with more than 10 per cent of any class of shares have requested the company to obtain an audit, or to a company which at any time in the financial year is one of the following:

- a parent or a subsidiary;
- a public company;
- a banking or insurance company;
- a company enrolled on the list maintained by the Insurance Brokers Registration Council;
- an authorised person, or appointed representative, under the Financial Services Act 1986; or
- a special registered body as defined in section 117(1) of the Trade Union and Labour Relations Act 1992 or an employers' association as defined in section 122 of that Act.

2.12 Whilst this measure to exempt companies from audit undoubtedly removed certain burdens from smaller companies, it did not impact on the form which their financial statements should take nor reduce the compliance costs directly associated with accounts preparation. The financial statements of companies taking advantage of the audit exemption provisions still need to be drawn up in accordance with the requirements of the Companies Act and accounting standards.

2.13 Furthermore, whilst it is only some two years since the new audit exemption regime was introduced, the DTI is currently considering further changes. In January 1997, it published, for comment by 5 March 1997, its Consultative Document *Small companies audit exemptions: consultation on proposed amendments*. This paper proposes:

- to increase the threshold for total audit exemption to £350,000 and thus to drop the requirement for a report from a qualified independent accountant;
- to make technical amendments to the treatment of dormant companies so that they are entitled to automatic exemption without having to pass a special resolution; and
- to allow companies in small groups whose total turnover does not exceed the £350,000 threshold to be eligible for audit exemption.

While the DTI paper does not give any clues as to the possible timetable for introduction of these changes, it notes that there have been informal consultations on these proposals in 1996. These consultations, together with the relatively short period available for comment, may be indications that the DTI has these proposed amendments on a fast track.

Accounting simplifications

2.14 A recent minor milestone in the process of revising the required disclosure within the accounts prepared by companies was introduced by SI 1996 No 189, The Companies Act 1985 (Miscellaneous Accounting Amendments) Regulations 1996. These regulations ('the 1996 Regulations') implemented proposals which were contained in two DTI consultative documents issued in 1995:

- *Accounting simplifications*, which sought views on 50 proposals to simplify specific Companies Act 1985 accounting requirements; and
- *Tackling late payment: stating payment policies in the directors' report*, which contained proposals to require public companies, and large companies in groups headed by public companies, to state their payment policies in their directors' reports.

2.15 The various accounting simplifications introduced by the 1996 Regulations are tabulated in Annex 2 to this chapter. They apply to all limited companies, regardless of their size or business sector. Generally speaking the revisions are uncontentious and relatively minor. The consequent relaxation from accounting disclosures, in the main effective for year ends ending after 2 February 1996, will therefore not prove substantial in most cases. The revisions also remove certain anomalies relating to changing a company's accounting reference date, extend the availability of exemptions from audit and amend certain of the accounting provisions relating to insurance companies.

Late payment

2.16 Late payment is an issue which is frequently cited as an economic burden on small businesses. To tackle late payment, the 1996 Regulations introduced a new requirement for the directors' report of a public company, or a company which did not qualify as small or medium-sized and was at any time in the financial year a member of a group headed by a public company, to state the company's policy in respect of the payment of creditors. In June 1996 the DTI issued a further Consultative Document, *Tackling late payment: stating payment practice in the directors' report*, proposing disclosure within the directors' report of creditor days as a measure of a company's payment practice. This again applies solely to public companies and companies within a group headed up by a public company, which do not qualify as small or medium-sized. Whilst the disclosure requirements do not affect small companies, the thinking behind them is that the publication of such details will bring benefits to small companies by 'shaming' large companies into paying more promptly. Further changes to this regime have been introduced in a SI laid before Parliament in January1997. Larger companies will now have to give creditor days statistics in all directors' reports with effect from 24 March 1997.

Future changes

2.17 The June 1995 Consultative Document, *Accounting simplifications* noted above suggested an increase in the financial ceilings for qualification as small and medium-sized. A number of reasons for raising the thresholds were advanced, for example to ensure that UK companies were not at a competitive disadvantage compared with their European equivalents, to allow more companies to take advantage of available concessions and to relieve business of unnecessary burdens. However, the DTI concluded that any changes to the financial ceilings defining small and medium-sized companies would need to take account of the work that a Working Party of the Consultative Committee of Accountancy Bodies (CCAB) was undertaking on the application of accounting standards to small companies (this was the work being carried out on the FRSSE). Accordingly no changes were made to the ceilings at the time of introducing the regulations in 1996.

2.18 The *Accounting simplifications* document also sought views on the level of accounting disclosure required of small companies to improve the DTI's understanding of the problems faced by such companies, with a view to publishing a summary of the views expressed. Other ideas which have been mooted at the DTI and which are described below include:

- introducing a standard form of accounts for small companies; and
- having a more structured approach to the disclosures required in the Companies Act. One suggestion along these lines was that there should be a basic schedule for small companies, with additional schedules for larger or more complex companies. This proposal received considerable support and, as detailed below, has now been enacted in SI 1997 No 220.

A standard form of accounts

2.19 The DTI published its proposals for a standard form of accounts for small companies in a Consultative Document, *Small company accounts: a possible standard format*, in September 1996.

2.20 The draft standard format is aimed at small companies filing abbreviated accounts with the Registrar of Companies. It would therefore not be available for use by companies which are unable to take advantage of the exemptions contained in Schedule 8 to the Companies Act 1985 (i.e., public companies, large or medium-sized companies as defined by the Companies Act, banking or insurance companies, companies which are authorised persons under the Financial Services Act 1986, companies which are members of an ineligible group, or parent companies which do not head a small group).

2.21 A significant feature, and serious flaw, of the proposed format is that it is based purely on company law requirements and makes no reference to accounting standards. Accounting standards need to be applied for the accounts to be true and fair, which is a Companies Act requirement. They cannot therefore be ignored in practice as they have been for the present DTI exercise.

2.22 One possible solution would be for the financial statements to be drawn up in accordance with all relevant accounting standards and for there to be a requirement for the inclusion of a statement, along the lines of the requirement in paragraph 36A of Schedule 4 (which currently does not apply to small companies) confirming that the accounts have been prepared in accordance with applicable accounting standards and giving particulars and the reasons for any material departure from the standards.

2.23   In addition, and as discussed later in the book, one of the key elements of the FRSSE is the requirement to make sufficient disclosures to explain non-routine accounting transactions so that a true and fair view can be given. The adoption of a standard form approach to some extent goes against the spirit of this aspect of the FRSSE. Some may suggest that there should be an additional box or page for necessary additional disclosures to be made, but in practice it is difficult to imagine many companies providing such additional information.

2.24   This said, a standard format would be particularly useful for companies which are below the audit requirement threshold. The directors in such circumstances may prepare accounts without the assistance of external accountants or auditors; a format would be a useful checklist and accounts preparation template for the disclosures needed in the accounts.

Restructuring the Schedules to the Companies Act

2.25   In a separate initiative, to find a more structured approach to the Schedules within the Companies Act, the DTI issued in July 1996 a Consultative Document, *Accounting simplifications: re-arrangements to Companies Act Schedule on small company accounts*. These proposals have recently been enacted in SI 1997 No 220.

2.26   Hitherto, small companies have been able to take advantage of exemptions from disclosure available to them within Schedule 8 to the Companies Act 1985. As explained in Chapter 7 the form which the exemptions previously took was that certain of the Schedule 4 disclosures could be dispensed with. The disadvantage of this structure lay in the fact that a company wishing to avail itself of the exemptions in Schedule 8 must first have gone through the provisions for the generality of companies to identify those from which it could be exempt and those which it still needed to apply.

2.27   To remedy this situation the July 1996 Consultative Document included draft regulations which show the standard small company requirements, rather than presenting the requirements on an exemptions basis. The draft regulations did not propose any significant amendments or reductions in the required disclosures for small companies and, whilst it included the proposal to revise section 246 (so that, as explained in Chapter 8, the accounts of small companies must be true and fair, as well as comply with Schedule 8), the intention was to preserve the right of small companies to:

- draw up Schedule 8 accounts only; or
- add additional Schedule 4 requirements to the Schedule 8 minimum; or
- draw up full Schedule 4 accounts.

2.28 The only other amendments of note proposed in the Consultative Document were those which seek to remedy defects in, or make consequential amendments arising from, SI 1996 No 189, The Companies Act 1985 (Miscellaneous Accounting Amendments) Regulations 1996 discussed above. The provisions of SI 1996 No 189 are summarised in Annex 2 to this chapter.

The new Schedule 8

2.29 SI 1997 No 220, The Companies Act 1985 (Accounts of Small and Medium-sized Companies and Minor Accounting Amendments) Regulations 1997, was laid before Parliament on 5 February 1997. The key implementation date is 24 March 1997. For companies preparing financial statements for accounting periods ending on or before 24 March 1997, they may do so without regard to the new SI; in other words those accounts may be based on the old rules. For accounting periods ending thereafter, in effect 31 March 1997 year ends onwards, regard should be had to the new SI. In particular, this means that small companies will no longer have to consider various Schedules to the 1985 Act; instead they will follow the revised Schedule 8 (i.e., Schedule I to SI 1997 No 220) which sets out the requirements for the form and content of accounts by small companies. The new Schedule 8A (Schedule 2 to the SI) then sets out the requirements for small companies' abbreviated accounts prepared for filing purposes.

2.30 Appendix 3 sets out a disclosure checklist for a small company. This includes references to the legislation pre SI 1997 No 220 and to the new revised Schedules 8 and 8A.

Outstanding developments

2.31 As noted elsewhere in this chapter there are two DTI proposals affecting small companies which are outstanding. The first is the change proposed to the audit exemption regime. The second is the standard form for accounts.

2.32 To some extent the need for a standard form has been alleviated by the new Schedules which can act as a checklist for accounts preparation. But users may still find helpful a form which puts the law and the relevant accounting standards into effect. As it will be later in 1997 before the FRSSE is finalised progress on the standard form will hopefully take account of the FRSSE in its final form and therefore, to be a useful and practical tool, be later rather than sooner.

Annex 1

Table of Principal 1992 Company Law Amendments

Company law amendments Small and medium-sized company accounts (SI 1992 No 2452)		
Section	*Subject*	*Effect*
s242B	Delivery and publication of accounts.	Permitted the annual accounts to be shown in ECUs.
s246 (1A), (1B) and Schedule 8	Exemptions for small and medium-sized companies.	Modified the requirements of Part VII of the Companies Act 1985 and Schedule 8 in respect of the content of the annual accounts and directors' reports of small companies. The exemptions apply not only to the individual accounts of such companies but also to the group accounts where a small company prepares them. The detailed exemptions made available under the revisions to Schedule 8 are detailed in Chapter 8. The amendments restructured Schedule 8 so that: Part I – refers to small company accounts Part II – refers to small company directors' report Part III – refers to exemptions for small and medium-sized company accounts prepared for filing.
s247	Qualification of company as small or medium-sized.	Raised the thresholds for small and medium-sized companies (previous figures in brackets): *Small company* turnover – £2.8m (£2m) balance sheet total – £1.4m (£975,000). *Medium-sized company* turnover – £11.2m (£8m) balance sheet total – £5.6m (£3.9m).

Section	Subject	Effect
s249	Qualification of group as small or medium-sized.	Raised the thresholds for small or medium-sized groups (previous figures in brackets): *Small group* Aggregate turnover: – net £2.8m (£2m) – gross £3.36m (£2.4m). Aggregate balance sheet total: – net £1.4m (£1m) – gross £1.68m (£1.2m) *Medium-sized group* Aggregate turnover: – net £11.2m (£8m) – gross £13.44m (£9.6m). Aggregate balance sheet total: – net £5.6m (£3.9m) – gross £6.72m (£4.7m). The regulations also addressed two minor defects in the Companies Act 1985: – correcting the position whereby certain small and medium-sized companies were technically precluded from filing abbreviated accounts with the Registrar of Companies; and – restoring the exemption for small companies from the requirement to disclose the auditors' remuneration in the abbreviated accounts which may be delivered to the Registrar (the exemption was inadvertently removed by the Companies Act 1989).

Annex 2

Table of Accounting Simplifications

Accounting simplifications – the 1996 Regulations (SI 1996 No 189)		
Part VII of the Companies Act		
Section	*Subject*	*Effect*
s224	Accounting reference periods and accounting reference date.	Where a company is incorporated on or after 1 April 1996, its first Accounting Reference Date (ARD) will be the end of the month in which the anniversary of the date of incorporation falls. A company can elect to amend its ARD under s225.
s225	Alteration of accounting reference date.	The revisions simplify the rules relating to changing a company's ARD. The previous restriction, that changes in relation to a previous accounting reference period can be made only where it is to permit the ARD to coincide with that of a parent or subsidiary undertaking, will no longer apply. In addition, the distinction between previous and current accounting reference periods are largely repealed, although it remains the case that to change a previous (i.e., expired) accounting reference period the period for filing must not itself have expired.

It continues to be the case that the accounting reference period cannot be extended within five years of an extension of an earlier period unless certain conditions are met. These conditions are that the company is a subsidiary or parent of another company and the change is being effected to make the company's ARD coincide with a parent or subsidiary. The definition of parent or subsidiary in this context has now been extended from UK companies to a subsidiary or parent of an European Economic Area (EEA) undertaking. |

Part VII of the Companies Act (continued)		
Section	*Subject*	*Effect*
s228	Exemption for parent companies from preparing group accounts.	Under s228 a company is exempt from the requirement to prepare group accounts if it is itself a subsidiary of a parent established in the EEC provided certain conditions are met. Such conditions include disclosure of details of the parent. The revision to s228 means that where the parent is incorporated in GB the country of registration (e.g., England and Wales or Scotland) need not be given (the country of incorporation will continue to be required).
s246	Exemptions for small companies.	The statements by a company that it has taken advantage of the disclosure exemptions relating to the accounts and the directors' report applicable to small companies under s246(1A) and (1B) continue to be required above the signature of the directors or the company secretary but no longer need to be **immediately** above the signatures.
s247	Qualification of company as small or medium-sized.	One of the small and medium-size criteria is based on average numbers of employees. The average henceforth should be determined on a monthly basis rather than a weekly basis.
ss248 and 237	Exemption from preparing group accounts for small and medium-sized groups.	Where a company had taken advantage of the exemption from preparing group accounts, a separate report by the auditors confirming that the company was entitled to the exemption was required to be attached to the accounts. In future, auditors will be required to provide a report only if they believe the directors should not have taken advantage of the exemption.

Part VII of the Companies Act (continued)		
Section	*Subject*	*Effect*
s249B	Exemption from audit.	A company which is a subsidiary undertaking has not been able to take advantage of the exemption from audit available under s249A (for small companies with turnover below £90,000). A company will now be able to take advantage of the exemption, provided that throughout the period it has been dormant within the meaning of s250. The statements by a company to the effect that it has taken advantage of the exemptions from audit under s249 continue to be required at the foot of the balance sheet but no longer need be **immediately** above the director's signature.
s250	Dormant companies.	The exemption from appointing auditors, available to dormant private companies under s250 is extended to dormant public companies. The statement by a company that it has been dormant throughout the period no longer need be **immediately** above the signature but is still required at the foot of the balance sheet and directors' report.
Schedule 4 – Form and content of accounts		
Paragraph	*Subject*	*Effect*
paras 3(7), 51	Proposed dividends.	Require disclosure of the aggregate amount of proposed dividends on the face of the profit and loss account if not given in the notes (previously required in notes).
para 34	Revaluation reserve.	Makes it clear that amounts may be transferred to and from revaluation reserve in respect of the tax on any gain or loss credited or debited to that reserve, e.g., deferred tax on a revalued asset intended for disposal.
para 39	Allotments of shares.	Reasons for an allotment are no longer required to be disclosed.

	Schedule 4 – Form and content of accounts (continued)	
Paragraph	*Subject*	*Effect*
para 41	Debentures.	Reasons for the issue of debentures are no longer required to be disclosed. Details of power to reissue redeemed debentures are no longer required to be given.
para 45	Listed investments.	An analysis of listed investments between those listed on a recognised investment exchange (other than an overseas exchange) and those otherwise listed is no longer required.
para 48	Maturity of creditors.	It will still be a requirement to state the aggregate amount in respect of the following for each item within creditors: • repayable (other than by instalments) in more than five years; and • repayable by instalments any of which fall due after five years. However it is no longer a statutory requirement to give the amounts due for payment after five years (although this is required by FRS 4 para 33).
para 50	Capital expenditure commitments.	Capital expenditure authorised by the directors but not contracted for is no longer required to be disclosed.
para 53(2)	Analysis of interest expense.	The analysis of interest on loans, between loans repayable other than by instalments which fall due in more than five years and loans repayable by instalments, is no longer required. Interest need only be analysed between bank borrowings and other loans.
para 53(3)	Amount set aside for redemption of loans and share capital.	No longer required.
para 53(4)	Income from listed investments.	No longer required.

	Schedule 4 – Form and content of accounts (continued)	
Paragraph	*Subject*	*Effect*
para 53(5)	Income from rents.	No longer required.
para 53(6)	Charge in respect of hire of plant and machinery.	No longer required.
para 54	Tax.	No longer required to disclose basis on which charge to UK tax is computed.
para 55	Classes of business.	No longer required to disclose profit or loss before tax attributable to classes of business.
para 56	Particulars of staff.	Average numbers employed to be based on monthly rather than weekly numbers.
para 59	Amounts owed to/by group undertakings.	No longer required to analyse amounts between owed to/by subsidiaries and owed to/by parent and fellow subsidiaries.
para 94	Definition of pension costs.	Brought into line with practice of SSAP 24 cost.
	Schedule 4A – Group accounts	
Paragraph	*Subject*	*Effect*
para 1	Auditors' remuneration.	Makes it clear that s390A(3) should be applied as if the group were a single undertaking, i.e., the auditors' remuneration is that of all auditors and not just those of the parent undertaking.
para 13	Acquisitions.	It is no longer necessary to disclose the profit or loss of an acquired entity for its previous financial year and the period from the beginning of its financial year to the date of acquisition.
para 14	Goodwill written off.	Clarifies that the disclosure of the amount of cumulative goodwill written off does not include goodwill which has been written off through the profit and loss account in any year.

Schedule 5 – Companies not required to prepare group accounts		
Paragraph	*Subject*	*Effect*
para 1	Country of registration for GB subsidiaries.	The country of registration (i.e., England and Wales or Scotland) for GB subsidiaries need no longer be disclosed.
para 3	Financial information about subsidiaries.	The existing exemption from this disclosure where group accounts are not prepared by virtue of s228, is extended to subsidiaries which have been included by equity accounting.
para 4	Financial years of subsidiaries.	Where the year end of a subsidiary differs from its parent, this fact now needs to be disclosed only where financial information about subsidiaries is required to be given. It is no longer necessary to disclose the reasons for having different year ends.
para 5	Further financial information about subsidiaries.	The requirement to provide information in certain circumstances about qualifications in subsidiaries' accounts is repealed. The requirement to disclose in certain circumstances the valuation of subsidiaries by the equity method is repealed.
para 6	Debentures held by subsidiaries.	The disclosures surrounding debentures of a company held by its subsidiaries are no longer required.
paras 7, 8	Information about holdings in non-subsidiary undertakings.	Information about 10 per cent investments no longer need be given: the relevant disclosure threshold is raised to 20 per cent. The country of registration (i.e., England and Wales or Scotland) of GB undertaking need not be given.
para 10	Merger relief.	The disclosures, previously required when s131(2) merger relief has been applied on the allotment of shares, no longer apply.
para 11	Identification of parent undertaking drawing up accounts for a larger group.	If the parent is incorporated in GB its country of registration (i.e., England and Wales or Scotland) no longer needs to be disclosed.

Schedule 5 – Companies not required to prepare group accounts (continued)		
Paragraph	*Subject*	*Effect*
para 12	Identification of ultimate parent undertaking.	If the parent is incorporated in GB its country of registration (i.e., England and Wales or Scotland) no longer needs to be disclosed.

Schedule 5 – Companies required to prepare group accounts		
Paragraph	*Subject*	*Effect*
para 15	Information about subsidiaries.	The country of registration (i.e., England and Wales or Scotland) no longer needs to be given for GB incorporated subsidiary companies.
para 18	Non-consolidated subsidiaries.	Information about qualified auditors' reports thereon need not be given.
para 19	Financial years of subsidiary undertakings.	No information is now required to be given about subsidiaries that have different year ends from the parent.
para 20	Debentures held by subsidiaries.	This information no longer need be given.
para 22	Associated undertakings.	If it is a GB associate, disclosure of the country of incorporation (e.g., England and Wales or Scotland) need not be given.
paras 23, 24 and 27	Information about holdings in non-subsidiary undertakings which are not associated undertakings or joint ventures.	Information about 10 per cent investments no longer need be given: the relevant disclosure threshold is raised to 20 per cent. The country of registration of GB undertakings (i.e., England and Wales or Scotland) need not be given.
para 29	Merger relief.	The disclosures previously required when s131(2) merger relief has been applied on the allotment of shares no longer apply.
para 30	Identification of parent undertaking drawing up accounts for a larger group.	If the parent is incorporated in GB its country of registration no longer need be disclosed.

Schedule 5 – Companies required to prepare group accounts (continued)		
Paragraph	*Subject*	*Effect*
para 31	Identification of ultimate parent undertaking.	If the parent is incorporated in GB its country of registration no longer needs to be disclosed.

Schedule 7 – Directors' Report

Paragraph/ Section	*Subject*	*Effect*
para 1	Significant changes in fixed assets.	No longer required.
para 5A	Insurance for directors, officers or auditors.	No longer required.
s234	Health and safety.	The amendment removes the power of the Secretary of State to make regulations requiring disclosure of information about health and safety at work.
s234	Reserves.	It is no longer a requirement to disclose the amount to be transferred to reserves.
s234	Directors' report.	A requirement to disclose the company's policy on payment of creditors has been introduced for public companies and companies which do not qualify as small or medium-sized and are within a group the parent of which is a public company.

Banks

Schedule	*Subject*	*Effect*
Sch 9	Various.	The amendments to Schedule 9 are similar to those to Schedule 4.

Insurance companies *(the changes broadly correct anomalies in the implementation of the Insurance Accounts Directive)*		
Section	*Subject*	*Effect*
s268	Realised profits of insurance company with long-term business.	The revision clarifies that s268 continues to be effective in limiting distributable profits in respect of long-term insurance business to those which are derived from the surplus released from the company's long-term fund and have been allocated to shareholders in accordance with s30 of the Insurance Companies Act 1982.

Schedule 9A – Insurance companies		
Paragraph	*Subject*	*Effect*
	Various.	The amendments concern the accounts of insurance companies and groups so as to bring those provisions more closely into alignment with the provisions of the Insurance Accounts Directive. There are also consequential amendments to Sch 11 (modifications of Pt VIII where a company's accounts prepared in accordance with special provisions for banking and insurance companies).
para 21	Valuation.	Para 21 of 9A is deleted, thereby enabling some debt securities to be valued at amortised cost under para 24 at the same time as others are valued at current value.
para 54	Prior year.	Para 54 is amended to require disclosure of prior year figures for numbers shown in the notes to accounts to bring the Sch 9A requirements into line with their Sch 4 and 9 equivalents.
paras 66 and 84	Classification.	The revision amends paragraphs to substitute 'provisions for other risks and charges' for 'provisions for liabilities and charges'.
	Various.	Other amendments are similar to those being made in respect of Sch 4 noted above.

Annex 3

Table of Amendments for Small and Medium-Sized Company Accounts

Restructuring the Companies Act 1985 Schedules – the 1997 Regulations (SI 1997 No 220) *(Note: These are explained in more detail in Chapter 7)*		
Section	*Subject*	*Effect*
s246	Special provisions for small companies.	The section permits small companies to: – comply with the new Sch 8 or existing Sch 4 in its accounts for members; – omit various details from Schs 5 and 6 from such accounts; – omit various details from s234 and Sch 7 from the directors' report accompanying such accounts; – deliver accounts to the Registrar which omit a profit and loss account, directors' report and comply with Sch 8A.
s246	Special provisions for medium-sized companies.	The section permits a medium-sized company to deliver accounts to the Registrar of Companies which combine the items above 'gross profit' in the profit and loss account and omit the detail required by para 55 of Sch 4 (relating to particulars of turnover).
s247A	Cases where small or medium-sized company provisions are not available.	Sets out conditions for when the provisions under s246 cannot be adopted by 'public interest' companies.
s247B	Special audit report.	Where the company is to produce accounts which take advantage of the provisions in s246 (in respect of accounts for members, directors' report or accounts for filing) for small or medium-sized companies a special audit report is required. The report must refer to the fact that the accounts/report have been prepared in accordance with the relevant provision (i.e., s246(5) or s246(6) or s246A(3)).

25

Section	Subject	Effect
		This is required provided the directors have not taken advantage of the exemption from audit conferred by s249(1) or (2) and the company is not exempt by virtue of s250 from the obligation to appoint auditors.
		Where abbreviated accounts are produced for filing, the audit report need no longer give in full, the audit report on the full accounts. If that report was qualified then the special report should set out the qualification in full, together with any further material necessary to understand the qualification. If the audit report on the full accounts contained a statement required under s237(2) (accounts, records or returns inadequate or accounts not agreeing with records or returns), or s237(3) (failure to obtain necessary information and explanations) then these should be set out in full.
s248A	Group accounts prepared by small companies.	Where a company has prepared individual accounts in accordance with s246(2) or s246(3) (i.e., complying with Sch 8 or failing to comply with Sch 8 only in so far as they comply with the corresponding provisions of Sch 4) and is also preparing group accounts then such group accounts can also be prepared on the same basis, and need not give the information required by s246(3).
		In Sch 8, for group accounts, the following applies in the format to the balance sheet:
		'BIII Investments
		1. Shares in group undertakings
		2. Interest in associated undertakings
		3. Other participating interests
		4. Loans to group undertakings and undertakings in which a participating interest is held
		5. Other investments other than loans
		6. Others'.

Section	Subject	Effect
		Group accounts prepared in accordance with s248A are required to contain a statement in a prominent position, above the signature required by s233 that they have been prepared in accordance with the special provisions of Pt VII relating to small companies.
s171(5)(b) s247(5) s249C(b) s250 s260(b) s262A s269(2)(6) s276 Sch 4 para 48(1) Sch 9A para 68(1) Sch 4A paras 1(2) and 19(2) Sch 9, Pt II para 2(1)(a)	Various.	Consequential amendments.
Sch 8	Content of small company accounts.	Sets out the various disclosures necessary for a small company entitled to take advantage of the provisions in s246. These were previously set out as exemptions from the disclosures required under Schs 4, 5 and 6.
Sch 8A	Content of small company abbreviated accounts for filing.	Sets out the various disclosures necessary for a small company entitled to file abbreviated accounts by taking advantage of the provisions in s246. These were previously set out as exemptions from the disclosures required under Schs 4, 5, 6 and 7.

Chapter Three

Accounting Standards and Smaller Companies

Introduction

3.1 As set out in Chapter 1, in the early days of accounting standards exemptions had been given on a piecemeal basis to companies meeting certain size criteria. In the 1980s the debate on the application of accounting standards to smaller companies continued, fuelled partly by the changes introduced in the 1981 Companies Act and partly by the continuing increase in the number of accounting standards. When the Accounting Standards Committee reviewed its processes in 1983, its report *Review of the standard-setting process* reiterated the Committee's view that future standards should apply to all accounts intended to give a true and fair view. However, the report acknowledged that exemptions might arise as a result of applying a cost-benefit test. It recognised that in judging whether a standard should be applied universally, the following additional information could be helpful:

1 the main purposes for which the accounts of small companies are used;
2 the burden imposed on small companies by accounting standards; and
3 the level of compliance with existing standards.

The 1985 research

3.2 To find some of the answers to those questions, the ASC requested that a research study be carried out. The resultant publication *Small company financial reporting* by BV Carsberg, MJ Page, AJ Sindall and ID Waring was published in 1985. The authors' major recommendations were as follows:

- *'we do not believe that a case exists for exemptions from all accounting standards of all companies below a certain size or of all private companies;*
- *the standards most suitable for universal application are those dealing with fundamental topics that must be dealt with one way or another in the basic accounts;*
- *where a standard would have minor importance for a small company, because small companies rarely undertake the transactions dealt with*

> by the standard, consideration should be given to the exemption of small companies and the limitation of scope should be given prominent display – for example, on the cover of the standard;
> - the application to small companies of other standards, particularly standards dealing with complex issues, extending the scope of existing accounting practice, should be the subject of special study so that the Accounting Standards Committee is informed about the potential costs and benefits of application to small companies. The Committee should be prepared to give exemptions to small companies if the evidence indicates that costs would exceed benefits; and
> - the professional accounting bodies should consider whether or not additional steps need to be taken to maintain compliance with standards and inform members of the scope and requirements of existing statements'.

3.3   At this time, the government was also concerned about burdens on business and was taking various steps to investigate how those burdens might be reduced. Therefore, prompted by the continuing interest in the topic and the general political climate, the ASC set up a Working Party in October 1986 to investigate the application of accounting standards to small companies.

The 1988 ASC Statement

3.4   The Accounting Standards Committee accepted, in February 1988, the report of the Working Party which it had set up in 1986. Its conclusion was that on the basis that company law requires small companies to present financial statements that give a true and fair view, the then existing standards had many benefits and few incremental costs. Accordingly there appeared to be neither reason nor demand to reduce the application of accounting standards to small companies. In reaching that conclusion, the Working Party had consulted widely and most consultees supported this position.

3.5   That said, the ASC recognised that there could be situations in the future in which new standards would be inappropriate for small companies either on conceptual grounds or, more likely, for reasons of practicability. It was also recognised that applying all standards to all companies, the universality concept, could hinder the ASC from making progress in the regulation of large and publicly accountable enterprises. Therefore, the ASC undertook to continue to consider specifically each new accounting standard.

3.6   But what the ASC meant by small was not as defined in company law. In a paper released in July 1988 the ASC clarified what it would generally consider as 'small' for determining whether or not to apply accounting standards. The criteria adopted was that relaxations, as specified in accounting standards, would be available to companies if they were not public companies and met two or more of the following criteria:

(a) turnover does not exceed £80 million;
(b) balance sheet totals do not exceed £39 million; and
(c) average number of persons employed in the year does not exceed 2,500.

These criteria represented those adopted in company law for the definition of a medium-sized company but scaled up by a factor of 10. Whilst the ASC accepted that these were arbitrary, it was its best attempt at determining what might be considered public interest entities and those which were not by virtue of their size.

3.7 As events turned out, these ASC definitions of an entity which was publicly accountable and one which was not and thus eligible for relief from accounting standards were used on only two occasions. The first was in the revised SSAP 13 *Accounting for research and development*; the second in SSAP 25 *Segmental reporting*.

Accounting standards and the ASB

3.8 In 1990, the Accounting Standards Committee was replaced with the new Accounting Standards Board, no longer a creature of purely the accountancy bodies. Funded by the accountancy profession, the financial community and the government, the ASB develops, issues and withdraws accounting standards on its own authority.

3.9 Whilst the ASB was allowed a brief honeymoon period by commentators during 1991 and 1992, the problem of the application of accounting standards to smaller entities remained unresolved and the piecemeal application was unsatisfactory. The ASB exempted small companies from its first FRS on cash flow statements. However, subsequent standards, such as FRS 3 *Reporting financial performance* and FRS 4 *Capital instruments*, which extended significantly disclosure requirements, did not contain specific exemptions. In this period also, corporate reporting requirements were being increased because of developments such as those emanating from the Cadbury Report on corporate governance matters. There was a general feeling of 'standards overload'.

3.10 Meanwhile, the momentum from government to reduce the burdens especially on smaller businesses continued. Therefore in late 1993, the ASB asked the Consultative Committee of Accountancy Bodies to establish a Working Party with the following terms of reference:

> *'The Board like its predecessor the Accounting Standards Committee, examines, on a standard by standard basis, whether exemptions from all or part of the standard should be provided for certain types of enterprise on the grounds of size or relative lack of public interest. The Working Party is asked to recommend to the Board, on the basis of a wide consultation, appropriate criteria for making such exemptions.'*

The CCAB Working Party

3.11 In its two and a half years of existence, this Working Party issued two papers. The November 1994 Consultative Document *Exemptions from standards on grounds of size or public interest* can perhaps best be summarised as a proposed 'quick fix'. Its main proposals were that:

1 with recent changes in company law, there should be no additional requirement for small companies to comply with the full body of accounting standards;

2 there should be a presumption that most small companies are exempt from accounting standards. Future standards should be reviewed on the basis of what is essential for small companies, using a number of specific criteria;

3 exemptions from accounting standards and UITF Abstracts should be based primarily on size, using the Companies Act definition of a small company; and

4 compliance with five particular standards and one UITF Abstract should continue for small companies.

3.12 The criteria proposed in the report to determine whether a standard should apply to small companies were as follows.

1 Is the standard likely to be regarded as of general application and an essential element of GAAP for all entities?

2 Would the standard be likely to lead to a transaction being treated in a way that would be readily recognised by the proprietor or manager of the business as corresponding to their understanding of the transaction?

3 Does the standard result in disclosures that are likely to be meaningful and comprehensible to a reasonably intelligent user of the accounts, such as the proprietor or manager of the business?

4 Are the disclosures likely to be visible to many users of the accounts, given that a large number of companies file abbreviated accounts?

5 Do the requirements of the standard significantly augment the treatment prescribed by legislation?

6 Is the treatment prescribed by the standard identical to that already used, or expected to be used, by the Inland Revenue in computing taxable profits?

7 Does the standard provide the 'least cumbersome' method of achieving

the desired accounting treatment and/or disclosure for an entity that is not complex?

8 Does the standard provide guidance that might be expected to be widely relevant to the transactions of small companies, and is it written in terms that can be understood by such businesses?

9 Are the measurement methods prescribed in the standard likely to be reasonably practical for small companies?

A preponderance of negative answers would result in exemption from the standard.

3.13 Through consideration of these criteria, the Working Party tentatively concluded, as set out in its November 1994 paper, that the following standards and one UITF Abstract would remain applicable for all companies:

- SSAP 4 *Accounting for government grants*;
- SSAP 9 *Stocks and long-term contracts*;
- SSAP 13 *Accounting for research and development*;
- SSAP 17 *Accounting for post balance sheet events*;
- SSAP 18 *Accounting for contingencies*; and
- UITF Abstract 7 *True and fair view override disclosures*.

3.14 The results of the November 1994 consultation, which produced some 112 responses, were that broadly three-quarters of respondents agreed that the present arrangements, whereby accounting standards and UITF Abstracts apply to all entities with few exceptions, cause problems. The clear message to the Working Party was that the status quo was not an acceptable option.

3.15 It was also clear from the consultation that the use of the small company criteria in company law had support. Whilst some commentators would have preferred the threshold to be much lower, others thought it should be at the medium-sized level or indeed applicable for all private companies.

3.16 But there was not clear support for the proposed 'quick fix' solution. Four recurring themes or issues were identified in examining the respondents' comments. The first was that the cost of considering and then complying with accounting standards was outweighing the potential improvement in information content in the financial statements. This issue had become very clear in the 1990s as the ASB's new Financial Reporting Standards were generally much longer than the existing SSAPs.

3.17 The second issue was that the standards themselves were in need of some refreshment. They had been developed by different people and committees over a period of some 25 years. While a codification exercise would benefit all users of accounting standards, it was recognised that this, whilst potentially of use in clarifying certain current difficulties, would not give a solution to the problems caused by the application of almost all standards to smaller entities.

3.18　Thirdly, whilst the quick fix solution did have some support, it was recognised that exempting smaller entities from some standards would solve some problems but in doing so would create others, particularly where there were interrelationships between different accounting standards.

3.19　The fourth issue, and perhaps the most serious one, was that guidance would still be necessary on measurement issues to determine whether financial statements of smaller entities give a true and fair view. The absence of any form of guidance on measurement might lead to unacceptable treatments being adopted.

The 1995 paper

3.20　In considering the responses to the 1994 Consultative Document, it had been noted that a few commentators were supporting the development of a specific accounting standard for smaller entities. The Working Party also noted the ideas which the DTI was considering in its Consultative Document *Accounting simplifications*. As evidenced in the recent Statutory Instrument, company law has now been revised so that all the accounting rules for small companies are given in one Schedule, contrasting with the previous situation in which the legislation was drafted for all and then exemptions given, thus making it quite complicated for small companies to work out what applied to them and what did not.

3.21　The extension of this thinking into accounting standards resulted in the conclusion that piecemeal application of particular standards to smaller companies was a flawed approach. Furthermore, it led to discussions on marginal cases, rather than a focus on determining what should apply to the generality of small companies. This led to the conclusion that a specific Financial Reporting Standard to meet the sector's needs should be developed.

3.22　To prove that the proposed approach of a Financial Reporting Standard for Smaller Entities (FRSSE) was feasible, practical and capable of delivering benefits to smaller entities, a draft FRSSE was produced and issued for comment as part of the paper *Designed to fit – A Financial Reporting Standard for Smaller Entities*. Published in December 1995, comments were sought by 29 March 1996. The responses were generally positive. The concept of a FRSSE received support, from commentators such as the accountancy bodies, users such as the Inland Revenue and many more firms than the previous piecemeal application of accounting standards proposal had done.

3.23 The Working Party therefore recommended in July 1996 that the ASB should proceed with the development of the FRSSE. This proposal was accepted by the Board which published in December 1996 its Exposure Draft of the FRSSE for comment by 14 March 1997. Assuming that no major difficulties emerge, the expected timetable is that the ASB issues the new standard in the autumn of 1997.

Chapter Four

The FRSSE

Introduction

4.1 At the end of Chapter 3, it is noted that the idea of a FRSSE was conceived, developed, promoted, supported and then accepted by the ASB. In reporting these activities so quickly, it may seem that the FRSSE has had a painless birth. But this masks a number of issues regarding the FRSSE's structure and contents and how these might be changed in the future. This chapter therefore discusses the FRSSE's structure, the major issues and the mechanisms for change.

The structure of the FRSSE

4.2 There has been no public dissension from the view that the ASB is the right body to issue the FRSSE. By virtue of SI 1990 No 1667, The Accounting Standards (Prescribed Body) Regulations 1990, the ASB is the body which issues applicable accounting standards to which companies must have regard. Thus, the ASB already has appropriate authority to issue an authoritative accounting standard.

4.3 Furthermore, because the ASB presently carries out this task on behalf of all companies, the risks of big GAAP and little GAAP becoming out of step in the future would be reduced if there was a single body responsible for both. Therefore, with the ASB being considered the appropriate body to assume responsibility for the FRSSE, it has been drafted in a similar format to that adopted for other Financial Reporting Standards.

4.4 Whilst the draft FRSSE issued as an Exposure Draft by the ASB in December 1996 looks similar to other ASB publications, there are a few differences. For example, other accounting standards place the definitions section before the Statement of Standard Accounting Practice. However, whilst other accounting standards have relatively only a few definitions because they focus on single topics, the FRSSE defines some 70 terms. Therefore, the definitions section has sensibly been placed after the accounting guidance. But what this highlights is the absence of a generally accepted glossary of accounting terms in the United Kingdom at this time.

4.5 The International Accounting Standards Committee developed a glossary as part of its 1990s revision project. The UK's Auditing Practices Board similarly issued a glossary of terms when it carried out its codification exercise in 1995. The importance of a common lexicon is something which the accountancy profession has recognised as important in the past. It is perhaps to be hoped that in due course the ASB will issue a comprehensive glossary so that accounting terms have the same meaning regardless of the context or individual standard in which they appear. As with other standards, such a glossary would need to be subject to periodic revision in the same way as dictionaries are constantly updated and revised.

4.6 A consequence of having so many terms defined in the FRSSE is that, within the text of the Statement of Standard Accounting Practice, terms which are explained in the Definitions section are highlighted in bold text. It can be argued that the list of defined terms is excessive. While precise definitions may be necessary to curb the activities of loophole spotters or pedants there is an argument that accounting standards are not written for, and are certainly not read by, the person who does not have any accounting knowledge (albeit standards are designed to benefit this community by producing consistent accounting practice). Therefore, on the presumption that the reader of the FRSSE has some accounting knowledge, definitions of terms such as 'consolidated financial statements' or a 'foreign enterprise' may be unnecessary.

Major issues

4.7 In preparing the draft FRSSE, there have been issues on which agreement was readily obtained and others which have been, and continue to be, controversial.

4.8 The FRSSE may be applied to all financial statements intended to give a true and fair view of the financial position and profit or loss (or income and expenditure) of all entities that are:

- small companies (or groups) as defined in companies legislation; or
- entities that would also qualify as such if they had been incorporated under Companies Act legislation.

4.9 By restricting the scope in this way the draft FRSSE continues the approach within the Companies Act 1985 whereby certain companies, such as insurance, banking or authorised persons under the Financial Services Act in which there is a public interest, are unable to take advantage of exemptions from disclosure.

4.10 Furthermore it is a logical extension of the availability of company law exclusions for small companies generally, such as those relating to the preparation of consolidated accounts and from accounting disclosures, for there to be an accounting standard drawn up specifically for small companies principally to reduce the required level of disclosure.

4.11 More controversial have been the questions on whether:
- the FRSSE should be capable of application to small groups;
- there should be a requirement for cash flow information; and
- there should be specific requirements for related party disclosures.

Application to groups

4.12 In the draft FRSSE issued as part of *Designed to fit* in December 1995, the Working Party took the view that the FRSSE should be capable of application only to single entity accounts. This was because the Companies Act 1985 provides an exemption from consolidation to small groups. In practice, companies which can take advantage of this exemption do so. If consolidated accounts are requested, typically they are prepared in a non-statutory format. Furthermore, given that compliance with the FRSSE is a voluntary alternative to compliance with all other accounting standards, if a small group wished to prepare its statutory consolidated accounts then it could do so by applying in full all existing accounting standards.

4.13 A minority of commentators on the 1995 draft asked that the FRSSE be made capable of application to groups. Whether this request was driven by a genuine need because statutory consolidated accounts were being prepared for small groups or as an intellectual challenge to the Working Party is not known. Therefore, the Working Party recommended to the ASB that this should be a matter of specific consultation in December 1996.

4.14 Clearly to include all requirements affecting consolidated accounts within the FRSSE would result in a significant extension in its length. Therefore, the Working Party has proposed that where a small entity is preparing consolidated financial statements it should also follow the requirements set out in FRSs 2, 6, 7 and, as they apply for consolidated financial statements, FRS 5, SSAPs 1 and 22, and UITF Abstract 3. This mechanism has the advantage of allowing the FRSSE to be followed by small groups while not extending significantly its overall length.

4.15 However, there may be disadvantages. The first is that it disturbs the concept of the FRSSE as a free-standing accounting standard. Thus, preparers and others interested in such financial statements may have to look to other accounting standards. Another possible disadvantage is that when new accounting standards are being written, which impact on consolidated financial statements, regard will have to be given to all sizes of company. This erodes the advantage that in producing the FRSSE there will be a clear regime for smaller entities, thus allowing other accounting standards to focus on the needs of larger ones.

4.16 A third disadvantage, which will probably not become visible for some years, is that the FRSSE will have to be more complex to deal with situations in which items arise both in single and consolidated accounts. There is already evidence of this in the changes which had to be made, for example, to the guidance on its specific areas such as deferred tax and goodwill in the main section of the FRSSE.

Cash flows

4.17 A second contentious area has been whether cash flow information should be required. The ASB gave small companies an exemption from preparing a cash flow statement when it issued its first Financial Reporting Standard in 1991. The exemption has proved popular; small companies invariably take advantage of this exemption and rarely provide cash flow statements in their published financial statements. But given that cash flow is undoubtedly a critical issue in businesses of all sizes it is difficult to see why small companies should be exempt.

4.18 The Working Party's membership was split on this subject. Those in favour of requiring the cash flow statement argued that it was a statement to which users would easily relate, its inclusion would be educative and it would reinforce how vital management of cash flow is in such businesses. Others took the view that the costs of preparing such a statement outweighed the benefits. The information would be of limited value as it would be prepared some months after the year end and because in many small businesses the transactions are relatively straightforward such a statement would add little to what was already apparent from the balance sheet and the profit and loss account. Furthermore, as managers in small businesses realised how important it was to manage cash effectively, they did so by using mechanisms not necessarily identical to the structure required in FRS 1.

4.19 In this debate on cash flows, it should perhaps be recognised that the authors of the FRSSE did not start with a clean sheet of paper. Company law, backed up by the EU Company Law Directives, imposes certain requirements for balance sheet and profit and loss account information on small companies. If a clean start could be made to design small company reporting from scratch then perhaps the cash flow statement would be the only one that was required, with information on other items being given in notes.

4.20 The subject of cash flows was one on which the Working Party sought particular comment in December 1995. The majority of commentators favoured continuation of the exemption. But others, who represented users of the financial statements, were strongly opposed and wished to see cash flow information being presented. Therefore, the ASB has again asked for comment on whether there is support for the deletion of the requirements for cash flow information as contained in *Designed to fit*.

Related parties

4.21 The third, and curiously perhaps the most difficult, issue has been whether the requirements of FRS 8 *Related party disclosures* should apply to small companies. The background to this debate is clearly set out in paragraphs 12 to 14 of Appendix V of the FRSSE. Related party disclosures were proposed in *Designed to fit* and a clear majority of commentators thereon argued that they were unnecessary. However, the ASB has taken the view at this time that such disclosures are in fact often more important in respect of smaller entities than others. Accordingly the main provisions of FRS 8 have been reflected in the draft FRSSE issued for comment. The problems of applying these provisions are discussed further in Chapter 6.

A structure for change

4.22 It was recognised in the original paper, *Designed to fit*, that any accounting standard for small companies would need to be responsive to changes in financial reporting practices for the generality of companies. For this reason the ASB is proposing to establish an advisory committee to assume responsibility for advising on financial reporting in smaller entities and thus for the FRSSE. The committee is likely to meet regularly and to report to the ASB as necessary.

4.23 The intention is that the FRSSE be reviewed after two years of operation and that any revisions necessary as a result of developments in financial reporting or problems encountered in the application of the FRSSE would be proposed at that time. Any proposed changes, unless they are minor or inconsequential, will be subject to a consultative process, in all probability by the issue of an exposure draft, as with the revision to any other accounting standard.

Chapter Five

Policies and Profit and Loss Account Matters

Introduction

5.1 The authors of the FRSSE have thought to arrange in a logical manner the guidance within the Statement of Standard Accounting Practice. Matters of general application are dealt with first. The profit and loss account and related items such as the statement of total recognised gains and losses, foreign currency and taxation matters are considered next. The balance sheet topics are tackled in the order in which they generally appear in a vertical balance sheet; goodwill is first and capital instruments last. The remainder of the items within the standard accounting practice section are notes to the accounts, matters such as contingencies, post balance sheet events and related party disclosures. In this chapter, general policy matters and points regarding preparation of the performance statements are discussed.

Unincorporated entities

5.2 A perennial issue for standard setters in the UK is that whilst the standards apply to all financial statements intended to give a true and fair view of the financial position and results of all entities, a large proportion of entities complying with accounting standards also comply with detailed accounting rules in company law whilst others, the unincorporated entities, are not subject to that legal regime. To ensure that the accounting standards make sense for all entities, rules are often introduced which overlap with those in company law.

5.3 Dealing with unincorporated entities therefore presented something of a challenge to the authors of the FRSSE. Should the FRSSE repeat accounting rules to be found in company law? Should unincorporated entities be ignored completely on the grounds that the number of sole traders, partnerships and other unincorporated entities preparing 'true and fair' accounts are relatively small? In fact, what has been followed is a middle course. Paragraph 2 of the draft FRSSE introduces a new piece of guidance for unincorporated entities. They:

*'should have regard to the **accounting principles**, presentation and disclosure requirements in **companies legislation** (or other equivalent legislation) that, taking into account the FRSSE, are necessary to present a true and fair view'.*

5.4   The effect of this sentence must be that unincorporated entities, wishing to prepare true and fair view accounts, should adopt, to the extent that is applicable to them, one of the formats in company law for the profit and loss account and the balance sheet and the appropriate additional note disclosure. Some items will clearly be not applicable. For example, in a partnership's accounts there will be no share capital; but there should be information on the partners' accounts. Similarly, having regard to the company law formats would mean that assets would generally be ordered from the least liquid to the most liquid, in other words from intangible assets through to cash. A structure which added property and debtors together and motor cars and investments together would fall foul of the above requirement.

5.5   The reference to 'other equivalent legislation' is designed *inter alia* for unincorporated charities. They will naturally look to the Charities Act for guidance, rather than company law.

5.6   Experience suggests that the number of unincorporated entities wishing to prepare true and fair accounts is relatively small compared to the number of companies who are required to do so. It is expected that just short of a million companies would be entitled to adopt the FRSSE. Therefore, the above device of inserting one sentence to require unincorporated entities to have regard to matters of accounting principles, presentation and disclosure in company law is surely an example of the tail not wagging the accounting standards' dog.

A true and fair view

5.7   Paragraph 3 of the draft FRSSE is potentially the most powerful in the document. It contains three elements:
- the requirement to present a true and fair view;
- that regard should be had to the substance of any arrangement or transaction into which the entity has entered; and
- where applying the provisions of the FRSSE would be insufficient to give a true and fair view, then further explanation should be given in the notes to the accounts.

5.8   The second element is clearly designed to bring in the general requirement of FRS 5 *Reporting the substance of transactions* into the FRSSE. The third element is more intriguing.

5.9 It is extremely unlikely that accounting standards could give specific guidance on all transactions or arrangements likely to occur in practice. Furthermore, it is often recognised that they should not try to do so. Accounting standards should be written so that they deal with perhaps 80 per cent of cases, leaving those at the margins to be dealt with sensibly having regard to generally accepted accounting principles and the overriding requirement to give a true and fair view. In drafting the FRSSE, which is essentially a précis of existing accounting requirements, some existing requirements were going to be dropped or otherwise subsumed. Therefore, it is recognised that the third element of paragraph 3 would be useful in ensuring adequate explanation was given of the transactions or arrangements concerned and the accounting treatment adopted.

Relationship with other accounting standards

5.10 Some commentators on the *Designed to fit* paper suggested that, in the absence of guidance on particular transactions in the FRSSE, regard should be had to any guidance provided in the accounting standards applying to larger entities. This approach was presumably proposed to ensure that there would be identical accounting between larger and smaller entities. In particular, there would not be divergences of practice between the way a transaction was accounted for in a company with a turnover of £2.5 million compared to a similar transaction in a company with a turnover of £3 million, the former qualifying as a small company and the latter not. Such cases at the margins are always difficult to deal with but they are not new. In respect of the FRSSE, it is mirroring different treatments available in company law. For example, the company with the lower turnover can file abbreviated accounts which are significantly smaller than the financial statements for the shareholders. For the company with the larger turnover, which qualifies as a medium-sized company, the exemptions available in the filed accounts are very few. Company law also gives significant exemptions in respect of the shareholders' accounts for small companies.

5.11 The Working Party and the ASB has rejected the approach of requiring all other SSAPs, FRSs and UITF Abstracts to be followed where these provide guidance on transactions not covered in the FRSSE. If that route had been taken, then the FRSSE would not have achieved its purpose of reducing the burden on small companies. The burden would in fact have been increased as such companies would have had to comply with the FRSSE and then check all other authoritative accounting guidance. But such guidance cannot be completely ignored. The courts, if asked to determine whether financial statements do give a true and fair view, will presumably wish to know that the accounting practices adopted were acceptable. Thus, in the absence of specific guidance in the FRSSE, preparers and auditors should consider what is established and accepted practice. Hence the rubric at the start of the draft FRSSE states that:

> *'In the absence of guidance within the [draft] FRSSE, financial statements should be prepared using accepted practice and, accordingly, regard should be had to other Statements of Standard Accounting Practice, Financial Reporting Standards and Urgent Issues Task Force Abstracts, not as mandatory documents, but as a means of establishing current practice.'*

5.12 In using this statement, it is important to recognise that it is a two part entreaty. The first point is to establish accepted practice. As part of that process regard should be had, secondly, to other authoritative accounting statements. Paragraph 17 of Appendix V to the draft FRSSE also usefully recognises that over time little GAAP may diverge from big GAAP as new rules are established applying to larger entities. As both sectors currently apply essentially the same set of accounting rules then on implementation of the FRSSE what is accepted practice in one sector is going to be the same as in the other. An oft-quoted example of a divergence which may appear in the future is in accounting for financial instruments where the current proposals of marking to market fixed interest instruments might be considered onerous and unnecessary in respect of smaller entities.

5.13 Where the current tensions are likely to be is in respect of the fact that the entreaty to consider accepted practice and thus other authoritative accounting statements is not limited to matters of accounting treatment and could be said also to apply to disclosure. But such an approach would run contrary to much of what the FRSSE is seeking to achieve, namely a significant reduction in the disclosure and compliance burden on smaller entities. As the disclosure checklist at Appendix 3 of this book illustrates, a significant number of the existing disclosure requirements in accounting standards are dropped in the new FRSSE. It therefore is reasonable to presume that there should not be enthusiastic use of the above entreaty solely on disclosure of matters. The key point should be that in paragraph 3 of the FRSSE that adequate explanation should be given in the notes to the accounts of transactions or arrangements on which specific guidance is not given in the FRSSE.

Accounting policies

5.14 Individual accounting standards have usually contained a require-ment that the reporting entity sets out its accounting policy on the topic which is the subject of the individual standard. This is in addition to SSAP 2 *Disclosure of accounting policies* which contains the general rule that the accounting policies followed for dealing with items that are material or critical to determining results or position should be disclosed in the notes to the accounts. In practice, this double counting on accounting policies has led to disclosure of policies on items which are not necessarily either material or critical to the financial statements in question. Therefore, presumably to encourage preparers to focus on the major accounting policies, the FRSSE has retained the general requirement from SSAP 2 but has dropped all the detailed requirements on individual topics from the other accounting standards.

5.15 It has however retained the essence of UITF 7 *True and fair override disclosures*. Therefore, if an entity overrides a specific provision of company law, including the accounting principles set out therein, there should be full and detailed disclosure not only in the year of the override but in subsequent financial statements if the departure continues.

Reporting financial performance

5.16 FRS 3, *Reporting financial performance*, was made mandatory in respect of financial statements relating to accounting periods ending on or after 22 June 1993. The standard aimed to highlight a range of important components of financial performance and therefore required the profit and loss account to contain information on the activities of reporting entities analysed amongst:

- continuing;
- discontinued; and
- acquisition activities.

5.17 FRS 3 thus requires a layered format to be used for the profit and loss account such that the results of a company or group are analysed between continuing and discontinued operations down to the level of operating profit. The analysis of turnover and operating profit, at least, are required to be shown on the face of the profit and loss account. The analysis of the other statutory profit and loss account format items must be given in the notes if they are not disclosed on the face of the profit and loss account.

5.18 The FRSSE continues to apply many of the features of FRS 3. However, the FRSSE does not require the same level of analysis or the tiered approach to the profit and loss account as is required under FRS 3. There is no requirement to analyse the profit and loss account between continuing and discontinued activities, nor do the results relating to the acquisition of subsidiaries or separate businesses need to be separately disclosed, either on the face of the profit or loss account or in the notes to the accounts, other than as required under the Companies Act.

5.19   One of the significant impacts of FRS 3 has been the virtual abolition of the use of extraordinary items in UK reporting. Instead the focus of attention has moved to whether or not certain items can meet the definitions within paragraph 20 of FRS 3 and so be regarded as exceptional items which fall below the operating profit line.

5.20   The conditions for regarding an item which is exceptional and which falls below operating profit is restricted in the FRSSE to the same items in paragraph 20 of FRS 3, namely:
- profits or losses on the sale or termination of an operation;
- costs for fundamental reorganisation or restructuring having a material effect on the nature and focus of the reporting entity's operations; and
- profits or losses on the disposal of fixed assets.

5.21   The positioning of such exceptional items below operating profit is important for listed companies and those preparing a figure for earnings per share. The significance of a figure for earnings per share is perceived as less meaningful for smaller entities (indeed the accounting standard, SSAP 3 *Earnings per share* specifically applies only to listed companies). But this is not to say that a measure of sustainable earnings is not an important feature for companies or entities of any size. One of the basic methods of valuing a business is on the basis of its projected stream of anticipated future income. This can still be achieved since the FRSSE continues to recognise that matters which are exceptional or outside the company's normal operating activities should be separately and clearly disclosed either on the face of the profit and loss account or in the notes to the accounts.

5.22   To avoid another financial reporting abuse FRS 3 made it clear that the profit to be reported in the profit and loss account on a disposal of an asset should be calculated as the difference between proceeds and net book value rather than cost. The method of calculating the profit on the disposal of a fixed asset is the same under the FRSSE as under FRS 3.

Statement of total recognised gains and losses

5.23   The FRSSE requires a statement of total recognised gains and losses (STRGL) to be presented, with the same prominence as the profit and loss account, showing the total recognised gains and losses and their components. These components should be the gains and losses that are recognised in a period in so far as they are attributable to shareholders.

5.24   Where the only recognised gain or loss in the year is as a result of the items in the profit and loss account the big change from FRS 3 is that no additional sentence or statement need be made. For companies which have not revalued assets during the year a separate gains statement has generally not been needed and the statement to the effect that there is no statement has added nothing to the financial statements.

5.25 Given that small companies generally do not revalue fixed assets or record other gains or losses not recognised in the profit and loss account, a strong case can be put forward for dropping altogether in the FRSSE the requirement for a separate statement of total recognised gains and losses. The Working Party did not propose this to the ASB, although it did drop FRS 3's requirements to give:

- a note of historical cost profits and losses; and
- a reconciliation of movements in shareholders' funds.

5.26 Perhaps the reasons for retaining the STRGL are partly political. The STRGL is one of the four primary financial statements. Its role in UK financial reporting is not currently well defined and the ASB has indicated, as part of the debate over its draft Statement of Principles, that it intends to consider more fully the separate roles of the profit and loss account and the STRGL. It would perhaps have been inopportune to pre-empt that discussion by dropping now the STRGL from small companies, albeit in practice that is likely to be the result of the FRSSE's guidance.

Accounting for value added tax

5.27 The FRSSE does not repeat the principal requirement of FRS 5 that turnover shown in the profit and loss account should exclude VAT on taxable outputs. This is presumably for two reasons. The first is that SSAP 5 was issued in April 1974, shortly after the introduction of VAT into the tax system. Accordingly, it was an urgent issue of its day, which with over 20 years' experience is no longer such an issue. The more obvious reason is that the requirement in SSAP 5 has been overtaken by company law which introduced in 1981 a definition of turnover which makes clear that it is after deduction of VAT and other sales taxes.

Chapter Six

Balance Sheet and Notes Matters

Introduction

6.1 This chapter considers the topics commonly associated with balance sheet items and notes to the accounts. Unlike the matters discussed in Chapter 5, which were essentially simplifications of big GAAP, this chapter discusses two areas in which the accounting rules are tweaked. The more complex rules in existing standards have been simplified in respect of leasing transactions and arrangement fees on capital instruments. These tweaks should not alter significantly the results and positions as reported by a small entity adopting the FRSSE and one with identical transactions but following big GAAP. The topics discussed in this chapter follow the order in which they appear in the FRSSE.

Goodwill

6.2 SSAP 22 *Accounting for goodwill* has been incorporated in the FRSSE except for the disclosure requirements which have been dropped. Of course, with the ASB expected to issue a new financial reporting standard on goodwill and other intangible assets, based on FRED 12, later in 1997, this is the part of the FRSSE which is likely to be subject first to revision considerations. This does not necessarily mean that there should be an hiatus the moment the new financial reporting standard based on FRED 12 appears.

6.3 The Working Party recognised in its *Designed to fit* paper that there could be a time delay between the two sectors of larger and smaller entities. The Working Party suggested that the FRSSE should be reviewed periodically at perhaps two-year intervals. Presumably, the Working Party was trying to avoid the situation in which the FRSSE appeared to be ever changing or at least amended perhaps two or three times a year as new rules were developed applying to larger entities. It has been argued elsewhere that instead of the present practice of new accounting regulations being implemented at different dates throughout the year, there should be an agreement that accounting standards and changes in company law should be introduced with effect from a standard date, say 31 December each year. The Working Party was presumably arguing for such a feature in respect of the FRSSE. It recognised that this could mean that the two sectors would be slightly out of step for short periods. For example, the provisions on accounting for goodwill in the FRSSE may be the extant guidance for the next two or three years, with the new rules reflecting the new financial reporting standard being introduced at its first biennial review.

6.4 In practice, this seemingly out of step implementation for big GAAP and little GAAP should not upset the accounting purists. Piecemeal implementation of new accounting standards has been a feature for many years. Furthermore, the implementation provisions in some financial reporting standards are generous so that the impact of the new standards is delayed for perhaps some 18 months.

6.5 The FRSSE's provisions on goodwill are an example of an area in which dealing with groups has meant potentially more complexity within the standard. In the *Designed to fit* document, the goodwill provisions dealt with cases in which a single company bought an unincorporated business. The Working Party extended these sections to deal with groups in the draft FRSSE published in December 1996. While this process was relatively simple, because of the way in which SSAP 22 was drafted, incorporating the principal requirements from a standard based on FRED 12 may be more challenging.

Research and development

6.6 Whilst many smaller entities do not undertake research and development activities, for those that do the accounting is often a contentious matter. Whilst for many of the largest companies in the UK the practice is to write off research and development expenditure as it is incurred, for other entities the pressure is to recognise that in incurring this expenditure they are creating an asset from which there will be benefit in future years. Of course, this capitalisation policy means that the immediate write-offs are avoided, thus protecting realised, and thus potentially distributable, profits in early years of new projects. Therefore, SSAP 13 *Accounting for research and development* was one of the standards which the Working Party proposed in its November 1994 consultation that should continue to apply. The major provisions of SSAP 13 have therefore been incorporated in the FRSSE. The present relief in SSAP 13 from the requirements to disclose the amounts charged to profit and loss account and movements on deferred development expenditure which are available to companies meeting the criteria for medium-sized companies in which the financial thresholds are multiplied by a factor of 10 is clearly retained for small entities as defined in the FRSSE.

Leases and hire purchase contracts

6.7 The section on accounting for leases in the FRSSE is unusual in two respects. The first, as noted above, is that one of the measurement rules in the existing SSAP 21 has been simplified. The second unusual feature is that there are reasonably extensive disclosure requirements for both lessees and lessors in the FRSSE.

6.8 The simplification in the FRSSE is in respect of rentals payable under finance leases. In SSAP 21, these are apportioned between the finance charge and the reduction of the outstanding obligation for future amounts payable. The finance charge is then allocated to accounting periods over the lease term to produce a constant periodic rate of charge on the remaining balance of the obligation. The Guidance Notes to SSAP 21 allow this to be done on an actuarial basis or on the sum of the digits basis. The FRSSE takes this one stage further and allows the finance charges to be charged on a straight-line basis over the lease term. For those who wish to adopt a different basis or continue with the SSAP 21 calculations, then presumably this is allowed as the relevant paragraph in the FRSSE permits another systematic and rational basis to be adopted if this is more appropriate.

6.9 Also within the section on leases in the FRSSE is the main requirement in UITF 12 *Lessee accounting for reverse premiums and similar incentives*. Paragraph 96 of the FRSSE requires such incentives to be spread on a straight line basis over the shorter of the lease term or the period to the review date on which the rent is first expected to be adjusted to the prevailing market rate.

Associated companies

6.10 For single companies adopting the FRSSE, there will be a significant reduction in the compliance burden as they will no longer have to consider the provisions of SSAP 1 *Accounting for associated companies*. This does not mean that there will be a dearth of information on associated companies. Indeed, this may be the very area in which the provisions on disclosure of related party transactions and balances will hit. Early experience with FRS 8 generally is that transactions with associated companies are now having to be disclosed.

Stocks and long-term contracts

6.11 The principal requirements of SSAP 9 *Stocks and long-term contracts* are incorporated in the FRSSE. Furthermore, SSAP9's guidance notes on practical considerations in calculating stocks and long-term contracts are repeated as an appendix. This is a topic on which there have been consistent requests for guidance. The November 1994 proposal was that SSAP 9 would continue to apply to small companies. In the draft FRSSE in *Designed to fit* the present paragraphs 85 to 88 of the FRSSE were incorporated. Commentators then requested that the SSAP 9 guidance notes also be included and these were added into the FRSSE by the Working Party in making its recommendations to the ASB in July 1996. The susceptibility of this item to manipulation in financial reporting is presumably the reason why the request for clear rules has continued.

Other debtors

6.12 The FRSSE does not include the requirements of UITF Abstract 4 *Presentation of long-term debtors in current assets* that debtors due after more than one year should be disclosed in the notes to the accounts except in those instances where the amount is so material in the context of the total net current assets that it should be disclosed on the face of the balance sheet so that readers do not misinterpret the accounts. This requirement has been dropped presumably because it is essentially a disclosure matter. However, this is a case in which if there was such an example of a highly significant long-term debtor in a small entity's balance sheet it should be clearly explained for the financial statements to present a true and fair view of the state of affairs of the entity. Assuming these financial statements are subject to audit, then the recoverability of this long-term debtor may be an issue considered by the auditors as part of their review with the directors of the entity's ability to continue as a going concern. Therefore, it may be the subject of specific reference in a note on going concern or even in the auditors' report.

6.13 One issue which might be considered is whether such long-term debtors should be discounted to their present value. At present, discounting is not widely adopted in UK financial reporting. It is specifically applied in particular standards such as FRS 7 *Fair values in acquisition accounting*. If the long-term debtor arose on the sale of a fixed asset then there is a strong case for restricting the profit on sale to the difference between the carrying amount of the asset and the present value of the long-term debtor, assuming that this is not interest bearing. Whilst this might constitute acceptable and sensible accounting practice, it cannot be said that it is effectively required practice in the UK at this time. Indeed, it may be argued that given the propensity of smaller companies to adopt pure historical cost accounting this introduction of current value methodology would be at best uncomfortable. Furthermore, it is known that the ASB is working on a discounting paper but it will presumably be some years before discounting is widely used, assuming the UK moves in that direction. Therefore, for small entities, the expectation is that historical cost accounting prevails and appropriate explanation of long-term debtors is given in the notes to the accounts.

6.14 Factoring of debts is a relatively common activity amongst smaller entities. Factoring improves cash flow and, depending on the arrangements, may leave the task of debt collection to another party, thus allowing the proprietors of the business to focus on obtaining new sales and generally running the business. In response to commentators' request for guidance on debt factoring, the FRSSE issued in December1996 now contains the guid-ance extracted from FRS 5. This explains when the debtors should be retained on the entity's balance sheet, when they might be considered as sold to the factor and when a linked presentation should be adopted.

6.15 The difficulty with the discussion on debt factoring is that whilst it is faithfully extracted from FRS 5 it does not sit comfortably within the FRSSE. The language is that of continuing recognition, derecognition and linked presentation – terms which are not readily understandable. Perhaps one of the first tasks of the new advisory committee will be to introduce further synthesis within the FRSSE so that its language is clear and avoids wherever possible excessive jargon.

Deferred tax

6.16 The 1994 Consultative Paper suggested that smaller entities should be exempt from SSAP 15 *Accounting for deferred tax*. Presumably, in the absence of this standard, entities would return to 'flow through' accounting for taxation, in which they would account for what was payable in respect of that year's results and would merely disclose as a contingent liability any deferred tax. Another reason for perhaps excluding SSAP 15 was that at that time the ASB was beginning its review of SSAP 15.

6.17 Accounting for deferred tax remains a controversial subject. The response to the ASB's 1995 Discussion Paper was not supportive of a move to full provision but that is the direction which the International Accounting Standards Committee has taken in its 1996 revision of International Accounting Standard No 12. The ASB is expected to issue another paper on the subject in 1997.

6.18 The subject of deferred tax is controversial in small entities' financial statements. The views in this sector appear to be as polarised as those elsewhere. The Working Party in producing the FRSSE therefore took perhaps the only route available to it which was to maintain the status quo as set out in SSAP 15. Thus, the requirements for partial provision have been retained.

Pensions

6.19 The provisions in the FRSSE for accounting for pension costs have remained substantially unchanged between the ASB's Exposure Draft and those in the *Designed to fit* paper. In small entities, defined contribution schemes are relatively more popular than defined benefit schemes. The accounting in respect of the former is straightforward and the FRSSE usefully contains an illustration of the disclosures for both types of scheme in its Appendix III.

Capital instruments

6.20 The four paragraphs in the FRSSE on capital instruments clearly represent a significant reduction from the comparable 40 or so which appear in FRS 4. FRS 4's requirement to analyse shareholders' funds between the amounts attributable to equity interests and those attributable to non-equity interests is not required in the FRSSE. It has selected four points for attention. First, there is the principle in FRS 4 that instruments other than shares, which contain an obligation to transfer economic benefits, should be classified as liabilities. Whilst such instruments, such as convertible bonds, are possibly rarer in small companies, clearly there is an important principle in establishing the right figure for liabilities and that for share capital. Thus, this principle in FRS 4 is repeated in the FRSSE.

6.21 A second important principle in FRS 4 is that finance costs on debt should be allocated to periods over the term of the debt at a constant rate on the carrying amount. It can be argued that this principle is not needed in the FRSSE. The correct application of the accruals concept in company law should lead to the same answer. But occasionally there is pressure to follow the cash pattern and this is perhaps why the requirement is continued in the FRSSE.

6.22 One provision of FRS 4 is seen as particularly irksome. If an entity incurs an arrangement fee of £50,000 to secure a facility of say £½ million for a period of five years, then these are classified as issue costs and the debt is recorded at its net proceeds, in this case £450,000. This approach, while conceptually elegant, is criticised as managers look at their balance sheet, knowing they have a £½ million loan to repay but seeing only £450,000 in their balance sheet. In their view, the arrangement fee is exactly that and is a cost of that period. Therefore intuitively they would prefer to write-off the arrangement fee in the year and then record the loan at its full amount.

6.23 The FRSSE allows the intuitive approach to be adopted. The only exception is where the arrangement fee represents a significant additional cost of finance when compared with the interest on the facility. For example, if in the above example interest was being paid at 10 per cent per annum, the expected rate which an entity of this size would pay on such a facility over such a period, the arrangement fee may be taken to the profit and loss account immediately. If, on the other hand, the arrangement fee was £100,000 and the interest rate was only 5 per cent then it can be seen that in effect the arrangement fee represents interest. In this case, the spreading rule would apply.

6.24 The fourth element of FRS 4 which has been included in the FRSSE is the requirement to accrue dividends when they are calculated by reference to time. The exception of cases where the profits are insufficient to cover a dividend and the dividend rights are non-cumulative is continued in the FRSSE.

Related party disclosures

6.25 As noted in Chapter 4, one of the more controversial topics has been related party disclosures and the extent to which the provisions of FRS 8 *Related party disclosures* has to be reflected in the FRSSE. In short, the provisions have been in, out and then in again. The Working Party was split on this issue at the time that the *Designed to fit* paper was issued. To highlight the topic, disclosure requirements in respect of related party transactions were included in that paper. As Appendix V of the FRSSE published in December 1996 notes, a clear majority of the commentators on *Designed to fit* argued that these provisions were unnecessary given that:

- company law already picked up dealings in favour of directors and connected persons; and
- where there were material transactions with related parties, possibly executed at values other than fair values, then regard might be had to paragraph 3 of the draft FRSSE which would require adequate explanation of these transactions or arrangements to be given in the notes to the accounts.

6.26 The Working Party therefore concluded in July 1996 that there should not be any explicit related party disclosures in the Exposure Draft. However, the ASB disagreed, having noted that such disclosures were often more important in respect of smaller entities than others. Accordingly, the main provisions from FRS 8 have again been included in the Exposure Draft. The ASB has asked for particular comment on this issue.

6.27 In repeating the requirement for disclosure of related party transactions, the FRSSE also includes in its definitions sections the FRS 8 definitions of related parties and related party transactions. As a consequence, the disclosure net is wide. Transactions and balances with associated companies will be caught. Transactions with members of the close family or any partnerships, companies, trusts or other entities in which they have a controlling interest will be disclosable. Furthermore, what might be considered personal arrangements which individual shareholders or directors undertake on behalf of the company might be disclosed. For example, the company's overdraft facility may be secured by a personal guarantee from a company director. FRS 8 explains that its definition of a related party transaction includes guarantees and the provision of collateral security. Therefore, the performance of this service by a company director is caught within the wording of the FRSSE and accordingly would be disclosable. Any doubt in this matter has been removed by the insertion of paragraph 138 in the FRSSE, dealing specifically with directors' personal guarantees in respect of borrowings.

6.28   Given that FRS 8 is a new Financial Reporting Standard, it is perhaps surprising that the ASB is keen to apply it at this time to small entities. A different approach would have been to allow large companies to implement FRS 8 so that the ASB can see how it was operating in practice. It might then have more knowledge to determine how best to apply the requirements for disclosure of related party transactions to small companies.

Chapter Seven

Modified and Abbreviated Accounts

Introduction

7.1   Under the Companies Act 1985 there are concessions available to 'small' and 'medium-sized' companies when preparing their financial statements. The concessions have been introduced in a piecemeal fashion, producing a Byzantine mix of three separate tiers of information relevant to some, but not all, companies below the small companies' size threshold, together with a possible exemption from producing group accounts. Medium-sized companies share the option of not preparing group accounts, but the Act affords them exemptions only in respect of the accounts prepared for filing and not in the necessary disclosures for the accounts prepared for members.

7.2   The DTI Consultative Document *Accounting simplifications: re-arrangements to Companies Act Schedule on small company accounts* issued in July 1996 was discussed in Chapter 2. The document proposed a revision to s246 (which grants the various disclosure exemptions to small and medium-sized companies) but retained the intention of permitting small companies to:

- draw up Schedule 8 accounts only;
- add additional Schedule 4 requirements to the Schedule 8 minimum; or
- draw up full Schedule 4 accounts.

7.3   The most recent change to the Companies Act 1985 and the available exemptions was brought about by The Companies Act 1985 (Accounts of Small and Medium-sized Companies and Minor Accounting Amendments) Regulations 1997, which implement the proposals in the DTI Consultative Document issued in July 1996. The Regulations were laid on 5 February 1997, coming into force on 1 March 1997. The critical date is 24 March 1997 in that a company may, with respect to a financial year ending on or before 24 March 1997 prepare and deliver to the Registrar of Companies such accounts, directors' and auditors' reports as were required under the preceding requirements of the Act. For accounting periods ending after 24 March the new regulations apply.

Modified and Abbreviated Accounts

7.4   The DTI announced in its Consultative Document (*Accounting simpli-fications*, issued in May 1995) that in 1993/94 of the estimated 870,000 small companies on the register only 308,800 filed abbreviated accounts. This relatively low response rate (35.5 per cent) was explained by the fact that the additional compliance costs (estimated at £100 to £250 over and above the cost of preparing accounts for members) would be justified only where there was a competitive or other advantage to be gained by not disclosing particular information. Given the relatively small sums involved the logical conclusion to draw is that the directors of the majority of small companies believe that the public filing of the full accounting details within their financial statements gives rise to no significant competitive disadvantage. Nonetheless the DTI has continued to permit abbreviated accounts to be filed, and has sought to make the exercise of preparing such accounts easier by revising Schedule 8, which contained the disclosure exemptions.

7.5   The new 1997 Regulations radically amend Schedule 8, in the sense of making it a self-contained Schedule applicable to small companies, so that reference will not be needed to Schedule 4 to allow a small company to prepare modified or abbreviated accounts. However, there are no significant revisions to the existing disclosure requirements – Schedule 8 therefore reproduces nearly all of those aspects of Schedule 4 which previously needed to be applied. In addition the Regulations amend s246 of the Act. This section now contains a number of the exemptions from other parts of the Act (such as references to Schedule 5), which were previously to be found in Schedule 8 Part I.

7.6   The revision of s246 and Schedule 8 is one in a series of measures outlined in Chapter 2 designed to reduce the burden on small businesses. It was generally perceived that the previous structure of exemptions in Schedule 8 was confusing, the DTI therefore sought to simplify matters. Whether the measure goes far enough is a moot point, but any step toward reducing the confusion is to be welcomed. The restructuring does have the possible additional effect of permitting further relaxations in disclosure for small companies easier to achieve. It also fits more neatly into the small company accounting regime being established under the FRSSE.

7.7   The exemptions available to small and medium-sized companies when preparing their financial statements are as follows.

Modified accounts

By virtue of s246(2), (previously s246(1A)) small companies may prepare accounts which take advantage of certain disclosure exemptions in s246 and Schedule 8 (previously Part I of Schedule 8). These can be used for circulation to members and for filing.

Modified reports

By virtue of s246(4), (previously s246(1B)) small companies may prepare a directors' report taking advantage of certain disclosure exemptions in s246 (previously Part II of Schedule 8). Again these can be used for circulation to members and for filing.

Abbreviated accounts

By virtue of s246(5), (previously s246(1)) small and medium-sized companies may file accounts with the Registrar of Companies, taking advantage of exemptions in s246, and providing the information set out in Schedule 8A. These exemptions apply only to accounts for filing with the Registrar and do not remove the obligation to prepare for circulation to members a full set of audited annual financial statements (although advantage can be taken of the exemptions relating to modified accounts and modified reports noted above).

Exemption from preparing group accounts

By virtue of s248 the parent companies of small and medium-sized groups need not prepare group accounts for a financial year in relation to which the group headed by that company qualifies, or is treated as qualifying, as a small or medium-sized group.

Exemption from specified disclosures

Small and medium-sized companies are exempt from the requirements of:

(a) paragraph 36A, Schedule 4, relating to the disclosure of compliance with applicable accounting standards;
(b) s390B, relating to the disclosure of non-audit remuneration by auditors and their associates; and
(c) Schedule 7, Part VI, relating to the disclosure of the Company's policy on payment of creditors.

Audit

Small companies may be able to dispense with the requirement for an audit of the annual financial statements, subject to the further conditions within s249B.

7.8 This chapter provides details of the exemptions available to small and medium-sized companies in respect of modified and abbreviated accounts described above, and explains the conditions which must be met for a company to take advantage of such exemptions.

Public interest companies

7.9 Certain classes of company in which there is a public interest are specifically excluded from taking advantage of the provisions relating to the preparation of modified or abbreviated accounts described in the exemptions above. A company is therefore excluded if it is, or was at any time during the financial year to which the accounts relate, either:

- a public company;
- a banking company (being an authorised institution under the Banking Act 1987);
- an insurance company (as defined in the Insurance Companies Act 1982);
- an authorised person under the Financial Services Act 1986; or
- a member of an ineligible group.

7.10 An ineligible group is defined in s247A as one which includes a parent or subsidiary which is either:

(a) a public company or a body corporate, other than a company (that is, a company subject to the Companies Act), which can offer its shares or debentures to the public. This might therefore include foreign parent companies that can offer their shares to the public; or

(b) an authorised institution under the Banking Act 1987;

(c) an insurance company to which Part II of the Insurance Companies Act 1982 applies; or

(d) an authorised person under the Financial Services Act 1986.

Qualifying as small or medium-sized

7.11 A company which does not trigger the 'public interest' exclusion will 'qualify' as small or medium-sized in the financial year to which the accounts relate if it meets certain relevant size criteria in the financial year in question and the preceding year (s247(1)). (For a newly incorporated company the required conditions need only be met in its first financial year.) A company will also be 'treated as qualifying' if:

- it 'qualified' in the preceding year; or
- it was 'treated as qualifying' in the preceding year.

7.12 Basically under the provisions a company will qualify if it meets the size criteria in two consecutive years but if, in a single year, a company fails to meet the required conditions its status would not be lost for that year. However, not meeting the size criteria in a second consecutive year will mean that the small or medium-size status is lost for that year. The company will then have to meet the size criteria for two consecutive years before the small or medium-sized status is regained. Table 1 illustrates the impact of these provisions.

Table 1	Meeting the size criteria in consecutive years	
Year	*Meets size criteria in year*	*Qualifies*
1*	X	N
2*	√	N
3	√	Y
4	X	Y+
5	√	Y+
6	X	N
7	X	N
8	√	N

+ = treated as qualifying

* NB This does not denote the company's first and second years of trading. There is a specific provision for a company's first year of trading – see **7.11**.

Size criteria

7.13 Small and medium-sized companies must satisfy at least two of the three criteria in Table 2.

Table 2	Size criteria for small and medium-sized companies
Small company	**Turnover** – not more than £2.8m **Balance sheet total** – not more than £1.4m **Average number of employees** – not more than 50
Medium-sized company	**Turnover** – not more than £11.2m **Balance sheet total** – not more than £5.6m **Average number of employees** – not more than 250

7.14 In applying these criteria:

● when comparing turnover, if the financial year of a company is not a period of 12 calendar months then the maximum figure of turnover set out within the table above should be proportionately adjusted – s247(4);

- the balance sheet total represents the sum of all assets, without any deduction for liabilities – s247(5); and
- for accounting periods ending after 2 February 1996, the average number of employees should be determined on a monthly basis (SI 1996 No 189). That is to say, the number of full and part-time employees with a contract of employment in each month of the financial year should be totalled and divided by the number of months to arrive at the average – s247(6). Prior to the implementation of SI 1996 No 189 (which has effect for annual statements ending on or after 2 February 1996) this average number was required to be calculated on a weekly basis.

Exception – parent companies

7.15 Further conditions apply where the company has subsidiary under-takings. A parent company (including an intermediate parent company) can only be treated:

- as a small company in relation to a financial year if the group headed by that company qualifies as a 'small group'; and
- as a medium-sized company in relation to a financial year if the group headed by that parent company qualifies as a 'medium-sized' group.

Small and medium-sized groups

7.16 The criteria for whether or not a group qualifies as small or medium-sized is significant other than in determining whether the parent itself can be treated as small or medium-sized. There is also an exemption available to the parent company of a small or medium-sized group permitting it not to prepare group accounts for a financial year in relation to which the group headed by that company qualifies as a small or medium-sized group and is not an ineligible group.

7.17 A group will qualify as small or medium-sized in the financial year to which the accounts relate if it meets the required size criteria in the year in question and the preceding year – s249(1). As explained above in the context of a company, the Companies Act will permit it to be 'treated as qualifying' if it qualified, or was 'treated as qualifying', in the preceding year.

7.18 The size criteria for small and medium-sized groups are set out in Table 3.

Table 3 Size criteria for small and medium-sized groups	
Small group	Turnover – not more than £3.36m gross (or £2.8m net) Balance sheet total – not more than £1.68m gross (or £1.4m net) Average number of employees – not more than 50
Medium-sized group	Turnover - not more than £13.44m gross (or £11.2m net) Balance sheet total – not more than £6.72m gross (or £5.6m net) Average number of employees – not more than 250

7.19   The gross criteria are applied by aggregating the relevant amounts from the accounts of a parent and its subsidiaries without making the set-offs and adjustments required by Schedule 4A (that is, the normal consolidation adjustments). The net criteria are applied after making consolidation adjustments and are likely to be relevant when there is significant intra-group trading which will be eliminated from the figures for consolidation. A group may qualify under either the gross or the net criteria.

7.20   When compiling the relevant figures, the amounts in respect of subsidiaries should be based on their financial statements for financial years that are co-terminous with those of the parent company or, where this is not the case, the last financial year ending before the year-end of the parent company – s249(5).

7.21   Having established whether or not the company qualifies as small or medium-sized, and whether it can take advantage of the exemption from preparing group accounts the next step is to consider the form which the company's individual accounts may take.

The content of financial statements

7.22   A small company can produce its report and accounts for its members which take advantage of some or all the specific exemptions in Parts I and II of Schedule 8. However, as with any company, it would be entitled to give more information than the required minimum. There is a further layer of detail which may be omitted from the abbreviated accounts prepared for filing with the Registrar of Companies. The permutations are shown in Table 4 on the next page.

Table 4					
	Can be applied by:		**Can be sent:**		
Financial statements prepared taking advantage of:	Small companies	Medium-sized companies	to members	for filing	Termed
– no disclosure exemptions	√	√	√	√	Full accounts
– limited exemptions from specific Companies Act disclosures	√	√	√	√	Full accounts
– s246(3) (accounts) and Schedule 8	√	X	}√	}√	Modified (or sometimes 'simplified') accounts
– s246(4) directors' report	√	X	}	}	
– s246(5), s246(6) and Schedule 8A	√		N/A – members must be sent one of the categories above	√	Abbreviated accounts
– s246A		√		√	

7.23 The remainder of this chapter explains the disclosure exemptions available for the preparation of modified and abbreviated accounts. Illustrative financial statements of a small company taking advantage of the available exemptions for modified accounts and abbreviated accounts are provided in Appendix 1 and Appendix 2, respectively.

Modified report and accounts for small companies

7.24 Small companies are able to take advantage of certain exemptions from disclosure when preparing the accounts and directors' report for circulation to members. If group financial statements are prepared for a small group they may also be prepared on the basis of these disclosure exemptions. Accounts which take advantage of such exemptions are termed 'modified accounts' (not to be confused with 'abbreviated accounts', which are relevant for filing purposes only).

Disclosure exemptions – modified accounts

7.25 A small company may take advantage of all or any of the various disclosure exemptions in s246(3) and the adoption of Schedule 8 for its individual accounts. The exemptions permit combinations of various sub-headings required under the formats within Schedule 4 to the Companies Act. For example:

- intangibles other than goodwill may be combined;
- tangible assets, other than land and buildings, under the sub-heading B.II in Schedule 4 may be combined;
- amounts to be reflected as shares in group undertakings may be combined with those for participating interests, and similarly loans to group undertakings may be combined with loans to undertakings in which the company has a participating interest (in both fixed and current asset investments);
- raw materials, work in progress and finished goods may be combined as a new item 'stocks' to be shown above 'payments on account';
- other debtors may be combined with called up share capital not paid, prepayments and accrued income;
- debenture loans, payments received on account, bills of exchange payable, other creditors including taxation and social security, and accruals and deferred income may be combined as 'other creditors';
- provisions for liabilities and charges (such as pensions and similar obligations) need not be sub-analysed between the different kinds of provision; and
- 'other reserves' need not be analysed into its components (such as the capital redemption reserve).

7.26 In addition, certain of the detail required to be given by way of note under Schedule 4 may be omitted. The following notes are among the more significant of those required under Schedule 4 but which are no longer required for small companies taking advantage of the exemptions in s246 and adopting Schedule 8:

Table 5	
Paragraph	Notes not required by s246(3) and Schedule 8
Schedule 4	
40	Detail as to number, the price paid and period exercisable where there are contingent rights to the allotment of shares.
44	The analysis of land and buildings between freehold and long and short leasehold.
47	The separate disclosure of deferred taxation from other provisions for taxation.
51(2)	Separate disclosure of the aggregate amount outstanding on loans provided by way of financial assistance for purchase of own shares.
51(3)	Separate disclosure of the aggregate amount recommended for dividends.
56	Particulars of staff (e.g., average numbers, analysis of wages, social security costs etc.).
Schedule 6	
1(3), 2, 3, 4, 5 and 7	The breakdown of the aggregate amount of directors' emoluments and details of chairman and highest paid director.

7.27   Where a small company has taken advantage of any of the exemptions in preparing individual financial statements it may also take advantage of all or any of the exemptions, as outlined above, in drawing up group accounts. Whilst many companies may be able to take advantage of the exemption from preparing group accounts some will elect to prepare accounts for the benefit of members.

7.28   Where the directors have taken advantage of the provisions available to small companies under s246(3), the balance sheet should contain above the signature required by s233 a statement that the accounts have been prepared in accordance with the special provisions of Part VII of the Companies Act 1985 relating to small companies.

Directors' report

7.29   Section 246(4) (previously s246(1B) and Part II of Schedule 8) also gives small companies exemptions from certain of the disclosures normally required within the directors' report. The report for a small company need not give the following information which is otherwise required under s234 or Schedule 7:

- fair review of business;
- amount to be paid as dividend;
- asset values;
- employee involvement; and
- miscellaneous disclosures required by paragraph 6 of Schedule 7 (important post balance sheet events, future developments, research and development and overseas branches).

7.30 Where the directors have taken advantage of the exemptions in s246(4), the directors' report should contain above the signature required by s234A a statement that the report has been prepared in accordance with the special provisions of Part VII relating to small companies.

7.31 There are no corresponding exemptions from disclosure in the directors' report for medium-sized companies.

Abbreviated accounts

7.32 Abbreviated accounts are accounts prepared by either small or medium-sized companies for filing at Companies House. Such financial statements are permitted to contain less information than those produced for shareholders. The required minimum content of abbreviated accounts will depend on whether the company is small or medium-sized.

Small company

7.33 If the company is a small company then the exemptions relating to small companies within s246(5) permit it to file abbreviated accounts comprising only an abbreviated version of its balance sheet and certain specified notes.

7.34 The abbreviated accounts for a small company therefore do not need to contain a directors' report nor a profit or loss account.

7.35 The abbreviated balance sheet, indicating on the face the name and signature of the director signing the accounts on behalf of the Board, needs to show only those items to which a letter or roman numeral is assigned in the formats within Schedule 4. The following matters must be disclosed on the face of the balance sheet or in an accompanying note:

1   the aggregate amount of debtors due after more than one year;
2   where format 2 has been used, the aggregate amount of creditors due within one year and the aggregate amounts of creditors due after more than one year (this information is already disclosed in format 1);

7.36 Of the detailed information required by Part III of Schedule 4, Schedule 5 and Schedule 6, only the following need be disclosed in applying the exemptions in s246(5) and (6) and Schedule 8A:

Table 6	
Paragraph	**Required disclosure**
Schedule 4	
36	Accounting policies.
38	Share capital.
39	Particulars of allotments.
42	Fixed assets (but only in so far as it relates to those items that do not have Arabic numerals).
48(1) & (4)(a)	Particulars of debts and the amount (but not the nature of security given).
58(1)	Basis of conversion of foreign currency.
58(2)	Corresponding amounts for previous financial year.
Schedule 5 – All information with the exception of:	
4	Financial years of subsidiary undertakings.
6	Shares and debentures of the company held by subsidiary undertakings.
Schedule 6	
Of the information required by Schedule 6 to be given in the notes to the accounts, the information detailed in paragraphs 1 to 14 (directors' emoluments, pension contributions and compensation for loss of office) need not be given. However, details of loans and other transactions with directors must still be disclosed.	

7.37 A statement of cash flows is not a Companies Act disclosure requirement but a requirement of an accounting standard (FRS 1), applicable only to accounts intended to show a true and fair view. Since abbreviated accounts do not purport to show a true and fair view, a statement of cash flows may be omitted. Moreover, FRS 1 specifically exempts from its requirements any company that would be eligible to file abbreviated accounts as a small company.

7.38 A pro forma set of abbreviated accounts for a small company is set out in Appendix 2.

Medium-sized company

7.39 The reductions in the level of disclosure for the abbreviated accounts of a medium-sized company available under s246A, (previously Section B of

Part III of Schedule 8) are far more limited than those applicable to small companies. A medium-sized company may file abbreviated accounts comprising a full (that is, unmodified) balance sheet, all notes to the accounts and the directors' report and an abbreviated version of its profit and loss account. The profit and loss abbreviations available are as follows:

- the figures for turnover and cost of sales may be combined into one figure for gross profit or loss (items 1, 2, 3 and 6 in format 1, and items 1 to 5 in format 2 within Schedule 4);
- the analysis of turnover by markets and by classes of business may be omitted.

Chapter Eight

Implications for Auditors and Accountants

Introduction

8.1 Under s235 of the Companies Act 1985 a company's auditors are required to state, in a report accompanying the financial statements and addressed to the members of the company, their opinion as to whether or not the accounts of the company (or group, if group accounts are prepared):

- give a true and fair view of:
    - its state of affairs at the end of the financial year; and
    - its profit or loss for the financial year; and
- have been properly prepared in accordance with the Act.

8.2 In forming their opinion, the auditors will need to consider the disclosures which the company should make by reference to the disclosure requirements of the Companies Act and relevant accounting standards. Both sources of disclosure need to be considered since, subject to the override discussed in **8.3** below, accounts cannot be true and fair or prepared in accordance with the Companies Act if they have not complied with the accounting requirements of the Act or with relevant accounting standards.

8.3 Where the directors believe a departure from an accounting standard or a Companies Act requirement is necessary to give a true and fair view then an 'override' can be applied. In such cases the Companies Act, UITF 7 (a pronouncement or 'Abstract' issued by the Urgent Issues Task Force) and the Foreword to Accounting Standards require the accounts to provide full disclosure of the departure and its effect. Where the auditors disagree with the departure they will need to refer to the matter, by way of a qualification, in their audit report.

8.4 We saw in Chapter 4 and Chapter 7 that small companies are entitled to take advantage of exemptions from certain disclosures in accounting standards (by applying the FRSSE) and the Companies Act (by applying s246 and Schedule 8). Clearly the directors and auditors will need to assess at an early stage whether the company is entitled to take advantage of the exemptions available. The directors are also required to include a statement on the balance sheet to confirm that the company is so entitled. Suggested wording for such a statement is shown in **8.35**.

Assessing whether the company is entitled to the exemptions

8.5 A key issue for directors and auditors alike will be to determine whether or not a company is entitled to take advantage of the exemptions afforded under s246 (enabling them to apply Schedule 8) and the FRSSE. To do this they will need to consider carefully the criteria outlined in Chapter 2 relating to small companies and to assess whether the various conditions have been met for the year under review.

8.6 Where the company meets the conditions the directors are required to make a positive statement, on the balance sheet, to the effect that the company is entitled to take advantage of the exemptions. If this conclusion were found to be invalid the accounts sent for filing should be rejected by the Registrar of Companies and potentially the directors could be liable to a fine and for the costs incurred in rectifying the situation.

8.7 Where the company's accounts are subject to audit and the auditors do not believe that the company is entitled to the exemptions then they would need to communicate this fact to their client as soon as practicable. In the unlikely event that the directors persevere with preparing accounts which are drawn up either under the FRSSE or s246 and Schedule 8 where the company is not entitled to those exemptions then the auditors would need to draw attention to this fact in their audit report.

8.8 In the annual reports published by the Registrar of Companies the point is frequently made that a number of companies have been found to be taking advantage of small company exemptions although they were not entitled to do so (one of the most common reasons being that the company was part of an ineligible group – see Chapter 7). Auditors who fail to draw attention to this and who have issued an unqualified report may be reported by the Registrar to the ICAEW, ICAS or other relevant accountancy body, for disciplinary action to be considered.

8.9 Where the company's accounts are not subject to audit, because the company has taken advantage of the exemptions in s249A (discussed in Chapter 7) the onus is placed solely on the directors to ensure that the relevant conditions for qualifying as a small company are met. Again the directors potentially would be liable to fines and for the cost of rectifying the situation. Any chartered accountants involved in the preparation of the accounts would potentially be liable to disciplinary action by their account-ancy body.

Ceasing to be entitled to the exemptions

8.10 As explained in Chapter 2, other than in the first year of trading a company will need to consider more than just the current year to establish if the company qualifies, or can be treated as qualifying, as a small company for the purposes of preparing modified or abbreviated accounts.

8.11 The provisions relating to qualifying and being treated as qualifying are designed to avoid a company constantly switching from preparing small or medium-sized company accounts in one year and not being able to take advantage of exemptions in the following year purely because its results, balance sheet or number of employees fall below and rise above the relevant thresholds in consecutive years. The rules basically provide for a 'one-off' year to be ignored.

8.12 Since entitlement to adopt the FRSSE is tied to the entitlement to prepare small company accounts, it follows that the same considerations will apply. A company will not lose its ability to prepare accounts under the FRSSE because of one particularly successful year. Since the company will lose its ability to prepare accounts under the FRSSE only after the second, or possibly third, year of not meeting the criteria the directors of the company in normal circumstances will have some advance warning that the FRSSE should not be adopted and can plan for this in the preparation of their financial statements.

8.13 The FRSSE does not specifically address the issue of what should happen when the company ceases being able to adopt the FRSSE, but it is a requirement of company law in both Schedule 4 and Schedule 8 that accounts are prepared on a comparable basis, so that comparative figures should be given and the previous years' figures, where necessary, restated to be on a consistent basis.

8.14 Ensuring such consistency is not purely a matter for the consideration of the auditors since the accounts are first and foremost the responsibility of the directors. Nevertheless the auditors may face practical problems in ensuring that the comparative figures are indeed comparable. Given that the FRSSE has largely retained the measurement aspects of current accounting standards, but has concentrated on reducing the levels of disclosure neces-sary, a significant restatement of comparatives is likely to be relatively rare. Furthermore, since the auditors will not be expressing an opinion on the prior year figures, their work on opening balances should be straightforward and that on checking comparatives may be able to be limited to analytical review, subject to meeting the standards in SAS 450.

8.15 Finally, assuming the company adequately explains the basis on which the accounts have been prepared and the auditors concur with this, then there would be no necessity for making reference in the auditors' report to the fact that the company is no longer entitled to úse the FRSSE.

Can modified accounts be true and fair?

8.16 Assuming that it is valid for the accounts to have been drawn up to take advantage of the various disclosure exemptions, the preparation of accounts which are abbreviated in some way then gives rise to the issue of whether the auditors (or indeed the directors) can conclude that such accounts:
- are still capable of giving a true and fair view; and
- have been prepared in accordance with the Act.

Application of accounting standards and the FRSSE

8.17 To be true and fair accounts must comply with accounting standards:

> *'accounting standards are authoritative statements of how particular types of transaction and other events should be reflected in financial statements and accordingly compliance with accounting standards will normally be necessary for financial statements to give a true and fair view'* – Foreword to Accounting Standards, paragraph 16.

8.18 Accounts drawn up by small companies in compliance with the FRSSE are still intended to permit their financial statements to present a true and fair view of the results for the period and the state of affairs of the company at the end of the period. But, as we have seen in Chapter 4, the FRSSE in many cases reduces the disclosure requirements of existing standards to a minimum.

8.19 The adoption of the FRSSE may therefore mean that not all of the disclosures which a company might otherwise need to make to reflect adequately its financial position or economic performance will be given. Where additional information is required for the accounts to give a true and fair view then the FRSSE requires that information to be given (as does s226(4) of the Companies Act). In this context, the FRSSE comments that to achieve a true and fair view:

> *'Where there is any doubt as to whether applying any provisions of the*

FRSSE would be sufficient to give a true and fair view, adequate explanation should be given in the notes to the accounts or the transaction or arrangement concerned as to the treatment adopted.'

8.20 Therefore, provided full disclosure of transactions not catered for under the FRSSE is made, a company can adopt the FRSSE and produce accounts which are capable of being true and fair and of being drawn up in accordance with the Companies Act. This leads to the next question, whether the same conclusion would hold for accounts prepared taking advantage of s246 and Schedule 8 (or the exemptions under the old Schedule 8 before its recent revision described in Chapter 7).

Schedule 8

8.21 It perhaps goes without saying that financial statements drawn up to comply with s246 and Schedule 8 will have been prepared in accordance with the Companies Act.

8.22 Whether such accounts can also be true and fair was an issue specifically addressed within the old Schedule 8. Paragraph 14(2) stated that the financial statements shall:

'not be deemed, by reason only of the fact that advantage has been taken of any exemptions set out in [Part I of Schedule 8] not to give a true and fair view as required by [The Companies Act 1985]'.

8.23 By the same token the Foreword to Accounting Standards recognises that the Companies Act disclosure requirements to some extent overlap with those of accounting standards. Accordingly where company law specifically permits disclosures not to be made the Foreword comments that:

'where accounting standards prescribe specific information to be contained in financial statements, such requirements do not override exemptions from disclosure given by law to, and utilised by, certain types of entity'.

8.24 In short, if information is not required by Schedule 8, or would be required to be given by an accounting standard but there is a specific exemption under company law from disclosing that information, then it is valid to omit it. But in neither case is this the same as saying that the resulting accounts will be true and fair.

8.25 A matter may have been omitted, because of an exemption, which is of such significance that it would need to be disclosed for the financial statements to give a true and fair view. So, in these circumstances would the auditors be obliged to qualify their opinion? Paragraph 14(3) of the old Schedule 8 resolved the question by providing that auditors merely had to state whether in their opinion the accounts of a small company taking advantage of the Schedule 8 exemptions had been properly prepared in accordance with the small company provisions of the Act.

8.26 The Auditing Practices Board (APB) also addressed this issue in a discrete, almost muted, way by using a footnote in SAS 600. The illustrative audit report in example 5 of that Standard (which was prepared in the context of the old Schedule 8 requirements) sets out the following opinion when reporting on a company incorporated in Great Britain, using the accounting exemptions available for small companies:

> *'In our opinion the financial statements give a true and fair view of the state of the company's affairs as at 31 December 19.. and of its profit [loss] for the year then ended and have been properly prepared in accordance with the provisions of the Companies Act 1985 applicable to small companies.'*

8.27 In the footnote to this example the APB advises that where the auditors consider that, were it not for paragraph 14(2) of the old Schedule 8, a true and fair view was not given because of the use of some or all of the exemptions, then the opinion could omit reference to 'true and fair', so that it was restricted to the following:

> *'In our opinion, the financial statements have been properly prepared in accordance with the provisions of the Companies Act 1985 applicable to small companies.'*

8.28 The revised Schedule 8 does not retain either paragraph 14(2) or 14(3). Instead the DTI amended s246(2) of the Act to the effect that when small companies take advantage of the right to draw up Schedule 8 accounts, references in s226 to compliance with the provisions of Schedule 4 *'shall be construed accordingly'*. In clarifying its position in the Consultative Document containing the proposed revisions, the DTI commented, somewhat cryptically:

> *'it is sufficiently clear that the provision of new section 246(2) ... applies the true and fair view without diminution and therefore no further embellishment is necessary'.*

8.29 In essence, the financial statements of a company, irrespective of whether or not it is taking advantage of Schedule 8, will now be **required** to be true and fair. This represents a subtle shift in the requirements for small companies adopting Schedule 8 although it has not been publicised as such.

8.30 As the changes to Schedule 8 are now made, neither the directors nor the auditors of a small company will need to agonise over whether the financial statements of a small company which have been drawn up under Schedule 8 and adopting the FRSSE can be true and fair or have been prepared in accordance with the Act. They can, and they should be, provided any additional disclosures necessary for a true and fair view are made.

Reporting

8.31   Because of the differences between the financial statements required of small companies adopting the FRSSE and Schedule 8 and the generality of companies it would be convenient to be able to make this distinction clear by having different forms of audit report applicable to small companies taking advantage of available exemptions and to other companies. This distinction has been made clear in the past by the required statement by the directors and by the auditors' report.

8.32   The logical extension of the subtle change referred to in **8.29** above, that in future all accounts need to be true and fair in all circumstances, is that the audit report on annual accounts of a small company taking advantage of the FRSSE and s246 and Schedule 8 will be expected to be expressed in true and fair terms, on the same basis as any other company complying with the Companies Act.

8.33   Although the revision to the Companies Act and the introduction of the FRSSE effectively admit the possibility of having two levels of true and fair it is unsatisfactory to have one standard report for two distinct reporting regimes. The APB will presumably need to revisit SAS 600 and delete the footnote to example 5 discussed in **8.27** above. But it is to be hoped that future APB guidance retains in its recommended 'standard' audit report the reference to the 'provisions of the Companies Act 1985 applicable to small companies'. This has proved helpful in the past in identifying and emphasising that the requirements for small companies are not the same as for larger companies, and the case for its retention is underlined by the introduction of the FRSSE.

Form of report

8.34   An example audit report on the annual accounts of a small company taking advantage of the FRSSE is included in the illustrative financial statements in Appendix 1.

8.35   This form of report is consistent with the statement which the directors should make on the balance sheet when they have taken advantage of the provisions within the revised s246 and Schedule 8 relating to small companies. An example of such a directors' statement is as follows:

> *'In preparing the accounts, the directors have taken advantage of the special provisions of Part VII of the Companies Act 1985 relating to small companies.'*

8.36 The FRSSE suggests that in addition a sentence to confirm that the accounts have been prepared in accordance with the FRSSE is included within this statement (although the suggested wording in the FRSSE was drafted to accompany the directors' old statement concerning Part I of Schedule 8 prior to the recent revisions). An example of the combined statement, included in the illustrative small company financial statements in Appendix 1, is as follows:

> *'In preparing the accounts, the directors have taken advantage of the special provisions of Part VII of the Companies Act 1985 relating to small companies and have prepared the accounts in accordance with the Financial Reporting Standard For Smaller Entities.'*

Reporting on abbreviated accounts

8.37 By virtue of ss246(5), 246(6) and 246(A)(3), small or medium-sized companies are entitled to file abbreviated accounts with the Registrar of Companies.

8.38 Where this is proposed, provided that the directors have not taken advantage of the exemption from audit under s249A or that the company has not exempted itself from appointing auditors by virtue of s250, the auditors will need to consider whether in their opinion the requirements for exemption are satisfied. Assuming the auditors are satisfied they are required to provide the directors of the company with a special report (for delivery to the Registrar with the abbreviated accounts), stating that in their opinion:

- the company is entitled to deliver abbreviated accounts prepared in accordance with ss246(5) and 246(6) or 246(A)(3); and that
- the accounts are properly prepared in accordance with those provisions.

8.39 Prior to the recent revision of s246 and Schedule 8, the special report, addressed to the directors, was required to reproduce the full text of the auditors' report on the full financial statements. Rather than reproduce the full text of the audit report the special report under the new s247B requires reference to the audit report on the full accounts only if that report was:

1 qualified; or
2 contained a statement under:

(a) s237(2) – accounts, records or returns inadequate or accounts not agreeing with the records and returns; or

(b) s237(3) – failure to obtain necessary information and explanations.

8.40 A copy of an example auditors' report on abbreviated accounts is included in the illustrative financial statements in Appendix 2.

Appendix 1

Example Financial Statements

Smallco Limited

Financial statements 31 December 1996
together with directors' and auditors' reports

Registered number: _____

KEY:
items underlined and in bold represent detail to be inserted when applying the FRSSE
items in italic represent detail to be deleted when applying the FRSSE

Directors' report

For the year ended 31 December 1996

Financial statements
The directors present their report and financial statements for the year ended 31 December 1996.

Directors' responsibilities
Company law requires the directors to prepare financial statements for each financial year which give a true and fair view of the state of affairs of the company and of the profit or loss of the company for that period. In preparing those accounts, the directors are required to:

- select suitable accounting policies and then apply them consistently;
- make judgments and estimates that are reasonable and prudent;
- state whether applicable accounting standards have been followed, subject to any material departures disclosed and explained in the accounts; and

The directors are responsible for keeping proper accounting records which disclose with reasonable accuracy at any time the financial position of the company and to enable them to ensure that the accounts comply with the Companies Act 1985. They are also responsible for safeguarding the assets of the company and hence for taking reasonable steps for the prevention and detection of fraud and other irregularities.

Principal activity
The principal activity of the company in the year under review was the manufacture and distribution of art and design equipment including software packages.

Results and dividends
The profit for the year after taxation amounted to £   (1995: £   ). The directors recommend a dividends of £   for the year (1995: £   ) which leaves a profit of £   to be retained.

Review of the business
Turnover increased by 15 per cent during the year and the directors believe that the trend will continue as export sales in Eire have increased by 25 per cent and now comprise 15 per cent of total turnover.

1   SMALLCO LIMITED

Directors' report (continued)

Future developments
The directors intend to take advantage of the single European market and open up further export markets in Europe and have opened negotiations with various European agencies to this end.

Market value of land and buildings
The land and buildings were revalued at 31 December 1996. The valuation of £   which as £   higher than the previous book value, is incorporated in the accounts.

Directors and their interests
The directors, all of whom served throughout the year, had the following interests in the £1 ordinary shares of the company at the beginning and the end of the financial year.

	1996	1995
Mr M. Clarke		
Mrs F. Mullen		
Miss J. Bennett		
Miss T. Green	_____	_____

Political and charitable contributions
During the year the company made a political contribution of £
to the XXX Party and various charitable donations totalling £

Auditors
In accordance with section 385 of the Companies Act 1985, a resolution proposing that [Firm] be reappointed auditors will be put to the Annual General Meeting.

This report has been prepared in accordance with the special provisions relating to small companies within Part VII of the Companies Act 1985.

[Address of registered office]   By order of the Board,

J. Bennett
Secretary

[Date]

2   SMALLCO LIMITED

Auditors' report

To the Members of Smallco Limited:

We have audited the financial statements on pages _ to _ which have been prepared on the basis of the accounting policies set out on pages _ to _.

Respective responsibilities of directors and auditors

As described on page _ the company's directors are responsible for the preparation of the financial statements. It is our responsibility to form an independent opinion, based on our audit, on those statements and to report our opinion to you.

Basis of opinion

We conducted our audit in accordance with Auditing Standards issued by the Auditing Practices Board. An audit includes examination, on a test basis, of evidence relevant to the amounts and disclosures in the financial statements. It also includes an assessment of the significant estimates and judgments made by the directors in the preparation of the financial statements and of whether the accounting policies are appropriate to the company's circumstances, consistently applied and adequately disclosed.

We planned and performed our audit so as to obtain all the information and explanations which we considered necessary in order to provide us with sufficient evidence to give reasonable assurance that the financial statements are free from material misstatement, whether caused by fraud or other irregularity or error. In forming our opinion we also evaluated the overall adequacy of the presentation of information in the financial statements.

Opinion

In our opinion the financial statements give a true and fair view of the company's state of affairs as at 31 December 1996 and of its profit for the year then ended and have been properly prepared in accordance with the provisions of the Companies Act 1985 applicable to small companies.

[Firm]

Chartered Accountants and Registered Auditors

[Address]

[Date]

3   SMALLCO LIMITED

Profit and loss account

For the year ended 31 December 1996

	Notes	1996 £	1996 £	1995 £
Turnover	2			
Existing operations		xxxx		
Acquisitions		xxxx		
			xxxx	xxx
Cost of sales			xxxx	xxx
Gross profit			xxx	xx
Distribution costs		xx		x
Administrative expenses		xx		x
			xx	x
Income from participating interest			x	x
Operating profit	3, 4			
Existing operations		xx		
Acquisitions		xx		
			xxx	xx
Interest receivable and similar income			xx	xx
Interest payable and similar charges			xx	x
Profit on ordinary activities before taxation			xx	x
Tax on profit on ordinary activities			x	x
Profit for the financial year			xx	x
Dividends paid or proposed *on equity and non-equity shares*	14		xx	x
Profit for the financial year			xx	x
Retained profit (loss) at the beginning of the year			xxx	xx
Retained profit carried forward			xxx	xxx

All the above results derive from continuing operations.

4   SMALLCO LIMITED

Statement of total recognised gains and losses and note of historical cost profits

For the year ended 31 December 1996

Statement of total recognised gains and losses

	1996	1995
	£	£
Profit for the financial year	xx	xx
Unrealised surplus on revaluation of properties	xx	xx
Total recognised gains and losses	xx	xx

Note of historical cost profits and losses

	1996	1995
	£	£
Reported profit on ordinary activities before taxation	xx	xx
Realisation of property revaluation gains of previous years	xx	xx
Difference between an historical costs depreciation charge and the actual depreciation charge for the year	xx	xx
Historical cost profit on ordinary activities before taxation	xx	xx
Historical cost retained profit for the year	xx	xx

5   SMALLCO LIMITED

Balance sheet
31 December 1996

	Notes	1996 £	1995 £
Fixed assets			
Intangible assets	5	xx	xx
Tangible assets	6	xx	xx
Investments	7	xx	xx
		xxx	xxx
Current assets			
Stocks	9	xx	xx
Debtors	10	xx	xx
Cash at bank and in hand		xx	xx
Creditors: Amounts falling due within one year	11	xx	x
Net current assets		xx	xx
Creditors: Amounts falling due after more than one year	12	x	x
Net assets		xxxx	xxxx
Capital and reserves			
Called up share capital	13	xx	xx
Share premium account		xx	xx
Revaluation reserve	14	xx	xx
Profit and loss account		xxx	xxx
Shareholders' funds	15	xxxx	xxxx

Analysis of Shareholders' funds:

Non-equity		x	x
Equity		xxx	xxx
		xxxx	xxxx

6   SMALLCO LIMITED

Balance sheet (continued)

These accounts have been prepared in accordance with the special provisions relating to small companies within Part VII of the Companies Act 1985 <u>and have been prepared in accordance with the Financial Reporting Standard for Smaller Entities.</u>

Signed on behalf of the Board

[Name]   Director

[Date]

7   SMALLCO LIMITED

Notes to financial statements

31 December 1996

1 Accounting policies

[Note the FRSSE requires the disclosure of accounting policies which are judged material or critical in determining profit or loss for the year and in stating the financial position – FRSSE paragraph 6. Certain accounting policies required to be disclosed under other accounting standards will therefore not need to feature in a company's accounts, but which can be deleted and which retained will depend on individual circumstances.]

The financial statements have been prepared in accordance with applicable accounting standards under the historical cost convention, modified by the revaluation of certain fixed assets.

(a) Consolidation

The company and its subsidiary undertaking form a small group as defined by statute and therefore, the company has availed itself of the exemption under section 248 of the Companies Act 1985 not to prepare group accounts. *These financial statements therefore present information about the company as an individual undertaking and not about its group.*

(b) Turnover

Turnover consists of invoiced sales net of returns, trade discounts and value added tax.

(c) Depreciation

Depreciation has been provided at the following rates in order to write off the assets on a straight-line basis over their estimated useful lives.

Freehold and long-leasehold buildings	– 2 per cent on cost or revalued amounts
Plant and machinery	– 10 per cent straight line
Fixtures and fittings	– 10 per cent straight line
Motor vehicles	– 25 per cent straight line
Goodwill and intangible assets	– 10 per cent straight line

(d) Revaluation of properties

Individual freehold and leasehold properties are revalued every [number] years with the surplus or deficit on book value being transferred to the revaluation reserve, unless a deficit (or its reversal) is expected to be permanent, in which case it is charged (or credited) to the profit and loss account.

8   SMALLCO LIMITED

Notes to financial statements (continued)

Where depreciation charges are increased following a revaluation, an amount equal to the increase is transferred annually from the revaluation reserve to the profit and loss account as a movement on reserves. On the disposal of a revalued fixed asset, any related balance in the revaluation reserve is also transferred to the profit and loss account as a movement on reserves.

(e) Investments

Fixed asset investments are shown at cost less provision for permanent diminution in value. Current asset investments are stated at the lower of cost and net realisable value.

(f) Leases

Assets held under finance leases, which confer rights and obligations similar to those attached to owned assets, are capitalised as tangible fixed assets and are depreciated over the shorter of the lease terms and their useful lives. The capital elements of future lease obligations are recorded as liabilities, while the interest element is charged to the profit and loss account over the period of the leases to produce a constant rate of charge on the balance of capital repayments outstanding. Hire purchase transactions are dealt with similarly, except that assets are depreciated over their useful lives.

Rentals under operating leases are charged on a straight-line basis over the lease term, even if the payments are not made on such a basis. Benefits received and receivable as an incentive to sign an operating lease are similarly spread on a straight-line basis over the lease term, except where the period to the review date on which the rent is first expected to be adjusted to the prevailing market rate is shorter than the full lease term, in which case the shorter period is used.

(g) Stocks and work in progress

Stocks and work in progress have been valued at the lower of cost and net realisable value.

(h) Taxation

Corporation tax payable is provided on taxable profits at the current rate. Advance corporation tax payable on dividends paid or provided for in the year is written off, except when recoverability against corporation tax payable is considered to be reasonably assured. Credit is taken for advance corporation tax written off in previous years when it is recovered against corporation tax liabilities.

9   SMALLCO LIMITED

Notes to financial statements (continued)

(i) Deferred taxation
Provision is made for deferred taxation using the liability method to take account of timing differences between the incidence of income and expenditure for taxation and accounting purposes except to the extent that the directors consider that a liability to taxation is unlikely to crystallise.

(j) Pension costs and other post-retirement benefits
The company operates a defined contribution scheme. The amount charged to the profit and loss account in respect of pension costs is the contributions payable in the year. Differences between contributions payable in the year and contributions actually paid are shown as either accruals or prepayments in the balance sheet.

(k) Foreign currencies
Transactions in foreign currencies are recorded at the rate of exchange at the date of the transaction or, if hedged, at the forward contract rate. Monetary assets and liabilities denominated in foreign currencies at the balance sheet date are reported at the rates of exchange prevailing at that date or, if appropriate, at the forward contract rate. Any gain or loss arising from a change in exchange rates subsequent to the date of the transaction is included as an exchange gain or loss in the profit and loss account.

(l) Research and development
Research expenditure is written off as incurred. Development expenditure is also written off, except where the directors are satisfied as to the technical, commercial and financial viability of individual projects. In such cases, the identifiable expenditure is deferred and amortised over the period during which the group is expected to benefit.

(m) Government grants
Government grants relating to tangible fixed assets are treated as deferred income and released to the profit and loss account over the expected useful lives of the assets concerned. Other grants are credited to the profit and loss account as the related expenditure is incurred.

2   Turnover
Turnover attributable to geographical markets outside the United Kingdom amounted to 15 per cent (1995 – 14 per cent) of total turnover.

3   Operating profit
Analysis of cost of sales, gross profit and expenses charged to arrive at the Company's operating profit.

10   SMALLCO LIMITED

Notes to financial statements (continued)

	1996 Existing Operations £	1996 Acquisition £	1996 Total Continuing activities £	1995 Total Continuing Activities £
Cost of sales	xx	x	xx	xx
Gross profit	x	x	xxx	xx
Distribution costs	x	x	xx	x
Administrative expenses	x	x	xx	x

4 Operating profit

Operating profit is stated after charging:

	1996 £	1995 £
Depreciation – owned assets	x	x
Depreciation – leased assets	x	x
Pension contribution	x	x
Auditors' remuneration	x	x
Directors' remuneration	x	x

5 Intangible fixed assets

	Goodwill £	Other intangible assets £	Total £
Cost			
1 January 1996	xx	xx	xxx
Additions	x	x	x
Disposals	x	x	x
31 December 1996	xx	xx	xxx
Amortisation			
1 January 1996	x	x	x
Disposals	x	x	x
Charge for the year	x	x	x
31 December 1996	x	x	x

11   SMALLCO LIMITED

Notes to financial statements (continued)

Net book value

31 December 1996	xx	xx	xx
31 December 1995	xx	xx	xx

Other intangible assets comprise development expenditure which has been capitalised in accordance with generally accepted accounting practice and are therefore treated, for dividend purposes, as a realised loss.

6 Tangible fixed assets

	Land and buildings £	Plant and machinery £	Total £
Cost or valuation			
1 January 1996	xxx	xxx	xxx
Additions	xx	xx	xx
Revaluation	x	x	x
Disposals	x	x	x
31 December 1996	xxx	xxx	xxx
Depreciation			
1 January 1996	xx	xx	xx
Disposals	x	x	x
Charge for the year	xx	xx	xx
31 December 1996	xx	xx	xx
Net book value			
31 December 1996	xxx	xxx	xxx
31 December 1995	xxx	xxx	xxx
Leased assets included above:			
Net book value			
31 December 1996	–	x	x
31 December 1995	–	x	x

Land and buildings were revalued during the year by A Surveyor, FRICS, on the basis of existing use value.

12   SMALLCO LIMITED

Notes to accounts (continued)

The historical cost of land and buildings included at a valuation of £ (1995 – £   ) was £   (1995 – £   ) and aggregate depreciation thereon would have been £   (1995 – £   ).

7 Investments

	Subsidiary undertaking and participating interests £	Listed investments £	Total £
Cost			
1 January 1996			
Additions			
31 December 1996			

Subsidiary undertaking and participating interests
The company's investment in its subsidiary company represents the acquisition of the whole of the ordinary share capital of Subsid Limited, which provides promotional services. At 30 September 1996 the aggregate share capital and reserves of Subsid Limited were £   (1995 – £   ) and the profit for the year to that date was £   (1995 – £   ).

The company's investment in its participating interest represents xx per cent of the share capital of Assoc Limited which provides design services. At 31 December 1996 the aggregate share capital and reserves of Assoc Limited were £   (1995 – £   ) and the profit for the year was £   (1995) – £   ).

Listed investments
Listed investments comprise investments which are listed on The London Stock Exchange. The market value of these investments was £   at 31 December 1996 (1995 – £   ).

8 Acquisition in year
On [date] the company acquired the business of Brothers Co for £X in cash. The following table sets out the book values of the identifiable assets and liabilities acquired for their fair value to the company:

13   SMALLCO LIMITED

Notes to accounts (continued)

	Book value	Revaluation	Accounting policy alignment	Other significant items	Fair value to company
	£	£	£	£	£
Fixed assets	x	x			x
Stocks	x		x		x
Bank loan	x			x	x
Net assets	x	x	x	x	x
Goodwill					x
					x
Satisfied by:					
Cash consideration					x

9 Stocks

	1996	1995
	£	£
Raw materials	xxx	xxx
Finished goods and goods for resale	xx	xx
	xxxx	xxxx

10 Debtors

	1996	1995
	£	£
Trade debtors	xxx	xxx
Amounts owed by group undertakings and undertakings in which the company has a participating interest	xx	xx
Other debtors	xx	xx
	xxxx	xxxx

Debtors include an amount of £   falling due after more than one year (1995 – £   ).

14   SMALLCO LIMITED

Notes to accounts (continued)

11 Creditors: Amounts falling due within one year

	1996 £	1995 £
Bank loans and overdrafts (secured)	xx	xx
Trade creditors	xx	xx
Amounts owed to group undertaking and undertakings in which the company has a participating interest	xx	xx
Other creditors, including taxation and social security costs of £ (1995 – £)	xx	xx
	xxx	xx

The bank loans and overdraft are secured on the freehold property.

12 Creditors: Amounts falling due after more than one year

	1996 £	1995 £
Amounts owed to group undertaking and undertakings in which the company has a participating interest	xx	xx
Other creditors	xx	xx
	xx	xx

Included with other creditors is an amount of £   due in more than five years.

13 Called up share capital

	1996 £	1995 £
Authorised		
Ordinary shares of £1 each	xxxx	xxxx
7 per cent Cumulative Preference shares of £1 each	xxx	xxx
	xxxx	xxxx
Allotted, called up and fully paid		
Ordinary shares of £1 each	xxx	xxx
7 per cent Cumulative Preference shares of £1 each	xxx	xxx
	xxxx	xxxx

15   SMALLCO LIMITED

Notes to accounts (continued)

The 7 per cent Cumulative Preference shares are redeemable at par at the option of the company at 1 January 1999 and on each anniversary of that date. *The Cumulative Preference Shareholders have no voting rights, on a winding up they are entitled to the repayment of capital of up to £1 per share in priority to the Ordinary Shareholders.*

14 Revaluation reserve

	1996 £	1995 £
1 January 1996	xx	xx
Revaluation of fixed asset in year	x	–
31 December 1996	xx	xx

No deferred tax has been provided by the company in respect of the revaluation reserves since the directors consider that no liability to taxation will arise in the foreseeable future.

15 *Reconciliation of movements in shareholders' funds*

	1996 £	1995 £
Balance brought forward	xxx	xxx
Recognised gains and losses	xx	xx
Balance carried forward	xxx	xxx

16 Dividends

	1996 £	1995 £
Proposed dividend on Ordinary shares *(equity)*	x	x
Dividend paid on 7 per cent Preference shares *(non-equity)*	x	x

17 Financial commitments
The company had no capital commitments, either authorised or contracted for at the year end. **The company was committed to paying £**

16   SMALLCO LIMITED

Notes to accounts (continued)

<u>(1995 – £   ) under operating leases entered into at 31 December 1996.</u>

Annual commitments under non-cancellable operating leases are as follows:

	1996		1995	
	Land and buildings	Other	Land and buildings	Other
	£	£	£	£
Expiry date				
– within one year	x	x	x	x
– between two and five years	x	x	x	x
– after five years	x	x	x	x
	xx	xx	xx	xx

18 Related party transactions

During the year the company purchased goods in the ordinary course of business from Assoc Ltd, an associated undertaking, at a cost of £.... (1995–£ ...). Amounts owed to associated undertakings amounted to £x at 31 December 1996 (1995- £x).

19 Controlling party

Mr Clarke, a director, and members of his close family control the company as a result of controlling directly or indirectly x per cent of the issued Ordinary share capital.

17   SMALLCO LIMITED

Appendix 2

Example Abbreviated Accounts

Smallco Limited

Abbreviated accounts 31 December 1996

Registered number: _____

Abbreviated accounts: these comprise an
abbreviated balance sheet, notes to the accounts,
a directors' statement and a special report by the
auditors.

KEY:
items underlined and in bold represent detail to be inserted when applying the FRSSE
items in italic represent detail to be deleted when applying the FRSSE

Auditors' Report

To the directors of Smallco Limited pursuant to section 247B of the Companies Act 1985:

We have examined the abbreviated accounts on pages _ to _ together with the financial statements of Smallco Limited prepared under s226 of the Companies Act 1985 for the year ended 31 December 1996.

Respective responsibilities of directors and auditors

The directors are responsible for preparing the abbreviated accounts in accordance with Schedule 8A to the Companies Act 1985. It is our responsibility to form an independent opinion as to the company's entitlement to the exemptions claimed in the directors' statement on page _ and whether the abbreviated accounts have been properly prepared in accordance with that Schedule.

Basis of opinion

We have carried out the procedures we considered necessary to confirm, by reference to the audited financial statements, that the company is entitled to the exemptions and that the abbreviated accounts have been properly prepared from those financial statements. The scope of our work for the purpose of this report does not include examining or dealing with events after the date of our report on the full financial statements.

Opinion

In our opinion the company is entitled to deliver abbreviated accounts prepared in accordance with section 246 of the Companies Act 1985 and the abbreviated accounts on pages _ to _ have been properly prepared in accordance with that provision.

[Firm]

Chartered Accountants and Registered Auditors

[Address]

[Date]

1   SMALLCO LIMITED

Appendix 2

Balance sheet
31 December 1996

	Notes	1996 £	1995 £
Fixed assets			
Intangible assets	1	xx	xx
Tangible assets	2	xx	xx
Investments	3	xx	xx
		xxx	xxx
Current assets			
Stocks		xx	xx
Debtors	4	xx	xx
Cash at bank and in hand		xx	xx
Creditors: Amounts falling due within one year	5	xx	x
Net current assets		xx	xx
Creditors: Amounts falling due after more than one year	6	x	x
Net assets		xxxx	xxxx
Capital and reserves			
Called up share capital	7	xx	xx
Share premium account		xx	xx
Revaluation reserve		xx	xx
Profit and loss account		xxx	xxx
Shareholders' funds		xxxx	xxxx

These accounts have been prepared in accordance with the special provisions relating to small companies within Part VII of the Companies Act 1985.

Signed on behalf of the Board

[Name]   Director

[Date]

2   SMALLCO LIMITED

Notes to financial statements

31 December 1996

1 Accounting policies

[Note the FRSSE requires the disclosure of accounting policies which are judged material or critical in determining profit or loss for the year and in stating the financial position – FRSSE paragraph 6. Certain accounting policies required to be disclosed under other accounting standards will therefore not need to feature in a company's accounts, but which can be deleted and which retained will depend on individual circumstances.]

The financial statements have been prepared in accordance with applicable accounting standards under the historical cost convention, modified by the revaluation of certain fixed assets.

(a) Consolidation

The company and its subsidiary undertaking form a small group as defined by statute and therefore, the company has availed itself of the exemption under section 248 of the Companies Act 1985 not to prepare group accounts. *These financial statements therefore present information about the company as an individual undertaking and not about its group.*

(b) Turnover

Turnover consists of invoiced sales net of returns, trade discounts and value added tax.

(c) Depreciation

Depreciation has been provided at the following rates in order to write off the assets on a straight-line basis over their estimated useful lives.

Freehold and long-leasehold buildings	– 2 per cent on cost or revalued amounts
Plant and machinery	– 10 per cent straight line
Fixtures and fittings	– 10 per cent straight line
Motor vehicles	– 25 per cent straight line
Goodwill and intangible assets	– 10 per cent straight line

(d) Revaluation of properties

Individual freehold and leasehold properties are revalued every [number] years with the surplus or deficit on book value being transferred to the revaluation reserve, unless a deficit (or its reversal) is expected to be permanent, in which case it is charged (or credited) to the profit and loss account. Where depreciation charges are increased following a revaluation, an amount equal to the increase is transferred annually from the revaluation reserve to the profit and

3   SMALLCO LIMITED

loss account as a movement on reserves. On the disposal of a revalued fixed asset, any related balance in the revaluation reserve is also transferred to the profit and loss account as a movement on reserves.

(e) Investments
Fixed asset investments are shown at cost less provision for permanent diminution in value. Current asset investments are stated at the lower of cost and net realisable value.

(f) Leases
Assets held under finance leases, which confer rights and obligations similar to those attached to owned assets, are capitalised as tangible fixed assets and are depreciated over the shorter of the lease terms and their useful lives. The capital elements of future lease obligations are recorded as liabilities, while the interest element is charged to the profit and loss account over the period of the leases to produce a constant rate of charge on the balance of capital repayments outstanding. Hire purchase transactions are dealt with similarly, except that assets are depreciated over their useful lives.

(j) Pension costs and other post-retirement benefits
The company operates a defined contribution scheme. The amount charged to the profit and loss account in respect of pension costs is the contributions payable in the year. Differences between contributions payable in the year and contributions actually paid are shown as either accruals or prepayments in the balance sheet.

(k) Foreign currencies
Transactions in foreign currencies are recorded at the rate of exchange at the date of the transaction or, if hedged, at the forward contract rate. Monetary assets and liabilities denominated in foreign currencies at the balance sheet date are reported at the rates of exchange prevailing at that date or, if appropriate, at the forward contract rate. Any gain or loss arising from a change in exchange rates subsequent to the date of the transaction is included as an exchange gain or loss in the profit and loss account.

Rentals under operating leases are charged on a straight-line basis over the lease term, even if the payments are not made on such a basis. Benefits received and receivable as an incentive to sign an operating lease are similarly spread on a straight-line basis over the lease term, except where the period to the review date on which the rent is first expected to be adjusted to the prevailing market rate is shorter than the full lease term, in which case the shorter period is used.

4   SMALLCO LIMITED

Notes to financial statements (continued)

(g) Stocks and work in progress
Stocks and work in progress have been valued at the lower of cost and net realisable value.

(h) Taxation
Corporation tax payable is provided on taxable profits at the current rate. Advance corporation tax payable on dividends paid or provided for in the year is written off, except when recoverability against corporation tax payable is considered to be reasonably assured. Credit is taken for advance corporation tax written off in previous years when it is recovered against corporation tax liabilities.

(i) Deferred taxation
Provision is made for deferred taxation using the liability method to take account of timing differences between the incidence of income and expenditure for taxation and accounting purposes except to the extent that the directors consider that a liability to taxation is unlikely to crystallise.

(l) Research and development
Research expenditure is written off as incurred. Development expenditure is also written off, except where the directors are satisfied as to the technical, commercial and financial viability of individual projects. In such cases, the identifiable expenditure is deferred and amortised over the period during which the group is expected to benefit.

(m) Government grants
Government grants relating to tangible fixed assets are treated as deferred income and released to the profit and loss account over the expected useful lives of the assets concerned. Other grants are credited to the profit and loss account as the related expenditure is incurred.

5   SMALLCO LIMITED

Notes to accounts

1 Intangible fixed assets

	Goodwill £	Other intangible assets £	Total £
Cost			
1 January 1996	xx	xx	xxx
Additions	x	x	x
Disposals	x	x	x
31 December 1996	xx	xx	xxx
Amortisation			
1 January 1996	x	x	x
Disposals	x	x	x
Charge for the year	x	x	x
31 December 1996	x	x	x
Net book value			
31 December 1996	xx	xx	xx
31 December 1995	xx	xx	xx

2 Tangible fixed assets

	Land and buildings £	Plant and machinery £	Total £
Cost or valuation			
1 January 1996	xxx	xxx	xxx
Additions	xx	xx	xx
Revaluation	x	x	x
Disposals	x	x	x
31 December 1996	xxx	xxx	xxx
Depreciation			
1 January 1996	xx	xx	xx
Disposals	x	x	x
Charge for the year	xx	xx	xx
31 December 1996	xx	xx	xx

6   SMALLCO LIMITED

Notes to accounts (continued)

Net book value

31 December 1996	xxx	xxx	xxx
31 December 1995	xxx	xxx	xxx

Land and buildings were revalued during the year by A Surveyor, FRICS, on the basis of existing use value.

The historical cost of land and buildings included at a valuation of £ (1995 – £   ) was £   (1995 – £   ) and aggregate depreciation thereon would have been £   (1995 – £   ).

3   Investments

	Subsidiary undertaking and participating interests £	Listed investments £	Total £
Cost			
1 January 1996			
Additions			
31 December 1996			

Subsidiary undertaking and participating interests
The company's investment in its subsidiary company represents the acquisition of the whole of the ordinary share capital of Subsid Limited, which provides promotional services. At 30 September 1996 the aggregate share capital and reserves of Subsid Limited were £   (1995 – £   ) and the profit for the year to that date was £   (1995 – £   ).

The company's investment in its participating interest represents xx per cent of the share capital of Assoc Limited, a company registered in England and Wales, which provides design services. At 31 December 1996 the aggregate share capital and reserves of Assoc Limited were £   (1995 – £   ) and the profit for the year was £   (1995 – £   ).

Listed investments
Listed investments comprise investments which are listed on The London

7   SMALLCO LIMITED

Notes to accounts (continued)

Stock Exchange. The market value of these investments was £   at 31 December 1996 (1995 – £   ).

4   Debtors

Debtors include an amount of £   falling due after more than one year (1995 – £   ).

5   Creditors: Amounts falling due within one year

The Company's bank loans and overdrafts are secured on its freehold property.

6   Creditors: Amounts falling due after more than one year

Included within other creditors is an amount of £   due in more than five years.

7   Called up share capital

	1996 £	1995 £
Authorised		
Ordinary shares of £1 each	xxxx	xxxx
7 per cent Cumulative Preference shares of £1 each	xxx	xxx
	xxxx	xxxx
Allotted, called up and fully paid		
Ordinary shares of £1 each	xxx	xxx
7 per cent Cumulative Preference shares of £1 each	xxx	xxx
	xxxx	xxxx

The 7 per cent Cumulative Preference shares are redeemable at par at the option of the company on 1 January 1999 and on each anniversary of that date.

8   SMALLCO LIMITED

Appendix 3

Companies' Accounts Disclosure Checklist

This checklist may be used for private companies that qualify as small within the meaning of s246 and s247 Companies Act 1985. It is assumed that the company wishes to take full advantage of all available disclosure exemptions in the accounts drawn up both for shareholders and for filing and would therefore elect not to prepare group accounts.

The checklist is a summary and is current at 1 January 1997. Whilst the intention has been to provide explanation and guidance where helpful, reference should be made to the specific provisions of the Act, Accounting Standard or Exposure Draft.

Principal sections:	Questions
General	1–14
Directors' report	15–25
Profit and loss account	26–63
Statement of gains and losses	64–66
Balance sheet	67–79
Notes to the accounts	80–134
Other disclosures/additional notes	135–187
Abbreviated accounts	188–201
Forming an opinion	202–207

Key: **Items in bold represent new requirements proposed by the draft FRSSE.**

Items in italics represent items which would not be required were the draft FRSSE to be adopted.

In the checklist, to avoid unnecessary duplication, the references are to the FRSSE rather than to the draft FRSSE.

Sources – references are to Accounting Standards, company law requirements etc. (s or Sch refer to the section or Schedule number of the Companies Act 1985 unless otherwise indicated). The number in parenthesis following an accounting standard relates to the relevant paragraph. The column headed up 'Old ref' refers to the existing accounting standard and Schedule 4 (or old Schedule 8 references). The column headed up 'New ref' refers to references in the draft FRSSE and to the new Schedule 8 and Schedule 8A and revisions to the Companies Act 1985 introduced by The Companies Act 1985 (Accounts of Small and Medium-sized Companies and Minor Amendments) Regulations 1997 SI 1997 No 220.

Disclosure Checklist

Client:	Small Company Limited
Year end:	
Completed by:	Reviewed by:

No.	Disclosure item	Old ref	New ref	Complies?	Comments
	General				
1	The financial statements should present a true and fair view of the results for the period and of the state of affairs at the end of the period. To achieve this, the accounts should in normal circumstances comply with generally accepted accounting principles. [The FRSSE also comments that to achieve such a view, regard should be had to the substance of any arrangement or transaction, or series of such into which the entity has entered. Where there is any doubt as to whether applying any provisions of the FRSSE would be sufficient to give a true and fair view, adequate explanation should be given in the notes to the accounts of the transaction or arrangement concerned and the treatment adopted.]	s226	FRSSE(3)		
2	The financial statements should state that they have been prepared in accordance with the FRSSE.		FRSSE(4)		
3	Where a change from one of the formats prescribed in Schedule 4 to another is adopted, disclose details and reasons in a note to the first accounts in which the new format is adopted.	Sch 4:2(2)	Sch 8:2(2)		
4	Corresponding amounts for the previous year should be disclosed for each item in the profit and loss account, balance sheet and notes to the financial statements (exceptions to thisrule are noted, where appropriate, in the checklist).	Sch 4:4(1) Sch 4:58(2)	Sch 8:4(1) Sch 8:4(2) Sch 8:51(2)		

No.	Disclosure item	Old ref	New ref	Complies?	Comments
5	Where corresponding amounts have been adjusted to make them comparable, disclose details and reasons.	Sch 4:4(2) FRS 3(62)	Sch 8:4(2) Sch 8:51(2) FRSSE(15)		
6	Assets or income should not be set off against liabilities or expenditure respectively (debit and credit balances should be aggregated into a single net item only where they do not constitute separate assets and liabilities).	Sch 4:5 FRS 5(29)	Sch 8:5		
7	The financial statements should be approved by the Board of Directors and signed on the company balance sheet on behalf of the Board by a director of the company.	s233(1) s233(2)			
8	Disclose the date on which the financial statements are approved by the directors.	SSAP 17(26)	FRSSE (134)		
9	Disclose the name of the director signing the balance sheet.	s233(3)			
10	The directors' report should be approved by the Board of directors and signed by a director or the company secretary on its behalf. The name of the director or company secretary so signing should be stated.	s234A			
11	The copy of the financial statements delivered to the registrar must state in a prominent position the registered number of the company, be signed by the directors and registered auditors as appropriate and comply with the requirements prescribed by regulations to enable clear copies to be made.	s706 s234A s236			
12	The balance sheet should contain, above the signature, the following: (a) a statement to the effect that advantage has been taken, in the preparation of the accounts, of special exemptions available to small companies; and (b) a statement of the grounds on which, in the directors' opinion, the company is entitled to those exemptions. The directors' report should contain, above the signature, a statement to the effect that advantage has been taken,	s246(1A) s246(1B)			

No.	Disclosure item	Old ref	New ref	Complies?	Comments
	in the preparation of the report, of special exemptions available to small companies. If advantage has been taken of the exemptions available in the directors' report but not in the accounts then a statement similar to that described in (b) should appear above the signature in the directors' report.				
13	Where the company is a charity but does not include the word 'charity' or 'charitable' in its name, the fact that it is a charity should be disclosed in the financial statements.	s68 Charities Act 1993			
14	Where the company is a registered charity and its gross income in its last financial year exceeded £10,000, the fact that it is a registered charity should be stated in the financial statements.	s5 Charities Act 1993 (SI 1995 No 2696)			

No.	Disclosure item	Old ref	New ref	Complies?	Comments
	Directors' Report				
15	Principal activities of the company (and of its subsidiary undertakings) during the period and any significant changes should be given.	s234(2)			
16	An indication of the difference between book value and market value of land and buildings of the company (or any of its subsidiary undertakings) if significant should be given.	Sch 7:1			
17	The names of all of the persons who were directors during the period should be given. Note: Although there is no statutory requirement to do so, it is conventional to disclose the names of directors who have been appointed or who have retired after the year end and also the names of the directors due for re-appointment at the AGM.	s234(2)			
18	Disclose interests of persons who were directors at the year end (with comparatives at the beginning of the year or date of appointment if later), as recorded in the Register of Directors' Interests and including those of spouse and children under 18, in shares, options to acquire shares, debentures and loan stock of the company or any group company: (a) name of company; (b) number of shares and amount of debentures; (c) description of shares etc; (d) negative statement if no such interests. Note: This information may alternatively be given in the notes to the financial statements. The following interests do not have to be notified to the company for inclusion in the register: (a) Directors' nominee shareholdings in wholly owned subsidiaries of a body corporate (s324(6)). (b) Directors of wholly owned	Sch 7:2A			

No.	Disclosure item	Old ref	New ref	Complies?	Comments
	subsidiaries of companies incorporated in Great Britain, who are also directors of the holding company, need not disclose interests in these subsidiaries to the subsidiaries themselves (SI 1985 No 802). (c) Interests of the directors of wholly owned subsidiaries of companies incorporated outside Great Britain in companies incorporated outside Great Britain (SI 1985 No 802). (d) Directors' holdings as trustees of trusts over which the Public Trustee is also a trustee (SI 1985 No 802). (e) Directors' holdings as trustees or beneficiaries of a pension fund or scheme (SI 1985 No 802). (f) Interests in shares which arise solely on account of a limitation in the right to dispose of a share imposed by the memorandum or articles of association (SI 1985 No 802).				
19	Give details of directors' rights to subscribe for shares in, or debentures of, group companies. State, in respect of each group company, the number of shares and amount of debentures for which rights were granted to or exercised by any director or his immediate family in the financial year. Further disclosure requirements derived from UITF Abstract 10 in respect of directors' share options are contained in the section of the checklist dealing with directors' emoluments.	Sch 7:2B			
20	Disclose the total UK charitable contributions of the group. (Not required for wholly owned subsidiaries of companies incorporated in Great Britain or if aggregate charitable and political contributions are not more than £200.)	Sch 7:3–5			
21	Disclose the total UK political contributions of the group together with, in respect of any amount over £200, a statement of the amount and the name of the political party or	Sch 7:3–5			

No.	Disclosure item	Old ref	New ref	Complies?	Comments
	person paid. (Not required for wholly owned subsidiaries of companies incorporated in Great Britain or if aggregate charitable and political contributions are not more than £200.)				
22	In respect of any acquisition by the company of its own shares disclose:	Sch 7:7 Sch 7:8			
	(a) Number and nominal value of shares purchased, aggregate consideration paid by the company and the reasons for the purchase.				
	(b) Number and nominal value of shares acquired or charged during the financial year.				
	(c) Maximum number and nominal value of such shares held during the year.				
	(d) Number and nominal value of such shares disposed of or cancelled during the year and, where applicable, the amount or value of the consideration in each case.				
	(e) In each case above, state the percentage of the called-up share capital which they represent and, in each case where shares have been charged, the amount of the charge.				
	Note: These disclosure requirements apply where own shares are:				
	(a) purchased by the company or acquired by the company by forfeiture or surrender in lieu of forfeiture; or				
	(b) acquired by the company otherwise than for valuable consideration; or				
	(c) acquired by a nominee of the company without financial assistance from the company, or by any person with financial assistance from the company and, in either case, the company has a beneficial interest in the shares; or				
	(d) made subject to a lien or charge under s150 of the Consequential Provisions Act.				

No.	Disclosure item	Old ref	New ref	Complies?	Comments
23	Where a UK partner or employee of the Firm acts as a trustee of a trust, or trusts, which hold securities in the company, disclose details of the investment unless the aggregate of all relevant trustee shareholdings is less than 1 per cent of the issued capital of the company. This disclosure may alternatively be made in the notes to the financial statements or the audit report.	Guide to Professional Ethics, stat.1.201 Paras 4.42–4.47			
24	The directors' report should refer to the resolution to re-appoint the auditors at the AGM or to the fact that there is an elective resolution in force under s386 and the auditors are deemed to be re-appointed (this is not actually a requirement, but disclosure is customary).				
25	A statement of directors' responsibilities, complying with the minimum requirements of SAS 600, should be set out in the directors' report or elsewhere in the annual report.	SAS 600(20–23)			

No.	Disclosure item	Old ref	New ref	Complies?	Comments
	Profit and Loss Account				
26	The format of the profit and loss account should comply with one of the formats set out in the Schedules to the Act. All items listed in the prescribed formats must be shown in a company's accounts unless there is no amount for that item for both the current year and the immediately preceding year. Profit and loss items may be combined on the face of the profit and loss account if they are not material or if the combination facilitates the assessment of the company's state of affairs but, in this latter case, the individual amounts must be disclosed in a note. The order, arrangement and headings of the profit and loss account items should be adapted where the special nature of the company's business requires such adaptation.	Sch 4:1 Sch 4:3(5) Sch 4:4(3) Sch 4:3(4) Sch 4:86 Sch 4:3(3)	Sch 8:1 Sch 8:3(5) Sch 8:4(3) Sch 8:3(4) Sch 8:56 Sch 8:3(3)		
27	Where any amount relating to any preceding financial year is included in any item in the profit and loss account, state the effect.	Sch 4:57(1)	Sch 8:50		
28	*Disclose separately down to the operating profit level, the aggregate results of each of:* *(1) continuing operations;* *(2) acquisitions in the period (as a component of continuing operations); and* *(3) discontinued operations (including acquisitions discontinued in the period).* *The minimum disclosure on the face of the profit and loss account is the analysis of turnover and operating profit.* *The analysis of each of the other statutory profit and loss account format items should be given by way of note where not shown on the face of the profit and loss account. These disclosures to be made separately for each material acquisition and for other acquisitions in aggregate – FRS 6(23), FRS 6(28).*	FRS 3(14)			

No.	Disclosure item	Old ref	New ref	Complies?	Comments
29	*Disclose separately in a note the results of operations which although not discontinued (as defined in FRS 3) are in the process of discontinuing. They should not be classified as discontinued. This is not a requirement of FRS 3 but may be appropriate in some cases if the results are material.*	FRS 3(41)			
30	*Disclose in the notes, in respect of the first full year in which an acquired operation is included, its results for that period, together with comparative figures. This is not a requirement of FRS 3 but may be appropriate in some cases if it would be useful to users of the financial statements.*	FRS 3(38) FRS 6(83)			
31	*Where it is not practicable to determine the post-acquisition results of an operation to the end of the current period, an indication should be given of the contribution of the acquisition to turnover and operating profit of the continuing operations. If an indication cannot be given, this fact and the reasons for it should be stated. These disclosures to be made separately for each material acquisition and for other acquisitions in aggregate – FRS 6(23), FRS 6(29).*	FRS 3(16)			
32	*Where interest or tax is allocated between continuing and discontinued operations, the method and underlying assumptions used in making the allocations should be disclosed.*	FRS 3(14)			
33	*The analysis of comparative figures between continuing and discontinued operations:* *(1) need not be made on the face of the profit and loss account;* *(2) should be based on the status of an operation in the current year; and* *(3) need not refer to the results of acquisitions in the prior period.* *The corresponding amounts for continuing operations must include only amounts relating to operations which are classified as continuing in the current period. Corresponding amounts for discontinued operations*	FRS 3(64) FRS 3(30)			

No.	Disclosure item	Old ref	New ref	Complies?	Comments
	must include amounts for operations which were shown as discontinued in the prior period and amounts previously included in continuing operations, but which have been discontinued in the current period.				
34	The following exceptional items, including provisions in respect of such items, should be shown separately on the face of the profit and loss account after operating profit and before interest *and should be identified individually as relating to either continuing or discontinued operations:* (1) profits or losses on the sale or termination of an operation; (2) costs of a fundamental reorganisation or restructuring having a material effect on the nature and focus of the reporting entity's operations; and (3) profits or losses on the disposal of fixed assets. Where the net amount of (1) or (3) is not material, but the gross profits or losses are material, the relevant heading should still appear on the face of the profit and loss account with a reference to a related note analysing the profits and losses.	FRS 3(20)	FRSSE(11)		
35	*With respect to the three 'para 20' exceptional items which are to be shown on the face of the profit and loss account, give relevant information (in a note) regarding the effect of these items on the tax charge and the minority interest.* *As a minimum the related tax and minority interests should both be shown in aggregate, but if the effect of the tax and minority interests differs for the various categories of items, further details should be given.*	FRS 3(20)			
36	All other exceptional items (i.e., except FRS 3 paragraph 20 or FRSSE paragraph 11 items) should be: (1) credited or charged in arriving at the profit or loss on ordinary activities; (2) included under the statutory format headings to which they	Sch 4:57(3) FRS 3(19)	Sch 8:50(3) FRSSE(10)		

No.	Disclosure item	Old ref	New ref	Complies?	Comments
	relate; (3) shown individually or as an aggregate of items of a similar type; (4) disclosed by way of note or on the face of the profit and loss account if necessary in order to give a true and fair view; (5) described adequately to enable their nature to be understood; and (6) *attributed to continuing or discontinued operations as appropriate.*				
37	*Gains and losses arising on the repurchase or early settlement of debt should be disclosed in the profit and loss account as separate items within or adjacent to interest payable and similar charges.*	FRS 4(64)			
38	*Provisions arising from decisions to sell or terminate operations.* *In the year following that in which provision is made, the results of the operations should be shown under each of the statutory format headings with the utilisation of the provision analysed between:* *(1) operating loss; and* *(2) loss on sale or termination of operation;* *and disclosed on the face of the profit and loss account immediately below the relevant items.*	FRS 3(18)			
39	The amount of the profit or loss on ordinary activities before taxation should be shown on the face of the profit and loss account.	Sch 4:3(6)	Sch 8:3(6)		
40	The effect of a fundamental change in the basis of taxation should be included in the tax charge or credit for the period and separately disclosed on the face of the profit and loss account.	FRS 3(23)	FRSSE(29)		
41	(1) Aggregate dividends paid and proposed (on the face of the profit and loss account). (2) Aggregate dividends proposed (on the face or in the notes). (3) *Aggregate dividends for each class of shares (on the face or in the notes).*	Sch 4:3(7) FRS 4(59)	Sch 8:3 (7)(b)		

No.	Disclosure item	Old ref	New ref	Complies?	Comments
	In each case dividends to exclude related ACT or tax credit SSAP 8(24) and FRSSE (45). Where shares are issued or proposed to be issued as an alternative to cash dividends (a scrip dividend), the value of such shares should be deemed to be the amount receivable if the cash alternative had been chosen – FRS 4(48).				
42	Any extraordinary profit or loss should be shown separately after profit or loss on ordinary activities after tax but before appropriations. Extraordinary items should be separately disclosed.	FRS 3(22)	FRSSE(13)		
43	Transfers to or from reserves (i.e., from or to the profit and loss account) should be shown on the face of the profit and loss account.	Sch 4:3 (7)(a)	Sch 8:3 (7)(a)		
44	*Where an acquisition, or sale or termination, has a material impact on a major business segment, this should be disclosed and explained.* *These disclosures to be made separately for each material acquisition and for other acquisitions in aggregate – FRS 6(23), FRS 6(28).*	FRS 3(15)			
45	Turnover should comprise the amounts derived from the provision of goods and services falling within the company's ordinary activities, after deduction of trade discounts, value added tax and any other sales tax. *If in rare circumstances it is desired to show gross turnover including VAT, the VAT relevant to that turnover should be shown as a deduction in arriving at turnover for statutory reporting purposes.*	s262(1) SSAP 5(8)			
46	*Disclose aggregate rentals receivable in respect of:* *(1) finance leases and HP contracts; and* *(2) operating leases.* *Disclose cost of assets acquired for the purpose of letting under finance leases and HP contracts.*	SSAP 21(60)			

No.	Disclosure item	Old ref	New ref	Complies?	Comments
47	Depreciation and other amounts written off tangible and intangible fixed assets. Show separately: (a) depreciation; (b) provisions for permanent diminution in value; (c) write-back of such provisions; and (d) amounts in respect of assets held under finance leases and HP contracts.	Sch 4:8 (Note 17) SSAP 21(49) SSAP 21(50)	Sch 8:8 (Note 14) FRSSE(71)		
48	Effect on depreciation charge of any change from one method of depreciation to another, and the reason for change in the year of change, if material.	SSAP 12(26)	FRSSE(72)		
49	Effect on depreciation charge of any revaluation of assets, in year of revaluation, if material.	SSAP 12(27)	FRSSE(73)		
50	Disclose auditors' remuneration for audit work, including expenses and benefits in kind (stating the nature and estimated money value of benefits in kind).	s390A			
51	*Disclose the net amount of exchange gains and losses on foreign currency borrowings less deposits, identifying separately:* *(1) the amount offset in reserves; and* *(2) the net amount charged/credited to profit and loss account.*	SSAP 20(60)			
52	Show separately any income or interest derived from group undertakings which is included in Income from other fixed asset investments or Other interest receivable and similar income. Note: Group undertakings include parent undertakings, subsidiary undertakings and fellow subsidiary undertakings.	Sch 4:8(15)	Sch 8:8(12)		
53	*For associated undertakings disclose:* *(1) aggregate share of profits less losses before tax of the associated undertakings, including the latters' own subsidiaries and associated undertakings;*	SSAP 1(19) SSAP 1(22) SSAP 1(32)			

No.	Disclosure item	Old ref	New ref	Complies?	Comments
	(2) *aggregate share of net profits less losses retained; and* (3) *any amounts written off goodwill relating to associated undertakings.* *Do not include share of associated undertakings' turnover, depreciation etc.* Note: 1. *The above applies to consolidated accounts – except where it is exempt from the requirement to prepare group accounts, or would be exempt if it had subsidiaries, an investing company which does not prepare consolidated financial statements should show the information required by SSAP 1 paras 19–23 by preparing a separate profit and loss account or by adding the information in supplementary form to its own profit and loss account in such a way that its share of the profits of the associated companies is not treated as realised for the purposes of the Act (SSAP 1 para 24).* 2. SSAP 1 is not addressed by the FRSSE, except that the user is cross referred to it if group accounts are to be prepared.				
54	*If the results of one or more associated undertakings are so material for a true and fair view of the investing company or group, show in respect of associated undertakings the following totals:* (1) *turnover;* (2) *depreciation;* (3) *total profits before tax; and* (4) *investing group's share of profits before tax.* Note: SSAP 1 is not addressed by the FRSSE, except that the user is cross referred to it if group accounts are to be prepared – FRSSE (140).	SSAP 1(23) SSAP 25(36)			

No.	Disclosure item	Old ref	New ref	Complies?	Comments
55	*For each associated company:* *(1) give an indication of the nature of its business;* *(2) disclose the use of non-coterminous accounts with facts and dates;* *(3) when an investment in a company (other than a subsidiary or proportionately consolidated joint venture) is 20 per cent or more of the equity voting rights but is not accounted for as an associated company, then disclose the accounting treatment adopted and the reason for it. Disclosure is not required if it would be harmful to the business;* *(4) where the holding is less than 20 per cent of the equity voting rights but the investment is accounted for as an associate then disclose the basis on which significant influence is exercised.* Note: SSAP 1 is not addressed by the FRSSE, except that the user is cross referred to it if group accounts are to be prepared – FRSSE (140).	SSAP 1(37) SSAP 1(38) SSAP 1(49)			
56	Show separately: (a) provisions for temporary diminution in value; (b) provisions for permanent diminution in value; and (c) the reversal of any such provisions.	Sch 4:19	Sch 8:19		
57	Show separately the amount of interest and similar charges payable to group companies (i.e. holding companies, subsidiaries and fellow subsidiaries) other than those companies which are included in the company's consolidated accounts.	Sch 4:8(16)	Sch 8:8(13)		
58	*Tax attributable to the share of profits of associated undertakings.* *The above applies to consolidated accounts – except where it is exempt from the requirement to prepare group accounts, or would be exempt if it had subsidiaries, an investing company*	SSAP 1(20)			

No.	Disclosure item	Old ref	New ref	Complies?	Comments
	which does not prepare consolidated financial statements should show the information required by SSAP 1 paras 19–23 by preparing a separate profit and loss account or by adding the information in supplementary form to its own profit and loss account in such a way that its share of the profits of the associated companies is not treated as realised for the purposes of the Act (SSAP 1 para 24). Note: SSAP 1 is not addressed by the FRSSE, except that the user is cross referred to it if group accounts are to be prepared – FRSSE (140).				

59	(1) *Show separately as a component of taxation charge (or credit):*
	  (a) *the charge for deferred tax; and*
	  (b) *any adjustments to balance on deferred tax resulting from changes in tax rates and allowances.*
	(2) Amount of unprovided deferred tax in respect of period analysed into major components in a note.
	(3) *Show separately deferred tax relating to extraordinary items as part of tax on extraordinary items.*
	(4) Under the FRSSE:
	  (A) For companies subject to taxation in the UK the following items should be included in the taxation charge in the profit and loss account and, where material, should be separately disclosed:
	    (a) the amount of UK corporation tax specifying:
	      – the charge for corporation tax on the income of the year;
	      – tax attributable to franked investment income;
	      – irrecoverable advance
		SSAP 8(22)
		SSAP 15(33)
		SSAP 15(34)
		SSAP 15(35)
		SSAP 15(36)
			FRSSE(28)
			FRSSE(29)
			FRSSE(37)
			FRSSE(42)		

No.	Disclosure item	Old ref	New ref	Complies?	Comments

	corporation tax; and
	     – relief for overseas taxation.
	  (b) the total overseas taxation, relieved and unrelieved, specifying that part of the unrelieved overseas taxation which arises from the payment or proposed payment of dividends.
	  (B) Any special circumstances that affect the overall tax charge or credit for the period, or may affect those of future periods, should be disclosed by way of note to the profit and loss account and their individual effects quantified. The effects of a fundamental change in the basis of taxation should be included in the tax charge or credit for the period and separately disclosed on the face of the profit and loss account.				

60	*Disclose the total amount in respect of each of:* *(1) dividends on equity shares;* *(2) participating dividends (FRS 4(13));* *(3) other dividends on non-equity shares;* *(4) any other appropriation on non-equity shares.* *Where any of the above includes amounts relating to non-equity shares, and disclosure of this is not given on the face of the profit and loss account, the caption must state that non-equity amounts are included.* *All dividends and other finance costs of non-equity shares should be reported as an appropriation of profit – FRS 4(43)(44).* Under the FRSSE, all dividends (there is no reference to non-equity) should be reported as appropriations of profit in the profit and loss account.	FRS 4(59)	FRSSE(121)		

No.	Disclosure item	Old ref	New ref	Complies?	Comments
61	(1) Show prior year adjustments (and attributable taxation) arising from changes in accounting policies or the correction of fundamental errors by restating amounts for the preceding year and adjusting the opening balance of reserves for the cumulative effect. (2) Where practicable disclose the effect of prior year adjustments on the results: (a) for the current period; and (b) for the preceding period. If the current year effect is immaterial or similar to the quantified effect on the prior year, a statement to that effect will suffice. If it is not practicable to give the current year effect, state that fact together with reasons. A change in accounting policy may only be made if it gives a fairer presentation of the result and financial position.	FRS 3(29) UITF 14 Sch 4:15	FRSSE(14) FRSSE(15) Sch 8:15		
62	*Where there is a material difference between the result as disclosed in the profit and loss account and the result on an unmodified historical cost basis:* *(1) a note of the historical cost profit or loss for the period should be given* *(2) the note should include:* *(a) a reconciliation of the reported profit on ordinary activities before taxation to the equivalent historical cost amount; and* *(b) the retained profit for the year reported on an historical cost basis;* *(3) the note should immediately follow the profit and loss account or the statement of recognised gains and losses.*	FRS 3(26)			
63	The geographical analysis may be limited to a statement of the percentage of turnover attributable to markets outside the UK.	Sch 4:55(2)	Sch 8:49		

No.	Disclosure item	Old ref	New ref	Complies?	Comments
	Statement of Recognised Gains and Losses				
64	A primary statement (having the same prominence as the profit and loss account, balance sheet and cash flow statement) should be presented showing the total of recognised gains and losses and its components. Notes: 1. The components should be the gains and losses that are recognised in the period insofar as they are attributable to shareholders. 2. The write off of goodwill ab initio against reserves is not a recognised loss. 3. *If there are no recognised gains and losses other than the profit or loss for the period include a statement to this effect immediately below the profit and loss account.*	FRS 3(27) FRS 3(57)	FRSSE(16)		
65	*Disclose that all of the results are derived from continuing operations.* *Example of wording (at foot of profit and loss account or in notes):* *All operations of the [company/group] continued throughout both periods and no operations were acquired or discontinued.*	FRS 3(14)			
66	The cumulative effect of prior year adjustments should be noted at the foot of the statement of total recognised gains and losses.	FRS 3(29)	FRSSE(14)		

No.	Disclosure item	Old ref	New ref	Complies?	Comments
	Balance Sheet				
67	The format of the balance sheets should comply with one of the formats set out in Schedule 4. All items listed in the prescribed formats must be shown in a company's accounts unless there is no amount for that item for both the current year and the immediately preceding year. Balance sheet items to which Arabic numbers are assigned in the formats may be combined on the face of the balance sheet if they are not material or if the combination facilitates the assessment of the company's state of affairs but, in this latter case, the individual amounts must be disclosed in a note. The order, arrangement and headings of the balance sheet items should be adapted where the special nature of the company's business requires such adaptation.	Sch 4:1 Sch 4:3(5) Sch 4:4(3) Sch 4:3(4) Sch 4:86 Sch 4:3(3)	Sch 8:1 Sch 8:3(5) Sch 8:4(3) Sch 8:3(4) Sch 8:56 Sch 8:3(3)		

68	For each item under intangible fixed assets state (comparatives not required):
	
	(1) The aggregate purchase price or production cost, or valuation determined under one of the alternative accounting rules, as at the beginning and end of the financial year. *Cost of intangible fixed assets and other items disclosed should include irrecoverable VAT (where practicable and material – but see note).*
	(2) The effect on any amount shown in the balance sheet in respect of each fixed asset item as a result of any:
	   (a) revaluation made during the year in accordance with the alternative accounting rules;
	   (b) acquisitions during the year;
	   (c) disposals during the year; and
	   (d) transfers during the year.
		Sch 4:42
		Sch 4:58(3)
		SSAP 5(9)
		SSAP 12(18)
		SSAP 12(25)
		SSAP 12(27)
			Sch 8:40
			Sch 8:51(3)
			FRSSE(71c)
			FRSSE(73)
			FRSSE(65)		

No.	Disclosure item	Old ref	New ref	Complies?	Comments

	(3) In respect of provisions for depreciation or diminution in value:
	   (a) the cumulative amount of such provisions as at the beginning and end of the year;
	   (b) the amount provided during the year;
	   (c) the amount of any adjustments made during the year in consequence of the disposal of any asset;
	   (d) the amount of any other adjustments (e.g., exchange translation differences) made during the year;
	   (e) where assets have been revalued, the effect of the revaluation on the depreciation charge should, if material, be disclosed in the year of revaluation; and
	   (f) when asset lives have been revised and future results would be materially distorted, recognise the adjustment to accumulated depreciation as an exceptional item, with the nature and amount of the adjustment being disclosed.
	
	 Note: The FRSSE does not consider SSAP 5, but it may be appropriate for companies to continue with this SSAP 5 requirement to establish the cost of the asset concerned.				

69	For deferred development costs disclose:
	 (1) (a) period over which amounts capitalised are being written off; and
	   (b) reasons for capitalisation.
	 (2) *Show separately:*
	   (a) opening balance;
	   (b) movement during period; and
	   (c) closing balance.
	 (3) Any special reasons for not regarding unamortised amounts as reducing company's distributable profits.
		Sch 4:20(2) SSAP 13(32) s269(2)(b)	Sch 8:20(2)		

No.	Disclosure item	Old ref	New ref	Complies?	Comments
	Note: Development costs may only be shown in a company's balance sheet in special circumstances (Sch 4:20). Compliance with SSAP13 will usually be sufficient to meet this requirement. Development costs must be treated as a realised loss in the calculation of distributable profits unless there are such 'special circumstances' and the disclosure at (3) above is made (s269(2)).				
70	Concessions, patents, licences, trade marks and similar rights and assets ('other intangible assets'): Amounts in respect of assets shall only be included in a company's balance sheet under this item if either: (1) the assets were acquired for valuable consideration and are not required to be shown under goodwill; or (2) the assets in question were created by the company itself.	Sch 4:8 (Note 2)	Sch 8:8 (Note 3)		

71	(1) Amounts representing goodwill shall only be included to the extent that goodwill was acquired for valuable consideration.
	(2) *Where the amortisation treatment is selected, show purchased goodwill as a separate item in the balance sheet until written off:*
	  (a) *show the cost, accumulated amortisation, movements (including the amount amortised through profit and loss account) during the year, and the net book value at the beginning and end of the year;*
	  (b) *state the period selected for amortising the goodwill relating to each major acquisition and the reason for choosing that period.*
	
	Note: None of the SSAP 22 disclosure requirements have been included in the FRSSE.
		Sch 4:8 (Note 3) SSAP 22(45) Sch 4:21	Sch 8:8 (Note 2) FRSSE(48) Sch 8:21		

No.	Disclosure item	Old ref	New ref	Complies?	Comments

72	For each item under tangible fixed assets state (comparatives not required):
	
	(1) the aggregate purchase price or production cost, or valuation determined under one of the alternative accounting rules, as at the beginning and end of the financial year. Cost of tangible fixed assets and other items disclosed should include irrecoverable VAT (where practicable and material);
	(2) the effect on any amount shown in the balance sheet in respect of each fixed asset item as a result of any:
	  (a) revaluation made during the year in accordance with the alternative accounting rules (including transfers of current assets to fixed assets at net realisable value);
	  (b) acquisitions during the year;
	  (c) disposals during the year;
	  (d) transfers during the year; and
	(3) in respect of provisions for depreciation or diminution in value:
	  (a) the cumulative amount of such provisions as at the beginning and end of the year;
	  (b) the amount provided during the year;
	  (c) the amount of any adjustments made during the year in consequence of the disposal of any asset;
	  (d) the amount of any other adjustments (e.g. exchange translation differences) made during the year;
	  (e) where assets have been revalued, the effect of the revaluation on the depreciation charge should, if material, be disclosed in the year of revaluation; and
	  (f) when asset lives have been
		Sch 4:42
		Sch 4:58(3)
		SSAP 12(22)
		SSAP 5(9)
		UITF 5(6)
		SSAP 12(25)(c)
		SSAP 12(18)
			Sch 8:40
			Sch 8:51(3)
			FRSSE(71(c))
			FRSSE(71(d))
			FRSSE(73)
			FRSSE(65)		

137

No.	Disclosure item	Old ref	New ref	Complies?	Comments
	revised and future results would be materially distorted, recognise the adjustment to accumulated depreciation as an exceptional item, with the nature and amount of the adjustment being disclosed.				
73	*(1) Show prominently the carrying value of investment properties;* *(2) Disclose changes in the value of investment properties as a movement on revaluation reserve.* Note: SSAP 19 and the requirements within the FRSSE relating to investment properties do not apply to charities – FRSSE(60). *In accordance with SSAP 19 investment properties (except leaseholds with an unexpired term of 20 years or less) will not be depreciated. This is a departure from the statutory accounting provisions and it will be necessary to disclose particulars of the departure, the reasons for it and its effect as required by s226 and s227 Companies Act 1985 unless the amount involved is not material (in which case this fact should be stated). In giving the disclosures required by law regard should be had to UITF Abstract 7.*	SSAP 19(13) SSAP 19(15) SSAP 19(12)			
74	*Where properties are valued on acquisition based on their trading potential disclose:* *(1) asset and treatment; and* *(2) that stated value does not exceed open market value.* Note: None of the SSAP 22 disclosure requirements have been included in the FRSSE.	SSAP 22(15)			
75	For assets held under finance leases and HP contracts disclose either by: (1) each major class of asset showing gross amount, accumulated depreciation and	SSAP 21(49) SSAP 21(50)	FRSSE(105)		

No.	Disclosure item	Old ref	New ref	Complies?	Comments
	depreciation charge allocated for the period; or (2) integrating with owned assets, disclosing net amount included in overall total and related depreciation charge for year.				
76	Disclose cost of assets held for rental under finance leases (applicable to lessors, whether asset acquired by purchase or finance lease).	SSAP 21(60)	FRSSE (107(b))		
77	The gross amounts of assets held for use in operating leases, and the related accumulated depreciation charges, should be disclosed.	SSAP 21(59)	FRSSE (107(a))		
78	For each item under fixed asset investments state (comparatives not required): (1) The aggregate cost, or valuation determined under one of the alternative accounting rules, as at the beginning and end of the financial year. *Cost of fixed asset investments should include irrecoverable VAT (where practicable and material but see note).* (2) The effect on any amount shown in the balance sheet in respect of each fixed asset item as a result of: (a) revaluation made during the year in accordance with the alternative accounting rules; (b) acquisitions during the year; (c) disposals during the year; and (d) transfers during the year. (3) In respect of provisions for depreciation or diminution in value: (a) the cumulative amount of such provisions as at the beginning and end of the year; (b) the amount provided during the year; (c) the amount of any adjustments made during the year in consequence of the disposal of any asset;	Sch 4:42 Sch 4:58(3) SSAP 5(9)	Sch 8:40 Sch 8:51(3)		

No.	Disclosure item	Old ref	New ref	Complies?	Comments
	(d) and the amount of any other adjustment (e.g., exchange translation differences) made during the year.				
	Note: The FRSSE does not consider SSAP 5, but it may be appropriate for companies to continue with this SSAP 5 requirement to establish the cost of the asset concerned.				
79	(1) *The amount at which the investing group's interest in associated companies should be shown in the consolidated balance sheet is the total of:* (a) *the investing group's share of the net assets, other than goodwill, of the associated companies stated, where possible, after attributing fair values to the net assets at the time of acquisition of the interest in the associated companies; and* (b) *the investing group's share of any goodwill in the associated companies' own financial statements; and* (c) *the premium paid (or discount) on the acquisition of the interest in the associated companies in so far as it has not already been written off or amortised.* *Item (a) should be disclosed separately but items (b) and (c) may be shown as one aggregate amount.* (2) *Details of associated companies' tangible and intangible assets and liabilities where so material that disclosure is of assistance in giving a true and fair view.* (3) *The totals of loans to and from associated companies should be separately disclosed in the consolidated financial statements.* (4) *Material trading balances due to/ from associated companies should be disclosed separately.*	SSAP 1(26) SSAP 1(30) SSAP 1(35) SSAP 1(27) SSAP 1(28) SSAP 1(29)			

No.	Disclosure item	Old ref	New ref	Complies?	Comments
	The above disclosure applies to consolidated financial statements. Except where it is exempt from the requirement to prepare group accounts, or would be exempt if it had subsidiaries, an investing company which does not prepare consolidated financial statements should show the information required by SSAP 1 paras 25–34 by preparing a separate balance sheet or by adding the information in supplementary form to its balance sheet. Note: SSAP 1 is not addressed by the FRSSE, except that the user is cross referred to it if group accounts are to be prepared.				

No.	Disclosure item	Old ref	New ref	Complies?	Comments
	Notes to the Accounts				
80	Where the company has at the end of the financial year a significant shareholding in an undertaking (which is not a subsidiary) which represents:	Sch 5:7–9			
	(a) 20 per cent or more of the nominal value of the allotted shares of any class of the undertaking's equity share capital, or				
	(b) more than 20 per cent of the book value of the investing company's total assets, state in relation to that other body:				
	(i) its name;				
	(ii) its country of incorporation, if not incorporated in GB;				
	(iii) the identity and proportion of the nominal value of each class of shares held (comparatives not required);				
	(iv) if it is unincorporated, the address of its principal place of business;				
	(v) the aggregate amount of its capital and reserves at the end of its most recent financial year ending with or before that of the investing company; and				
	(vi) its profit or loss for that period.				
	Note: The 20 per cent of assets test applies to the company's assets in relation to the company's investments and to the group's assets in relation to the group's investments.				
	Where the disclosures required would result in a statement of excessive length, they may be limited to the principal investments provided that it is indicated that it is so limited and full details must be attached to the company's next annual return – s231(5,6).				
	Information need not be disclosed with respect to an				

No.	Disclosure item	Old ref	New ref	Complies?	Comments
	undertaking which is established under the law of a country outside the UK or carries on business outside the UK, if in the opinion of the directors of the company the disclosure would be seriously prejudicial to the business of that undertaking, or to the business of the company or any of its subsidiary undertakings, and the DTI agrees that the information need not be disclosed. The fact that advantage has been taken of the exemption must be stated.				
	The information required by (v) and (vi) (aggregate capital and reserves and profit or loss) need not be given if:				
	(a) (i) the undertaking is not required by the Act (either as a company incorporated in Great Britain or as an overseas company) to file its accounts with the Registrar of Companies, and does not otherwise publish its accounts in Great Britain or elsewhere; and				
	(ii) the investing company or group holds less than one half in nominal value of its allotted share capital; or				
	(b) it is not material; or				
	(c) the company is:				
	(i) exempt from preparing group accounts by virtue of s228 (parent company included in the accounts of a larger group); and				
	(ii) the investment of the company in all undertakings in which it has such a holding is shown, in aggregate, in the notes to the accounts by way of the equity method.				
81	(1) Aggregate amount of listed investments included under each item of investments shown under fixed assets.	Sch 4:45	Sch 8:42		

No.	Disclosure item	Old ref	New ref	Complies?	Comments

	(2) For each item which includes listed investments disclose:
	    (a) the aggregate market value of the listed investments where it differs from their balance sheet amount; and
	    (b) both the market value and stock exchange value where the market value is taken as being higher than the stock exchange value.				

82	Show separately the nominal value of own shares held. Note: Own shares that are purchased or redeemed must be cancelled or redeemed immediately – s160(4), s162. A plc may not carry its own shares (acquired by forfeiture, surrender etc.) for more than three years and a non distributable reserve must be established equal to the carrying value of the shares – ss147-148. These restrictions do not apply to shares held by a subsidiary or by an ESOP trust accounted for in accordance with UITF13.	Sch 4:8 (Note 4)	Sch 8:8 (Note 4)		

83	Where the company departs from any of the historical cost accounting rules state:
	
	(1) the items affected and the basis of valuation adopted for each such item;
	(2) for each balance sheet item (except stocks) affected, state:
	    (a) the comparable amounts determined according to the historical cost accounting rules; or
	    (b) the differences between those amounts and the corresponding amounts actually shown in the balance sheet in respect of that item.
	
	Applies to both fixed and current assets.
		Sch 4:33(2)
		Sch 4:33(3)
			Sch 8:33(2)
			Sch 8:33(3)		

84	Fixed or current assets – disclosure where original cost unknown. Give particulars where the purchase	Sch 4:51(1)	Sch 8:47		

No.	Disclosure item	Old ref	New ref	Complies?	Comments
	price or production cost is unknown and for the first time is taken as being the value ascribed to it by the earliest available record of the company.				
85	State cumulative amount of interest included in determining the production cost of any fixed asset, indicating the balance sheet item affected.	Sch 4:26(3)	Sch 8:26(3)		
86	Where government grants are receivable, the following information should be disclosed: (1) the effects of grants on the results for the period and/or the financial position of the enterprise; (2) where the results are materially affected by government assistance other than capital grants, the nature and an estimate of the effect of that assistance; and (3) potential liabilities to repay grants except where the possibility of repayment is remote – SSAP 18 (16) (FRSSE(123)).	SSAP 4(28) SSAP 4(29)	FRSSE(77)		
87	(1) Where the amount of any fixed asset (other than listed investments) is arrived at on the basis of any of the alternative accounting rules (including transfers of current assets to fixed assets at net realisable value) disclose the following: (a) the years (so far as they are known to the directors) in which the assets were severally valued and the several values; (b) where assets have been valued during the year, the names of the valuers or particulars of their qualifications for so doing, and (whichever is stated) the bases of valuation used; and (c) for investment properties, disclose if the valuer is an employee or officer of the company or group. (2) Where, under the alternative	Sch 4:43(a) Sch 4:43(b) UITF 5(6) SSAP 19(12) Sch 4:31(3)	Sch 8:41 FRSSE(58) Sch 8:31(3)		

No.	Disclosure item	Old ref	New ref	Complies?	Comments
	accounting rules, the amount of any fixed asset investment is determined on any basis (other than at market value) which appears to the directors to be appropriate in the circumstances of the company, disclose in a note particulars of the method of valuation adopted and the reasons for adopting it.				
88	Consideration of fixed assets values for distribution rules. Where, for the purpose of the Act's distribution rules, fixed assets are not actually revalued in the balance sheet but their value is 'considered' by the directors, state that: (1) the directors have considered the value of fixed assets without actually revaluing them; (2) the directors are satisfied that the aggregate value of those assets at the time in question is or was not less than the aggregate amount at which they are or were for the time being stated in the company's accounts; and (3) that the assets affected are accordingly stated in the accounts on the basis that a revaluation of the company's fixed assets, which by virtue of s275(4) and (5) included the assets in question, took place at that time. In certain circumstances provisions which have properly been charged to the profit and loss account for accounting purposes may be ignored when calculating the amount of distributable profit for dividend purposes.	s275(6)			
89	*Sub-classify the main categories of stock and work in progress in a manner appropriate to the business. (This may result in an additional classification to that in the prescribed formats.)* Stock held subject to reservation of title – consider disclosure if a material proportion of stock is held subject to	SSAP 9(27)			

No.	Disclosure item	Old ref	New ref	Complies?	Comments
	reservation of title by the supplier, including whether, and the extent to which, the liability to the supplier is secured, and the nature of the security given – ICAEW Members' Handbook Volume II 2.404.				
90	Stocks and work in progress, other than long-term work in progress, should be stated at the total of the lower of cost and net realisable value of the separate items (or, if impracticable, groups of similar items).	Sch 4:14 Sch 4:22 Sch 4:23 Sch 4:27(2) SSAP 9(2) SSAP 9(26)	Sch 8:14 Sch 8:22 Sch 8:23 FRSSE(85) Sch 8:27		
91	Work in progress: (1) show separately by way of note under the heading 'long-term contract balances' costs incurred net of amounts transferred to cost of sales, less foreseeable losses; and (2) show separately as 'payments on account' the balance of such payments on account in excess of amounts matched with turnover or offset against long-term contract balances.	SSAP 9(30)(c)	FRSSE (88(b)) FRSSE (88(c))		
92	State cumulative amount of interest included in determining the production cost of any current asset, indicating the balance sheet item affected.	Sch 4:26(3)	Sch 8:26(3)		
93	Debtors: (1) for each item under debtors show separately the amount falling due after more than one year (but for small companies taking advantage of the exemptions in Part I of Schedule 8, disclose only the aggregate amount of debtors falling due after more than one year); and (2) *the amount of debtors due after more than one year should be disclosed on the face of the balance sheet where the amount is so material (in the context of total net current assets) that in the absence of such disclosures, readers may misinterpret the accounts.* Note: UITF 4 is not addressed in the FRSSE.	Sch 4:8 (Note 5) UITF 4(3)	Sch 8:8 (Note 5)		

No.	Disclosure item	Old ref	New ref	Complies?	Comments
94	Where a company acts as a lessor, separately disclose the net investment in (i) finance leases and (ii) hire purchase contracts as a debtor.	SSAP 21(58) SSAP 21(38)	FRSSE (107(c)) FRSSE(98)		
95	Pensions contributions: (1) prepaid pension contributions (for a defined contribution scheme); and (2) prepayments due to excess of amount funded over pension cost charged (for a defined benefit scheme).	SSAP 24(86–89)	FRSSE (110(c)) FRSSE (117(e))		
96	Long-term contracts – state separately under the heading 'amounts recoverable on contracts' the excess of recorded turnover over payments received on account.	SSAP 9(30)(a)	FRSSE (88(a))		
97	(1) Investments: aggregate the amount of listed investments under each item of investments shown under current assets; and (2) For each item which includes listed investments disclose: (a) the aggregate market value of the listed investments where it differs from their balance sheet amount; and (b) both the market value and stock exchange value where the market value is taken as being higher than the stock exchange value.	Sch 4:45	Sch 8:42		
98	*Capital instruments (creditors including convertible debt):* *(1) Brief description of the legal nature of any instrument where it is different from that normally associated with debt (e.g., subordinated or conditional repayment).* *(2) Where the amount payable, or the claim that would arise in a winding up, is materially different from that at which the instrument is stated, that amount should be stated (this may be summarised).* *(3) If further information is necessary to understand the commercial effect of an*	FRS 4(63) FRS 4(65)			

No.	Disclosure item	Old ref	New ref	Complies?	Comments
	instrument, that fact should be stated together with particulars of where the information may be obtained. In all cases the principal features should be stated.				
	The market value of capital instruments may be useful to users of financial statements as it provides an insight into the economic burden represented by the debt. Although not required by FRS 4, this disclosure should be considered where it would assist users – FRS 4(102).				
99	Convertible loans: (1) the amount attributable to convertible debt, included within liabilities, should be disclosed separately from that of other liabilities; and (2) *if, exceptionally, disclosure is in the notes rather than on the face of the balance sheet, the relevant caption on the face of the balance sheet should state that it includes convertible debt;* (3) *redemption date and amount payable on redemption;* (4) *number and class of shares into which it may be converted;* (5) *dates at which, or periods within which, conversion may take place; and* (6) *whether conversion is at the option of the holder or the issuer.*	Sch 4:8 (Note 7) FRS 4(25) FRS 4(54) FRS 4(62)	Sch 8:8 (Note 7)		
100	*An analysis of the maturity of debt should be given showing amounts falling due:* (1) *in one year or less, or on demand;* (2) *between one and two years;* (3) *between two and five years; and* (4) *in five years or more.* *Where the maturity of debt is assessed by reference to that of permitted refinancing facilities (FRS 4(35)) disclose the amount of the debt so treated, analysed by the earliest date on which the lender could demand repayment in the absence of the facilities.*	FRS 4(33) FRS 4(36)			

Appendix 3

No.	Disclosure item	Old ref	New ref	Complies?	Comments
101	For each item shown under creditors falling due after more than one year: (1) amount due for repayment, other than by instalments, after more than five years from the balance sheet date; and (2) amount repayable by instalments, any of which fall due after more than five years. Note: For small companies the disclosures in (1) and (2) may be given on an aggregate basis for all items shown under 'creditors'. The terms of repayment and rate of interest for each amount owed included in (1) or (2) above is generally required to be given, except where in the opinion of the directors, this would result in a statement of excessive length, in which case give only a general indication of the terms of repayment and rates of interest. This disclosure requirement does not however apply to small companies.	Sch 4:48(1) Sch 4:48(2) Sch 4:48(3) Sch 4:48(5)	Sch 8:44		
102	For each item shown under creditors falling due within one year or after more than one year (Sch 4:48(5)): (1) the aggregate amount of liabilities included on which any security has been given by the company; and (2) an indication of the nature of the security given (but note small companies need not disclose this).	Sch 4:48(4)(a) Sch 4:48(4)(b)			
103	Disclose the unamortised amount of discount or premium on debts (e.g., debentures), where this is not shown separately in the balance sheet.	Sch 4:24(2)	Sch 8:24(2)		
104	Payments received on account in respect of long-term contracts: Show the excess of the amounts: (1) matched with turnover; and (2) offset against long-term contract balances, under this heading.	SSAP 9(30)(b) Sch 4:8 (Note 8)	FRSSE (88(b))		

150

No.	Disclosure item	Old ref	New ref	Complies?	Comments
	(This must be shown under E3 or H3 in the prescribed formats in so far as they are not shown as identified deductions from stocks.)				
105	Obligations under finance leases and HP contracts: (1) disclose separately from other liabilities and obligations either on the balance sheet or in the notes; and (2) *analyse net obligations between amounts payable:* *(a) in the next year;* *(b) in the second to fifth years; and* *(c) after five years;* *either separately or combined with other liabilities and obligations; and* (3) *alternatively, analyse gross obligations as above separately from other liabilities and obligations with future finance charges deducted from the total.*	SSAP 21(51) SSAP 21(52)	FRSSE (105(b))		
106	Pension cost creditors: (1) amount of outstanding contributions; and (2) where the cumulative pension cost recognised in the profit and loss account has not been completely discharged by payments of contributions or directly paid pensions, show excess as a net pension provision.	SSAP 24(86) SSAP 24(87) SSAP 24(88)	FRSSE (117(e)) FRSSE (110(c))		
107	Taxation/social security: (1) show separately the amount included under items E8 and H8 (other creditors including taxation and social security) in the prescribed formats in respect of taxation and social security; (2) disclose separately the amounts included under liabilities in respect of mainstream corporation tax payable within and after more than 1 year; and (3) *where corporation tax is not payable within twelve months of balance sheet date, state the due date of payment.*	Sch 4:8 (Note 9) SSAP 8(14)	Sch 8:8 (Note 7)		

No.	Disclosure item	Old ref	New ref	Complies?	Comments
108	Advance Corporation Tax: (1) include ACT on proposed dividends as current tax liability; (2) deduct recoverable ACT on proposed dividends from deferred tax account, if any, otherwise show as a deferred asset; and (3) deduct recoverable ACT on dividends paid in period from appropriate mainstream corporation tax liability.	SSAP 8(15) SSAP 8(26) SSAP 8(27)	FRSSE(47)		
109	Disclose the amount of any arrears of fixed cumulative dividends and the period for which each class is in arrears.	Sch 4:49	Sch 8:45		
110	Movement on provisions. Where there is any movement on provisions disclose (comparatives not required – Sch 4:58(3)): (a) the amount of the provision as at the beginning and end of the financial year; (b) the amount transferred to or from the provisions during the year; and (c) the source and application of the amounts transferred. This is not required where the movement consists of the application of a provision for the purpose for which it was established.	Sch 4:46	Sch 8:43		
111	Deferred taxation: Provide the following information: (1) transfers to and from deferred tax in a note; (2) deferred tax balance analysed by its major components; (3) amount of any unprovided deferred tax analysed into its major components in a note; (4) *where potential deferred tax on a revalued asset is not shown because disposal of the asset and any subsequent replacement would not result in a tax liability, state that it does not constitute a timing difference and that tax has therefore not been quantified;*	SSAP 15 (37–42) FRS 2(54)	FRSSE(39) FRSSE(38) FRSSE(41) FRSSE(42) FRSSE(40) FRSSE(43)		

No.	Disclosure item	Old ref	New ref	Complies?	Comments
	(5) state assumptions made as to availability of group relief expected and payment therefor; (6) *state where deferred tax is not provided on earnings retained overseas;* (7) show separately any amounts arising from movements on reserves as part of those movements; (8) *tax effect of realising an asset the value of which differs materially from its book amount; and* (9) *the extent to which deferred tax has been accounted for in respect of the accumulated reserves of overseas subsidiaries and, where applicable, the reason for not making full provision.*				
112	*Material balance sheet provisions for post-retirement benefits other than pensions should be distinguished from other provisions in the notes to the accounts.*	UITF 6(9)			
113	Particulars of each material provision included under 'Other provisions' in the balance sheet (comparatives not required – Sch 4:58(3)).	Sch 4:46(3)	Sch 8:43(3)		
114	Long-term contracts Show the amount by which a provision for foreseeable losses exceeds the costs incurred (after transfers to cost of sales), as a provision for liabilities. (Where appropriate the foreseeable losses may have been set up as an accrual, in which case this excess should be classified as accruals within creditors.)	SSAP 9 (30)(d)	FRSSE (88(d))		
115	*The balance sheet should show the total amount of shareholders' funds.* *It is good practice to describe this total as 'equity shareholders' funds' if there are no non-equity interests to be disclosed in accordance with FRS 4.*	FRS 4(38)			
116	*Shareholders' funds (non-equity interests):* (1) *should be analysed between the amount attributable to equity interests and the amount attributable to non-equity*	FRS 4(40) FRS 4(54) FRS 4(55)			

No.	Disclosure item	Old ref	New ref	Complies?	Comments
	interests; (2) *if, exceptionally, disclosure is in the notes rather than on the face of the balance sheet the relevant caption on the face of the balance sheet should state that it includes non-equity interests;* (3) *the aggregate amount of non-equity interests should be analysed showing the amounts attributable to each class of non-equity shares and warrants for non-equity shares.*				
117	Share capital. Authorised, issued and paid up: (1) authorised share capital; (2) amount of allotted share capital and amount of called up share capital which has been paid up; and (3) number and aggregate nominal value of allotted shares of each class where more than one class of shares have been allotted.	Sch 4:38(1)(a) Sch 4:38(1)(b) Sch 4:8 (Note 12)	Sch 8:38(1)(a) Sch 8:38(1)(b) Sch 8:8 (Note 9)		
118	*A brief summary of the rights of each class of shares which should include:* (1) *dividends;* (2) *redemption dates and amounts;* (3) *priority and amounts receivable on a winding up;* (4) *voting rights; and* (5) *if rights vary according to circumstances, the circumstances and the variations.* *If necessary additional information to the above should be given to explain the classification of any class of share as equity or non-equity.* *Where warrants or convertible debt are in issue that may require the issue of a new class of shares, then the above information must also be given for that class.* *If further information is necessary to understand the commercial effect of an instrument, that fact should be stated together with particulars of where that information may be obtained. In all cases the principal features should be stated.*	FRS 4(56) FRS 4(57) FRS 4(58) FRS 4(65)			

No.	Disclosure item	Old ref	New ref	Complies?	Comments
119	Redeemable shares. In addition to the above, indicate: (1) earliest and latest dates on which the company has power of redemption; (2) whether redemption is required in any event or at option of company or shareholder; and (3) whether any (and if so what) premium is payable on redemption.	Sch 4:38(2)	Sch 8:38(2)		
120	Where the company has allotted any shares during the financial year disclose: (1) the classes of shares allotted; and (2) for each class of shares, the number allotted, their aggregate nominal value and the consideration received by the company.	Sch 4:39	Sch 8:39		
121	Number, description and amount of shares in the company held by its subsidiaries or their nominees.	Sch 5:6			
122	*Where the title of the preference, participating, or preferred ordinary shares issued before 6 April 1973 includes a fixed rate of dividend, incorporate the revised rate of dividend in the description of the shares.*	SSAP 8(28)			
123	Where there is any movement on reserves, disclose: (1) the amount of the reserves as at the beginning and end of the financial year; (2) any amount transferred to or from the reserves during the year; (3) the source and application respectively of any amounts transferred (including any related deferred taxation adjustments); and (4) *the net movements on reserves arising from exchange differences.* Comparatives not required.	Sch 4:46(1) Sch 4:46(2) Sch 4:58(3) SSAP 15(39) SSAP 20(60)	Sch 8:43(1) Sch 8:43(2) Sch 8:51(3) FRSSE(40)		

No.	Disclosure item	Old ref	New ref	Complies?	Comments
124	It is recommended that the analysis of reserves should distinguish between distributable and non-distributable reserves (where this is not evident from their description).				
125	*For reserves in associates, disclose the following:* *(1) investing group's share of post acquisition accumulated reserves of associated companies;* *(2) extent of any significant restrictions on the ability of associated companies to distribute their retained profits;* *(3) state where accumulated reserves of overseas associated companies are subject to further taxation on distribution; and* *(4) account for and disclose interests in movements on associated companies' reserves other than those accounted for in the profit and loss account (comparatives not required).* Note: SSAP 1 is not addressed by the FRSSE, except that the user is cross referred to it if group accounts are to be prepared.	SSAP 1(31) SSAP 1(40)			
126	*The investment property revaluation reserve should be displayed prominently.*	SSAP 19(15)			
127	State the treatment for taxation purposes of amounts debited or credited to the revaluation reserve.	Sch 4:34(4)	Sch 8:34(6)		
128	*A note should be presented reconciling the opening and closing totals of shareholders' funds for the period.* *If presented as a primary statement, the reconciliation should be shown separately from the statement of total recognised gains and losses.*	FRS 3(28) FRS 3(59)			
129	In respect of any contingent liability not provided for disclose: (1) the amount or estimated amount of that liability; (2) its legal nature (e.g., guarantee or performance bond); and (3) whether, and if so what, valuable security has been provided by the company in respect thereof.	Sch 4:50(2)	Sch 8:46(2)		

No.	Disclosure item	Old ref	New ref	Complies?	Comments
130	For material contingent losses not provided against and which are not remote (and for material contingent gains but only if it is probable that the gain will be realised) disclose: (1) the nature of the contingency; (2) the uncertainties which are expected to affect the ultimate outcome; (3) a prudent estimate of the net pre-tax financial effect (at date of approval of accounts by directors) or a statement that estimation is not practicable; and (4) an explanation of the taxation implications where necessary for a proper understanding of the financial position. Note: Where both the nature of, and the uncertainties that affect a contingency are common to a large number of similar transactions the disclosure of the financial effect may be based on a group of similar transactions – SSAP 18 (21), FRSSE (128).	SSAP 18 (16–21)	FRSSE (123–128)		
131	Aggregate or estimated amounts of: (1) capital commitments not provided for (*including where practicable any related irrecoverable VAT*); and (2) commitments in respect of finance leases and hire purchase contracts entered into but whose inception occurs after the balance sheet date. Note: The FRSSE does not consider SSAP 5, but it may be appropriate for companies to continue with this SSAP 5 requirement to establish the cost of the asset concerned.	Sch 4:50(3) SSAP 5(6) SSAP 21(54)	Sch 8:46(3) FRSSE (105(c))		
132	*Amounts of payments committed to be made during the next year in respect of operating leases analysed between commitments expiring:* *(a) within one year;* *(b) in the second to fifth years; and* *(c) after five years,*	SSAP 21(56)	FRSSE(106)		

No.	Disclosure item	Old ref	New ref	Complies?	Comments
	showing separately those in respect of land and buildings. Under the FRSSE, the lessee should disclose the payments that it is committed to make. (Note: unlike the above SSAP 21 requirements this disclosure is not limited to payments to be made in the next year. However an analysis is not required.)				
133	Particulars of any other financial commitments which: (a) have not been provided for; and (b) are relevant to assessing the company's state of affairs. Other than contingencies, capital commitments, operating lease commitments and pension commitments which are subject to specific disclosure requirements. Commitments made on behalf of group companies. Any commitments which are undertaken for or on behalf of or for the benefit of: (1) any holding company or fellow subsidiary of the company; or (2) any subsidiary of the company, shall be stated separately from other commitments and commitments within (1) shall be stated separately from those within (2). Sch 4:59A.	Sch 4:50(5)	Sch 8:46(5)		
134	Disclose particulars of any charge on the assets of the company to secure liabilities of another person and, where practicable, the amount secured.	Sch 4:50(1)	Sch 8:46(1)		

158

No.	Disclosure item	Old ref	New ref	Complies?	Comments
	Other Disclosures/Additional Notes to the Accounts				
135	State the accounting policies adopted by the company in determining the amounts to be included in respect of items shown in the balance sheet and in determining the profit or loss of the company (including such policies with respect to the depreciation and diminution in value of assets).	Sch 4:36 SSAP 2(18)	Sch 8:36 FRSSE(6)		
136	Disclose details and effects of, and reasons for, departure from any of the five fundamental *concepts*/**principles** (going concern, consistency, prudence, accruals, separate valuation).	Sch 4:15 SSAP 2(17)	Sch 8:15 FRSSE(5)		
137	If there are any departures from the Companies Act to give a true and fair view, the necessary disclosures should be made in accordance with s226(5) and UITF 7 or FRSSE (7, 8).	s226(5) UITF 7	FRSSE(5)		
138	*State the accounting policies which have been applied to stocks and long term contracts, in particular the method of ascertaining turnover and attributable profit.*	SSAP 9(32)			
139	For each major class of depreciable asset: (1) depreciation methods used; (2) useful lives or depreciation rates.	SSAP 12 (25(a)) SSAP 12 (25(b))	FRSSE (71(a)) FRSSE (71(b))		
140	*Research and development:* *Accounting policy for research and development expenditure to be clearly explained.*	SSAP 13(30)			
141	Foreign currency translation: (1) basis of translating foreign currencies for profit and loss account and balance sheet, *including the basis used for translating the financial statements of foreign enterprises;* (2) *the treatment accorded to exchange differences; and* (3) *where group operations in hyper-inflationary areas are material in the context of group results and net assets, state the accounting policy adopted to eliminate the distortions. When*	Sch 4:58(1), SSAP 20(59), UITF 9(7-8)	Sch 8:51(1)		

No.	Disclosure item	Old ref	New ref	Complies?	Comments
	an alternative method to either of those permitted in UITF 9 is considered appropriate to eliminate distortions, state the reasons for adopting the alternative method. **Note:** UITF 9 is not addressed in the FRSSE.				
142	*Lessees.* *Disclose policies adopted for accounting for operating leases and finance leases (including in each case hire purchase contracts).* *Additional disclosures are required where in exceptional circumstances reverse premiums or other incentives have not been agreed on a straight line basis over the lease term (or to the first market rent review) in accordance with UITF Abstract 12).* *Benefits received and receivable by a lessee, as an incentive to sign the lease, should be spread by the lessee on a straight line basis over the lease term or, if shorter than the full lease term, over the period to the review date on which the rent is first expected to be adjusted to the prevailing market rate. Where, exceptionally, the presumption can be rebutted that an incentive (however structured) is in substance part of the lessor's market return another systematic and rational basis may be used, with disclosure of the following:* *(a) an explanation of the specific circumstances that render the standard treatment specified by Abstract 12 misleading;* *(b) a description of the basis used and the amounts involved; and* *(c) a note of the effect on the results for the current and corresponding period of any departure from the standard treatment.* *The same disclosures also apply if in exceptional circumstances another method of spreading is used more accurately to adjust the rents paid to the prevailing market rate.*	SSAP 21(57)			

No.	Disclosure item	Old ref	New ref	Complies?	Comments
143	*Lessors.* *Disclose policies adopted for accounting for operating leases and finance leases (including in each case hire purchase contracts).* *Disclose in detail the policy for accounting for finance lease income.*	SSAP 21(60)			
144	*Explain accounting policy followed in respect of goodwill.* **Note:** None of the disclosure requirements of SSAP 22 have been included in the FRSSE.	SSAP 22(43)			
145	*Pension costs:* *(1) state accounting policy adopted for pension scheme contributions and in the case of defined benefit schemes state also funding policy, if different; and* *(2) either the full provision basis or the partial provision basis may be used in accounting for the deferred tax implications of pensions and other post-retirement benefits – the policy adopted should be disclosed.*	SSAP 24(87) SSAP 24(88) SSAP 15(32A)			
146	*Disclose accounting policy for government grants.*	SSAP 4 (28)(a)			
147	In respect of directors of the company disclose aggregate amount of emoluments (including benefits in kind and contributions to pension schemes).	Sch 6:1(1)			
148	In respect of directors (and past directors) of the company disclose aggregate compensation for loss of office, including the estimated amount of benefits in kind and stating the nature of such benefits, distinguishing amounts for office of director and other office.	Sch 6:8			
149	In respect of directors of the company disclose total of emoluments waived and number concerned.	Sch 6:6			
150	Aggregate amount of any consideration paid to, or receivable by, third parties for making available the services of any person: (1) as a director of the company; or (2) while a director of the company,	Sch 6:9			

No.	Disclosure item	Old ref	New ref	Complies?	Comments
	as director of any subsidiary undertaking, or otherwise in connection with the management of the affairs of the company or any of its subsidiary undertakings. Third parties are persons other than: (1) the director himself or a person connected with him or body corporate controlled by him; and (2) the company or any of its subsidiary undertakings. Includes estimated money value of benefits, the nature of which should be disclosed.				
151	*Directors' benefits from share options.* *In addition to the information specified by law, which is dealt with elsewhere in this checklist, the UITF has recommended increased disclosure in respect of directors' share options. These disclosures are set out in the Listing Rules (or Yellow Book) and are mandatory for listed companies but are regarded as best practice for other companies.* **Note:** UITF 10 is not addressed in the FRSSE.	UITF 10			
152	State the nature of the pension scheme (e.g., defined contribution or defined benefit).	SSAP 24(87)(a) SSAP 24(88)(a)	FRSSE (110(a)) FRSSE (117(a))		
153	In respect of a defined benefit scheme state: (a) whether the pension cost and provision (or asset) are based on advice from a professionally qualified actuary and, if so, the date of the most recent formal actuarial valuation or later formal review used for this purpose. *If the actuary is an employee or officer of a group company, the fact should be disclosed;* (b) the amount of any deficiency on a current funding level basis indicating the action being taken to deal with it in current and future accounting periods. (Note:	SSAP 24(88)(d) SSAP 24(88)(g) SSAP 24(89) SSAP 24(88)(h–k)	FRSSE (117(b–h))		

No.	Disclosure item	Old ref	New ref	Complies?	Comments
	Where there is more than one scheme a current funding level basis deficiency in one scheme cannot be set off against a surplus in another);				
	(c) outline of the most recent formal actuarial valuation or later formal review of the scheme on an ongoing basis (SSAP 24 stipulates the following content for such an outline, which is not reproduced in the FRSSE):				
	– *actuarial method used and description of the main assumptions;*				
	– *market value of scheme assets;*				
	– *percentage level of funding; and*				
	– *comments on material actuarial surplus or deficiency.*				
	(d) any commitment to make additional payments over a limited number of years;				
	(e) accounting treatment adopted in respect of a refund subject to deduction for tax which is not allocated over the average remaining service lives of current employees and a credit appears in the financial statements in relation to it;				
	(f) details of expected effects on future costs of any material changes in the groups and/or company's pension arrangements;				
	(g) whether the scheme is funded or unfunded;				
	(h) the pension cost charge for the period *together with explanations of significant changes in the charge compared to that in the previous accounting period.*				
	Note: If company or group has more than one pension scheme disclosure should be made on a combined basis, unless information about individual schemes necessary for proper understanding of accounts, but a deficiency in one scheme				

No.	Disclosure item	Old ref	New ref	Complies?	Comments
	cannot be set off against a surplus in another – SSAP 24 (89). Subsidiary exempt from disclosure of information required in (b) and (c) above if holding company registered in UK or Republic of Ireland – SSAP 24 (90), FRSSE (116).				
154	If the company is a subsidiary and a member of a group pension scheme disclose: (a) that it is member of a group scheme; (b) that contributions are based on pension costs across group as a whole; and (c) name of holding company in whose accounts particulars of actuarial valuation are contained.	SSAP 24(90)	FRSSE(116)		
155	*Pension schemes in respect of foreign operations should be dealt with in accordance with SSAP 24 or adjusted on consolidation to make the charge commensurate with the basis laid down therein, unless nature of commitment is very different from that which is customary in the UK and Ireland. If adjustment is impractical because of difficulties of obtaining the necessary actuarial information, the amount charged and the basis of the charge to profit and loss account should be disclosed.*	SSAP 24(91)			
156	Defined contribution scheme. Disclose the pension cost charge for the period.	SSAP 24(87)	FRSSE (110(b))		
157	Pension commitments. (1) Particulars of: (a) any pension commitments included under any provision shown in the company's balance sheet; and (b) any such commitments for which no provision has been made. (2) Where any such commitment relates wholly or partly to	Sch 4:50(4)	Sch 8:46(4)		

No.	Disclosure item	Old ref	New ref	Complies?	Comments
	pensions payable to past directors of the company, separate particulars of that commitment, so far as it relates to such pensions.				
158	Post-retirement benefits other than pensions should be accounted for on a SSAP 24 basis. Give the equivalent disclosures to those required by SSAP24 in respect of pension schemes including details of any important assumptions which are specific to the measurement of such benefits such as the assumed rate of inflation in the cost of providing benefits.	UITF 6(9)	FRSSE(108)		
159	For post balance sheet events which are either non-adjusting events of exceptional materiality or the reversal or maturity of transactions entered into before the year-end primarily in order to alter the appearance of the balance sheet, disclose: (1) nature of event; (2) estimate of its pre-tax financial effect (or statement that estimation is not practicable); and (3) explanation of taxation implications, where necessary for proper understanding of financial position.	SSAP 17(23–25)	FRSSE (131–133)		
160	With respect to the body corporate (if any) regarded by the directors as being the company's ultimate holding company state: (1) the name of that body corporate; and (2) its country of incorporation if outside Great Britain. [For periods commencing on or after 23 December 1995] When the reporting entity is controlled by another party disclose: (1) the related party relationship; (2) the name of that party; and if different (3) the name of the ultimate controlling party. If these parties are not known disclose that fact.	Sch 5:12 Sch 5:31 FRS 8(5)	FRSSE (139)		

No.	Disclosure item	Old ref	New ref	Complies?	Comments
161	Application of FRS 5. Disclosure of a transaction in the financial statements, whether or not it has resulted in assets or liabilities being recognised or ceasing to be recognised, should be sufficient to enable the user of the financial statements to understand its commercial effect. **Under the FRSSE, regard should be had to the substance of any arrangement or transaction or series of such entered into by the entity. Adequate explanation should be given in the notes to the accounts to ensure that the financial statements give a true and fair view. Other than for the conditions relating to linked presentations and factored debts as noted below, and to the extent that it may apply to any group accounts which are produced, FRS 5 has not been considered in the FRSSE.** Where a transaction has resulted in the recognition of assets or liabilities whose nature differs from that of items usually included under the relevant balance sheet heading, the difference should be explained. Where a transaction does not result in assets or liabilities being recognised in the financial statements but does give rise to guarantees, commitments or other rights and obligations, this information should be disclosed if it is necessary to give a true and fair view. Where an asset has been partially transferred, or transferred for part of its life, or all of its life but retaining some significant rights to benefits or exposure to risks, and the resulting gain or loss is uncertain, full provision should be made for any loss but recognition of any gain if it is in doubt should be deferred. The uncertainty should be disclosed if material.	FRS 5(24) FRS 5(30) FRS 5(31) FRS 5(94)	FRSSE(3)		
161 A	Linked presentation. Where a transaction qualifies for the linked presentation (see FRS 5(29) or FRSSE (90)): (1) show the finance deducted from	FRS 5	FRSSE(90)		

No.	Disclosure item	Old ref	New ref	Complies?	Comments
	the gross amount of the item on the face of the balance sheet within a single asset caption. The gross amounts of both the item and the finance should be shown on the face of the balance sheet – FRS 5(26), FRSSE (90); (2) the directors must state that the company is not obliged to support any losses and that it does not intend to do so – FRS 5(27); (3) disclose that the provider of finance has agreed in writing that it will seek repayment of the finance, as to both principal and interest, only to the extent that specific funds are generated by the specific item it has financed and that it will not seek recourse in any other form – FRS 5(27). Where the conditions are met for only part of the finance, adopt the linked presentation to the extent that they are met – FRS 5(27, 85). Where a linked presentation is used the net profit or loss recognised in each period should be included in the profit and loss account with separate disclosure of its gross components given in the notes, or on the face of the profit and loss account using a linked presentation if necessary to give a true and fair view – FRS 5(28, 88).				
161 B	*Quasi-subsidiaries.* *The assets, liabilities, profits, losses and cash flows of a quasi-subsidiary should be included in the consolidated financial statements of the group that controls it in the same way as if they were those of a subsidiary. Where an entity has a quasi-subsidiary but no subsidiaries and therefore does not prepare group financial statements, it should provide in its financial statements consolidated financial statements of itself and the quasi-subsidiary, presented with equal prominence to the reporting entity's individual financial statements – FRS 5(35, 99, 100).*	FRS 5			

No.	Disclosure item	Old ref	New ref	Complies?	Comments
161 C	*Consignment stock.* *Disclose the nature of the arrangement and the main terms under which any consignment stock is held, including the terms of any deposit – FRS 5(A11, A12). Where consignment stock is on balance sheet include the liability to the supplier in trade creditors, after deducting any deposit, and disclose the amount of consignment stock included in the balance sheet – FRS 5(A11).* *Where consignment stock is not on balance sheet include any deposit under 'other debtors' and disclose the amount of consignment stock held at the year end.*	FRS 5			
161 D	*Sale and repurchase agreements.* *Describe the main features of the arrangement, including the status of the asset and the relationship between the asset and the liability. If the arrangement is not in substance a financing transaction, give full disclosure in the notes.* *Where the substance of the transaction is that the seller has a new asset and/or liability (including a contingent asset or liability), recognise or disclose the new asset and/or liability on a prudent basis in accordance with SSAP 18 and describe the terms of any repurchase provisions (including any options) and/or guarantees.*	FRS 5			
161 E	Factored debts. Where the conditions for a linked presentation are met show the non-returnable proceeds deducted from the factored debts on the face of the balance sheet and disclose: (1) the main terms of the agreement; (2) the gross amount of factored debts outstanding at the balance sheet date; (3) the factoring charges recognised in the period, analysed as appropriate; and (4) the details set out above under 'linked presentation' – FRS 5(C19). (5) a note stating that the company is not required to support bad	FRS 5	FRSSE(90)		

No.	Disclosure item	Old ref	New ref	Complies?	Comments
	debts in respect of factored debts and that the factors have stated in writing that they will not seek recourse other than out of factored debts – FRSSE (90).				
	Where separate presentation is required disclose the amount of factored debts outstanding at the balance sheet date – FRS 5(C20), FRSSE (91).				
161 F	*Securitised assets.*	FRS 5			
	Where the conditions for a linked presentation are met show the non-returnable proceeds deducted from the securitised assets on the face of the balance sheet within a single caption and disclose:				
	(1) a description of the assets securitised;				
	(2) any income or expenses recognised in the period, analysed as appropriate;				
	(3) the terms of any options for the originator to repurchase assets or transfer additional assets to the issuer;				
	(4) the terms of any interest rate swap or interest rate cap agreement between the issuer and the originator that meet the conditions set out in paragraph D11 of Application Note D of FRS 5;				
	(5) the priority and amount of claims on the proceeds generated by the assets, including any rights of the originator to proceeds from the assets in addition to the non recourse amounts already received;				
	(6) the ownership of the issuer; and				
	(7) the details set out above under 'linked presentation' – FRS 5 (D22, D26).				
	Where more than one securitisation qualifies for the linked presentation they may not be aggregated on the face of the balance sheet unless they relate to assets which, were they not securitised, would be shown within the same balance sheet caption. The note disclosures may be aggregated only				

No.	Disclosure item	Old ref	New ref	Complies?	Comments
	where the securitisations are on similar terms and related to a single type of asset – FRS 5(D23, D26).				
	Where a separate presentation is required, disclose the gross amount of assets securitised at the balance sheet date - FRS 5(D24, D26).				
161 G	*Loan transfers.*	FRS 5			
	Where the conditions for a linked presentation are met show the non returnable proceeds deducted from the gross amount of loans on the face of the balance sheet and disclose:				
	(1) the main terms of the arrangement;				
	(2) the gross amount of loans transferred and outstanding at the balance sheet date;				
	(3) the profit or loss recognised in the period, analysed as appropriate; and				
	(4) the details set out above under 'linked presentation' – FRS 5(E23).				
	Where separate presentation is required, the notes should disclose the amount of loans subject to loan transfer arrangements that are outstanding at the balance sheet date – FRS 5(E24).				
162	*Shares held by an ESOP should be classified as 'own shares' within fixed assets where the shares are held for the continuing benefit of the sponsoring company's business; otherwise they should be classified as 'own shares' within current assets.*	UITF 13			
	Disclose sufficient information to enable readers to understand the significance of the ESOP in the context of the sponsoring company, including:				
	(1) a description of the main features of the ESOP including the arrangements for distributing shares to employees;				
	(2) the manner in which the costs are dealt with in the profit and loss account;				
	(3) the number and market value of the shares held by the ESOP and whether dividends on those				

No.	Disclosure item	Old ref	New ref	Complies?	Comments
	shares have been waived; and (4) *the extent to which these shares are under option to employees, or have been conditionally gifted to them.* Note: UITF 13 is not addressed by the draft FRSSE.				
163	In respect of loans to directors, disclose: (A) any loans, quasi-loans, credit transactions and any guarantee or security in connection therewith; (B) any agreement (by the company or a subsidiary) to enter into any such transaction; (C) any assignment to the company or an assumption by it of rights, obligations or liabilities under any such transaction which, had it been entered into by the company would have contravened the Act; and (D) any arrangement by the company whereby another party enters into any such transaction which if entered into by the company would have contravened the Act and whereby that other party obtains any benefit from the company or other group company, disclose separately for each transaction, arrangement or agreement: (a) a statement that it was made or subsisted during the period; (b) the name of the director and, where applicable, the connected person; (c) its principal terms; and additionally: (a) for a loan or agreement for a loan or an arrangement under (C) or (D) above in relation to a loan: (i) amount of the liability (principal and interest) at the beginning and end of the financial year;	Sch 6: 15–24			

No.	Disclosure item	Old ref	New ref	Complies?	Comments

	(ii) the maximum amount of the liability at any time during the period;
	(iii) amount of interest due but unpaid; and
	(iv) any provision in the accounts for non-recovery of all or part of the loan or any interest thereon;
	(b) for a guarantee or security or an arrangement under (C) above in relation to a guarantee or security:
	   (i) amount of the liability of the company (or subsidiary) at beginning and end of the financial year;
	   (ii) maximum amount for which company (or subsidiary) may become liable; and
	   (iii) any amount paid or liability incurred by company (or a subsidiary) in fulfilling a guarantee or in discharging any security;
	(c) for any other transaction (i.e., including quasi-loans and credit transactions), the value of the transaction or arrangement.				

164	For any transaction or arrangement (other than loans etc. – see previous question) in which a director (including a shadow director) or connected person had directly or indirectly a material interest, disclose (comparative amounts not required): (1) a statement that it was made or subsisted during the period; (2) its principal terms; (3) the name of the person for whom it was made (i.e., the other parties to the transactions) and where that person is connected with a director, the name of the director;	Sch 6: 15–27			

No.	Disclosure item	Old ref	New ref	Complies?	Comments
	(4) the name of the director with the material interest and the nature of the interest; (5) the value of the transaction or arrangement.				
165	In respect of transactions, arrangements and agreements by the company and, for holding companies, by their subsidiaries, for persons who at any time during the financial year were officers of the company (but not directors), under each of: (a) loans; (b) quasi-loans; and (c) credit transactions, in each case including related guarantees, security, arrangements for assignment or assumption, and indirect arrangements, disclose for each category the aggregate amounts outstanding at the end of the financial year (comparative amounts not required) and the number of officers for whom they were made.	Sch 6:29			
166	For material transactions with related parties (regardless of whether a price is charged) disclose: (1) names of the transacting parties; (2) description of the relationship between the parties; (3) description of the transactions; (4) amounts involved; and (5) other elements of the transactions necessary for an understanding of the financial statements. **Materiality of a related party transaction should be judged not only in terms of significance to the reporting entity, but also in relation to the other related party – FRSSE (135). This is less restricted than FRS 8 where the 'other party' considerations are limited to cases where that party is, or is an entity controlled by, a director, key manager or close family member – see FRS 8 (20). Disclosure is not required of emoluments in respect of services as an employee of the reporting entity and certain other parties (such as providers of finance,**	FRS 8(6)	FRSSE (135)		

Appendix 3

No.	Disclosure item	Old ref	New ref	Complies?	Comments
	utility companies etc) – see FRS 8 (3, 4) and FRSSE (137) which differ in the exemptions available.				
167	Personal guarantees given by the directors in respect of the reporting entity's borrowings.		FRSSE (138)		
168	In respect of amounts due to and from related parties disclose: (1) amounts at the balance sheet date; (2) provisions for doubtful debts at that date; and (3) amounts written off in the period. Disclosure may be on an aggregated basis (similar transactions by type of related party) unless disclosure of individual transactions is necessary for an understanding of the impact or required by law.	FRS 8(6)	FRSSE (135) FRSSE (136)		
169	Where the company holds subsidiary undertakings at the end of the financial year but is not required to prepare group accounts, there should be a statement: (1) that the financial statements present information about it as a single undertaking and not about its group; and (2) giving, or referring to a note giving, the reason why the company is not required to prepare group accounts.	Sch 5:1(4) FRS 2(22)			
170	If the company has taken advantage of the exemption for small and medium sized groups from the need to prepare group accounts and in the auditors opinion they were not entitled to do so, the auditors shall state this fact in their report.	s237(4A)			
171	If the company has taken advantage of the exemption not to prepare group accounts available to certain subsidiaries of an immediate parent undertaking established under the law of an EU member state: (1) the company should disclose in its individual accounts that it is exempt from the obligation to prepare and deliver group	s228(2)			

174

No.	Disclosure item	Old ref	New ref	Complies?	Comments
	accounts; and (2) the company should state within its individual accounts the name of the parent undertaking which draws up the group accounts; and also: (i) if the parent is incorporated outside GB, the country of incorporation; or (ii) if it is not incorporated, the address of the principal place of business.				
172	*If the reason for not preparing group accounts is that all subsidiary undertakings fall within the exclusions provided for in s229, state with respect to each subsidiary undertaking which of those exclusions applies.*	Sch 5:1(5) FRS 2(21d)			
173	In relation to each subsidiary undertaking, state: (1) the name of each subsidiary; (2) if incorporated outside GB, the country of incorporation; and (3) if unincorporated, the address of its principal place of business. Exemptions: (1) where the disclosures required would result in a statement of excessive length, they may be limited to: (a) principal subsidiaries; and (b) those subsidiaries excluded from consolidation by virtue of s229(3) and (4); provided that it is indicated that it is so limited and full details must be attached to company's next annual return – s231(5, 6). (2) if DTI approval is obtained, the disclosures required may be omitted in respect of an undertaking which is established outside the law of the UK or carries on business outside the UK where disclosure would be harmful. The fact of the omission should be stated.	Sch 5:1			
174	State in relation to each class of share held by the company in subsidiary undertakings:	Sch 5:2(1) Sch 5:2(2)			

No.	Disclosure item	Old ref	New ref	Complies?	Comments
	(1) the identity of the class; and (2) the proportion of the nominal value of the shares held. Exemptions: (1) where the disclosures required would result in a statement of excessive length, they may be limited to: (a) principal subsidiaries; and (b) those subsidiaries excluded from consolidation by virtue of s229(3) and (4); provided that it is indicated that it is so limited and full details must be attached to company's next annual return – s231(5, 6). (2) if DTI approval is obtained, the disclosures required may be omitted in respect of an undertaking which is established outside the law of the UK or carries on business outside the UK where disclosure would be harmful. The fact of the omission should be stated.				
175	Financial information. In respect of each subsidiary undertaking show: (1) the aggregate amount of capital and reserves at the end of its financial year; and (2) its profit or loss for the year. Note: This information is not required to be given if the company is exempt by virtue of s228 from the requirement to prepare group accounts, if the subsidiary is not required under the Companies Act to deliver its balance sheet (and does not otherwise publish it) and the company's holding is less than 50 per cent of the nominal value of the shares in the undertaking or if the subsidiary is included in the company's accounts by way of equity accounting. If the subsidiary's year is not coterminous with the company's financial year state the date on which	Sch 5:3 Sch 5:4			

No.	Disclosure item	Old ref	New ref	Complies?	Comments
	the subsidiary's last financial year ended. Exemptions: (1) where the disclosures required would result in a statement of excessive length, they may be limited to: (a) principal subsidiaries; and (b) those subsidiaries excluded from consolidation by virtue of s229(3) and (4); provided that it is indicated that the disclosures are so limited. Full details must be attached to company's next annual return – s231(5, 6). (2) if DTI approval is obtained, the disclosures required may be omitted in respect of an undertaking which is established outside the law of the UK or carries on business outside the UK where disclosure would be harmful. The fact of the omission should be stated.				
176	*State for all business combinations:* *(a) the names of the combining entities (other than the reporting entity);* *(b) whether the combination has been accounted for as an acquisition or a merger; and* *(c) the date of the combination.* *Comparatives not required.* *(a) and (b) need not be disclosed with respect to an undertaking which is established outside the UK or carries out business outside the UK, if disclosure would be seriously prejudicial and the Secretary of State agrees – Sch 4A:16.* Note: The FRSSE does not deal with group accounts.	Sch 4A:13(2) FRS 6(21)			
177	*For each material acquisition and for other acquisitions in aggregate disclosure:* *(a) the composition and fair value of the consideration given by the acquiring company and its subsidiary undertakings should be disclosed; and*	FRS 6(24), Sch 4A:13(3)			

No.	Disclosure item	Old ref	New ref	Complies?	Comments
	(b) the nature of any deferred or contingent purchase consideration should be stated, including, for contingent consideration, the range of possible outcomes and the principal factors that affect the outcome. *Comparatives not required.* *(a) need not be disclosed with respect to an undertaking which is established outside the UK or carries out business outside the UK, if disclosure would be seriously prejudicial and the Secretary of State agrees – Sch 4A:16.* Note: The FRSSE does not deal with group accounts.				
178	*Provide a table showing, for each class of assets and liabilities of the acquired entity:* *(a) the book values, as recorded in the acquired entity's books immediately before the acquisition and before any fair value adjustments;* *(b) the fair value adjustments, analysed into:* *(i) revaluations;* *(ii) adjustments to achieve consistency of accounting policies; and* *(iii) any other significant adjustments, giving an explanation for the adjustments; and* *(c) the fair values at the date of acquisition.* *The table should include a statement of the amount of purchased goodwill or negative goodwill arising on the acquisition.* *For each material acquisition and for other acquisitions in aggregate.* **Note:** *Comparatives not required.* *Need not be disclosed with respect to an undertaking which is established outside the UK or carries out business outside the UK, if disclosure would be seriously prejudicial and the Secretary of State agrees – Sch 4A:16.* The FRSSE does not deal with group accounts.	Sch 4A:13(5) FRS 6(25) SSAP 22(44)			

No.	Disclosure item	Old ref	New ref	Complies?	Comments
179	*In the fair value table identify separately:* *(a) provisions for reorganisation and restructuring costs that are included in the liabilities of the acquired entity; and* *(b) related asset write downs made in the twelve months up to the date of acquisition.* *For each material acquisition and for other acquisitions in aggregate.* **Note:** *Comparatives not required.* **The FRSSE does not deal with group accounts.**	FRS 6(26)			
180	*Disclose the method of dealing with goodwill arising on each acquisition during the period and whether it has been set off against merger reserve or other reserves or has been carried forward as an intangible asset.* **Note:** *Comparatives not required.* *When merger relief applies to the individual accounts of the acquirer, the difference between the fair value of the shares issued and their nominal value should be credited to a separate reserve in the consolidated accounts. Goodwill must still be calculated by comparing the fair value of the consideration given with the fair value of the net assets acquired but the 'merger reserve' will be available for writing off such goodwill* **The FRSSE does not deal with group accounts.**	SSAP 22(47), FRS 6(43), SSAP 22(22)			
181	*State if fair values of acquired assets and liabilities, or fair value of consideration, have been determined on a provisional basis, giving reasons.* *Disclose and explain material adjustments to provisional fair values determined in previous years (with corresponding adjustments to goodwill).* **Note:** *For each material acquisition and for other acquisitions in aggregate.*	FRS 6(27)			

No.	Disclosure item	Old ref	New ref	Complies?	Comments
	Comparatives not required. **The FRSSE does not deal with group accounts.**				
182	*Any exceptional profit or loss that is determined using the fair values recognised on acquisition should be disclosed in accordance with the requirements of FRS 3, and identified as relating to the acquisition.* **Note:** *For each material acquisition and for other acquisitions in aggregate.* *Comparatives not required.* *FRS 6 requires disclosure of exceptional profits or losses determined using fair values recognised on an acquisition. Examples include profits or losses on the disposal of acquired stocks where the fair values of stocks sold lead to abnormal trading margins after the acquisition; the release of provisions in respect of an acquired loss making long term contract that the acquirer makes profitable; and the realisation of contingent assets or liabilities at amounts materially different from their attributed fair values. In accordance with the requirements of FRS 3, exceptional items would be included in the profit and loss account format headings to which they relate, and would be disclosed by way of note, or on the face of the profit and loss account if necessary to give a true and fair view – FRS 6(85).* **The FRSSE does not deal with group accounts.**	FRS 6(30)			
183	*Show the costs incurred in reorganising, restructuring and integrating acquisitions. Such costs are those that:* *(a) would not have been incurred had the acquisition not taken place; and* *(b) relate to a project identified and controlled by management as part of a reorganisation or integration programme set up at the time of acquisition or as a*	FRS 6(31)			

No.	Disclosure item	Old ref	New ref	Complies?	Comments
	direct consequence of an immediate post acquisition review.				
	Note:				
	For each material acquisition and for other acquisitions in aggregate.				
	FRS 3 requires the profits or losses on the post acquisition sale or termination of an operation, or on the disposal of fixed assets, to be shown in the profit and loss account below operating profit. Post-acquisition integration, reorganisation and restructuring costs, including provisions in respect of them, would, if material, be reported as exceptional items; but only if the restructuring is fundamental, having a material effect on the nature and focus of the enlarged group's operations, would the costs be shown below operating profit as an item falling under para 20 of FRS 3. Paragraph 31 of FRS 6 requires that costs of reorganising, restructuring and integration that relate to an acquisition, whether relating to a fundamental restructuring or not, should be shown separately from other exceptional items – FRS 6(86).				
	The costs of reorganising, restructuring and integrating an acquired entity may extend over more than one period. For major acquisitions, therefore, management may wish to state in the notes to the financial statements the nature and amount of such costs expected to be incurred in relation to the acquisition (including asset write-downs) indicating the extent to which they have been charged to the profit and loss account. If part of these costs relate to asset write-downs (beyond any impairments recognised in adjusting to fair values on the acquisition) it may be useful to distinguish these from cash expenditure. An illustrative example of how such information might be shown is included as Appendix IV to FRS 6 – FRS 6(87).				
	The FRSSE does not deal with group accounts.				

No.	Disclosure item	Old ref	New ref	Complies?	Comments
184	*Movements on provisions or accruals for costs related to an acquisition should be disclosed and analysed between the amounts used for the specific purpose for which they were created and the amounts released unused.* **Note:** *For each material acquisition and for other acquisitions in aggregate.* *Comparatives not required.* **The FRSSE does not deal with group accounts.**	FRS 6(32)			
185	*For material acquisitions, the profit after taxation and minority interests of the acquired entity should be given for:* (a) *the period from the beginning of the acquired entity's financial year to the date of acquisition, giving the date on which this period began; and* (b) *its previous financial year.* **Note:** *Comparatives not required.* **The FRSSE does not deal with group accounts.**	FRS 6(35)			
186	*For substantial acquisitions:* (a) *Summarised profit and loss account of acquired entity from beginning of its financial year (giving date) to date of acquisition showing:* *Turnover* *Operating profit* *Exceptional items (para 20 of FRS 3)* *Profit before tax* *Taxation* *Minority interests* *Profit after tax and minority interests* *[Extraordinary items]* (b) *Profit after tax and minority interests of acquired entity for its previous financial year.* (c) *Statement of total recognised gains and losses of the acquired*	FRS 6(36)			

No.	Disclosure item	Old ref	New ref	Complies?	Comments
	entity from beginning of its financial year to date of acquisition. **Note:** *Comparatives not required.* *Information required to be on the basis of the acquired entity's accounting policies prior to the acquisition.* *Management may consider it helpful in explaining the impact of the acquisition to give, in addition, the same information restated onto the basis of the acquiring entity's accounting policies – FRS 6(89).* **The FRSSE does not deal with group accounts.**				
187	*In respect of each material disposal of a previously acquired business or business segment show:* *(1) the profit or loss on disposal;* *(2) disclose the amount of purchased goodwill attributable to disposal of a business as a separate component of the profit or loss on disposal, either on the face of the profit and loss account or by way of a note; and* *(3) the accounting treatment adopted and the proceeds where no profit or loss is recorded because the proceeds have been treated as a reduction in the cost of the acquisition.* *In respect of acquisitions in accounting periods commencing prior to 1 January 1989, if it is impossible or impracticable to ascertain the attributable goodwill on a disposal this should be stated and the reasons given.* Note: **The FRSSE does not deal with group accounts.**	SSAP 22(52) SSAP 22(53) UITF 3(10)			

No.	Disclosure item	Old ref	New ref	Complies?	Comments
	**Prescribed Formats for Abbreviated Accounts**
188	The balance sheet should accord with one of the prescribed formats.	Sch 8:17	Sch 8A:1		
189	A directors' report and profit and loss account are not required for small company abbreviated accounts.	Sch 8:18 Sch 8:20	s246(5)		
190	In the notes to the abbreviated accounts. State the accounting policies adopted by the company in determining the amounts to be included in respect of items shown in the balance sheet and in determining the profit or loss of the company (including such policies with respect to the depreciation and diminution in value of assets and including basis of conversion of foreign currency amounts into sterling).	Sch 4:36 SSAP 2(18) Sch 4:58(1)	Sch 8A:4 Sch 8A:9		

191	Intangible fixed assets for small company abbreviated accounts.
	
	Gross amounts, movements and depreciation.
	
	For each item under intangible fixed assets that does not have an Arabic numeral, i.e., for the aggregate of intangible fixed assets only, state (comparatives not required):
	
	(1) the aggregate purchase price or production cost, or valuation determined under one of the alternative accounting rules, as at the beginning and end of the financial year. Cost of tangible fixed assets and other items disclosed should include irrecoverable VAT (where practicable and material);
	(2) the effect on any amount shown in the balance sheet in respect of each fixed asset item as a result of any:
	  (a) revaluation made during the year in accordance with the alternative accounting rules;
	  (b) acquisitions during the year;
	  (c) disposals during the year; and
		Sch 4:42 Sch 4:58	Sch 8A:7 Sch 8A:9(3)(d)		

No.	Disclosure item	Old ref	New ref	Complies?	Comments
	(d) transfers during the year; and				
	(3) in respect of provisions for depreciation or diminution in value:				
	(a) the cumulative amount of such provisions as at the beginning and end of the year;				
	(b) the amount provided during the year;				
	(c) the amount of any adjustments made during the year in consequence of the disposal of any asset; and				
	(d) the amount of any other adjustments (e.g., exchange translation differences) made during the year.				

192	Tangible fixed assets for small company abbreviated accounts.
	
	Gross amounts, movements and depreciation.
	
	For each item under tangible fixed assets that does not have an Arabic numeral, i.e., for the aggregate of tangible fixed assets only, state (comparatives not required):
	
	(1) the aggregate purchase price or production cost, or valuation determined under one of the alternative accounting rules, as at the beginning and end of the financial year. Cost of tangible fixed assets and other items disclosed should include irrecoverable VAT (where practicable and material);
	(2) the effect on any amount shown in the balance sheet in respect of each fixed asset item as a result of any:
	    (a) revaluation made during the year in accordance with the alternative accounting rules;
	    (b) acquisitions during the year;
	    (c) disposals during the year; and
	    (d) transfers during the year;
		Sch 4:42
		Sch 4:58
			Sch 8A:7
			Sch 8A:9(3)(d)		

Appendix 3

No.	Disclosure item	Old ref	New ref	Complies?	Comments
	and (3) in respect of provisions for depreciation or diminution in value: (a) the cumulative amount of such provisions as at the beginning and end of the year; (b) the amount provided during the year; (c) the amount of any adjustments made during the year in consequence of the disposal of any asset; and (d) the amount of any other adjustments (e.g., exchange translation differences) made during the year. Note: There are additional requirements in respect of investment properties (see question 73). SSAP 19 and FRSSE (56–59) require such properties to be included in the balance sheet at open market value, and not subject to depreciation unless the asset is held on lease with 20 years or less to run. These requirements do not apply to charities.				
193	Fixed asset investments for small company abbreviated accounts. Gross amounts, movements and depreciation. For each item under fixed asset investments that does not have an Arabic numeral, i.e., for the aggregate of fixed asset investments only, state (comparatives not required): (1) the aggregate purchase price or production cost, or valuation determined under one of the alternative accounting rules, as at the beginning and end of the financial year. Cost of tangible fixed assets and other items disclosed should include irrecoverable VAT (where practicable and material); (2) the effect on any amount shown in the balance sheet in respect of	Sch 4:42 Sch 4:58	Sch 8A:7 Sch 8A:9(3)(d)		

186

No.	Disclosure item	Old ref	New ref	Complies?	Comments
	each fixed asset item as a result of any: (a) revaluation made during the year in accordance with the alternative accounting rules; (b) acquisitions during the year; (c) disposals during the year; and (d) transfers during the year; and (3) in respect of provisions for depreciation or diminution in value: (a) the cumulative amount of such provisions as at the beginning and end of the year; (b) the amount provided during the year; (c) the amount of any adjustments made during the year in consequence of the disposal of any asset; and (d) the amount of any other adjustments (e.g., exchange translation differences) made during the year.				
194	For small company abbreviated accounts disclose details of debtors falling due after more than one year.	Sch 4:8 (Note 5)	Sch 8A:2 (Note 1)		
195	For creditors in small company abbreviated accounts: Where: (1) security has been given, provide details of amounts; (2) there are amounts payable other than by instalments, after five years, provide details of aggregate amounts; and (3) if paid by instalments, and any instalments fall due after five years, show total due.	Sch 4:48	Sch 8A:8		
196	Authorised, issued and paid up capital in small company abbreviated accounts: (1) authorised share capital; (2) amount of allotted share capital and amount of called up share	Sch 4:8 (Note 12) Sch 4:38	Sch 8A:5		

No.	Disclosure item	Old ref	New ref	Complies?	Comments
	capital which has been paid up; (3) number and aggregate nominal value of allotted shares of each class where more than one class of shares have been allotted. For redeemable shares indicate: (1) earliest and latest dates on which the company has power of redemption; (2) whether redemption is required in any event or at option of company or shareholder; and (3) whether any (and if so what) premium is payable on redemption.				
197	Shares allotted during period for small company abbreviated accounts. Where the company has allotted any shares during the financial year disclose: (1) the classes of shares allotted; and (2) for each class of shares, the number allotted, their aggregate nominal value and the consideration received by the company.	Sch 4:39	Sch 8A:6		
198	Schedule 5 information for small company abbreviated accounts. All of the information required by Sch 5 (refer to checklist or full accounts), except for: (a) financial years of subsidiary undertakings (para 4); (b) **additional information about subsidiaries (para 5);** (c) shares and debentures held by subsidiaries (para 6); (d) **arrangements attracting merger relief (para 10).** Note: The regulations containing the proposed revision to s246 do not include the exemption from disclosing details under paras 5 or 10 of Sch 5.	Sch 8:19(2)	s246		
199	Schedule 6 information for small company abbreviated accounts. Disclose the information required by Part II and Part III of Sch 6, (refer to checklist or full accounts) i.e., transactions involving directors,	Sch 8:19(3)	s246		

No.	Disclosure item	Old ref	New ref	Complies?	Comments
	connected persons and officers of the company.				
200	Directors' statement for small company abbreviated accounts.	Sch 8:23	s246		
	Where the directors intend to take advantage of the exemptions under *Section A of Part III (small company) of Sch 8/***Sch 8 or Sch 8A**, the company's balance sheet should contain:				
	(1) a statement that *advantage has been taken of the exemption conferred by Section A of Part III of Sch 8/***the accounts are prepared in accordance with the special provisions of Part VII of the Companies Act 1985 relating to small companies**; and				
	(2) *a statement of the grounds on which in the directors opinion the company is entitled to the exemption.*				
	Note:				
	Does not apply where the company is exempt by virtue of s250 (dormant companies) from the obligation to appoint auditors – Sch 8:25 (s246(9), as revised).				
201	Auditors' report for small companies' abbreviated accounts:	Sch 8:24	s247B		
	(1) *the auditors shall provide the directors with a report stating whether in their opinion the company is entitled to those exemptions, and whether the documents proposed to be delivered in accordance with Schedule 8 have been properly prepared;*				
	(2) the accounts to be delivered should be accompanied by a special report of the auditors stating that in their opinion:				
	(a) the company is entitled to *the exemptions claimed in the directors statement/* **deliver abbreviated accounts prepared in accordance with s246(5) and/or s246(6)**; and				
	(b) the accounts to be delivered				

No.	Disclosure item	Old ref	New ref	Complies?	Comments
	are properly prepared in accordance with *Schedule 8*/that (those) provisions; *and which reproduces the full text of the audit report prepared under s235.* Under the new requirements of s247B the audit report on the abbreviated accounts should reproduce the report on the full accounts only if it contained a qualification. Where statements were made under s237(2) or s237(3) these also need to be included in the audit report on the abbreviated accounts; (3) the special report should be dated on, or as soon as possible after, the date of the report on the full financial statements. Notes: 1 Where the audit report under s235 is qualified, the special report should include any further information or material necessary to understand the qualification. 2 The above does not apply where the company is dormant and is exempt by virtue of s250 from the obligation to appoint auditors. 3 For further guidance see APB's Practice Note 8.				

No.	Disclosure item	Old ref	New ref	Complies?	Comments
	Forming an opinion				
202	Consider whether, otherwise than as noted elsewhere in completion of this checklist: (1) the financial statements give a true and fair view; (2) the financial statements have been properly prepared in accordance with the provisions of the Companies Act 1985; (3) proper accounting records have been kept; (4) proper returns adequate for audit have been received from branches not visited (where applicable); (5) the financial statements are in agreement with the accounting records and returns; (6) all information and explanations necessary for the purposes of the audit have been obtained; (7) the information given in the directors' report in relation to the financial year being reported upon is consistent with the financial statements; (8) any significant departures from accounting standards are adequately disclosed and are departures with which we concur.	s235(2) s237(1) s237(3) s235(3)			
203	There should be adequate disclosure of additional information necessary to show a true and fair view.	s226(4)	FRSSE(3)		
204	There should be adequate disclosure relating to going concern in order to give a true and fair view. There should be disclosure in the financial statements or accompanying information (e.g., the OFR) if the period to which the directors have paid particular attention in assessing going concern is less than one year from the date of approval of the financial statements.	SAS 130.5 SAS 130.7			
205	The audit report should comply with the requirements of SAS 600.				

No.	Disclosure item	Old ref	New ref	Complies?	Comments
206	The auditors' report and the copy of the auditors' report which is delivered to the Registrar of Companies must state the name of the auditors (partnership) and be signed by them (the copy delivered to the Registrar must have an original signature). Every copy of the auditors' report which is laid before the company in general meeting, or which is otherwise circulated, published or issued must state the names of the auditors.	s236			
207	Where a qualified audit report has been given, a written statement is required as to whether the qualification is material for determining whether a proposed distribution is permitted under s270 of the Act.	s271(4)			

Appendix 4

The Draft FRSSE

Contents

Appendices

[*Appendices VI and VII are not reproduced here.*]

[Draft] Financial Reporting Standard for Smaller Entities (FRSSE) is set out in paragraphs 1–217.

The Statement of Standard Accounting Practice set out in paragraphs 2–143 should be read in the context of the Objective as stated in paragraph 1 and the Definitions set out in paragraphs 144–217 and also of the Foreword to Accounting Standards.

In the absence of guidance within the [draft] FRSSE, financial statements should be prepared using accepted practice and, accordingly, regard should be had to other Statements of Standard Accounting Practice, Financial Reporting Standards and Urgent Issues Task Force Abstracts, not as mandatory documents, but as a means of establishing current practice.

Appendix V, 'The development of the Exposure Draft' reviews considerations and arguments that were thought significant by members of the Board in reaching the conclusions on the [draft] FRSSE.

© *The Accounting Standards Board Limited 1996*

Preface

The proposals in this Exposure Draft of a Financial Reporting Standard for Smaller Entities (FRSSE) have been developed to reflect comments received on the application of accounting standards to smaller entities, organised through the two consultation exercises carried out by a Working Party of the Consultative Committee of Accountancy Bodies (CCAB) set up at the request of the Accounting Standards Board. These consultation exercises consisted of the publication of:

- a Consultative Document 'Exemptions from Standards on Grounds of Size or Public Interest' issued for comment in November 1994; and
- a Paper 'Designed to fit – A Financial Reporting Standard for Smaller Entities' issued for comment in December 1995.

As explained in paragraph 31 of the Foreword to Accounting Standards, the issue of the Exposure Draft does not affect the application of extant accounting standards and UITF Abstracts, the requirements of which remain in force until superseded by the proposed standard.

Appendix V 'The development of the Exposure Draft' sets out the main issues raised and the responses given.

To assist readers of the Exposure Draft to understand the sources of the paragraphs in the proposed standard and the changes to the body of accounting standards and UITF Abstracts which the Exposure Draft proposes, Appendix VI provides a table of derivations. Appendix VII sets out simplifications that have been made in the Exposure Draft as compared with the existing body of accounting standards and UITF Abstracts.

Meeting the main concerns of the commentators

The comments received in the two consultative exercises demonstrated support for the proposition that the present arrangements, whereby all accounting standards and UITF Abstracts apply to all entities with few exceptions, cause problems. From the consultations begun in November 1994, there was clear support for relief from accounting standards to be based on size or a combination of size and public interest, with the use of the 'small company' ceiling in section 247 of the Companies Act 1985 being the most popular option. The acceptance of the use of this ceiling was reinforced in the second consultation, and accordingly is adopted in the proposed FRSSE.

However, a number of commentators asked that small groups, as well as single entities, should be eligible to use the proposed FRSSE. As small groups are not required by law to prepare consolidated accounts, experience is that not many do so, at least on a statutory basis. To import all the necessary requirements from accounting standards and UITF Abstracts into the proposed FRSSE to deal with consolidated accounts would add significantly to its length and complexity, yet it is expected that it would be of interest to only a relatively small percentage of entities. The proposed FRSSE therefore caters for small groups by specifying that users should apply those accounting standards that are specific to consolidation (for example, FRSs 2, 6 and 7) and UITF Abstracts that are written to cover group situations.

Two matters in the draft FRSSE issued in December 1995 attracted particular comment. These were the proposals:

- to require a summary cash flow statement;
- to import the majority of the related party disclosure requirements contained in FRS 8.

The cash flow statement proposal called for a simplified statement setting out the entity's inflows and outflows of cash in the period. Based on the requirements of FRS 1 (as revised in 1996), the cash flow statement for smaller entities would be as follows.

Example: Cash flow statement (1995 comparatives not illustrated here)

	1996 £
Cash flow from operating activities	68,890
Returns on investments and servicing of finance	5,820
Taxation	(29,220)
Capital expenditure	(15,250)
	30,240
Acquisitions and disposals	50
Equity dividends paid	(250)
	30,040
Management of liquid resources	300
Financing	70
Increase in cash	30,410

Some commentators suggested that the cash flow statement should be dropped because:

- FRS 1 exempts small entities from preparing such a statement and there is little or no evidence that such statements are being prepared voluntarily for inclusion in the statutory financial statements. FRS 1 (Revised 1996) maintains the exemption.

- for many small businesses in which transactions are straightforward, the cash flow statement adds little to what is already apparent from the balance sheet and the profit and loss account.
- the gap between the period-end and the date of finalising the financial statements may be of such length (up to ten months) as to limit the usefulness of any cash flow information.
- managers in small businesses are well aware of the need to manage cash effectively. Their mechanisms for doing so may be informal but little would be added by a requirement for a cash flow statement in annual financial statements prepared some months after a period-end.

Other commentators, who represent the main users of financial statements, were strongly opposed to dropping the proposed requirement. They argued that management of cash is crucial in small, as well as large, businesses and that a cash flow statement provided a useful focus for discussions with management as well as a reference point for subsequent more detailed analysis that they might require.

Having regard to the points made above, the CCAB Working Party recommended that the requirement for a cash flow statement should not be included in the Exposure Draft. The Board seeks comments on this issue.

The CCAB Working Party also recommended the deletion of the related party disclosures from the Exposure Draft, again in response to comments received. The arguments were that (i) companies legislation already requires extensive disclosures and (ii) the proposed FRSSE contains a requirement (paragraph 3) that, where there is any doubt whether applying any provisions of the proposed FRSSE would be sufficient to give a true and fair view, adequate explanation should be given in the notes to the accounts of the transaction or arrangement concerned. The Board's view is that related party disclosures are just as relevant to readers of smaller entities' accounts and accordingly the proposals in 'Designed to fit' have been retained.

The Board accepts the recommendations of the CCAB Working Party for maintaining the FRSSE. Subject to the comments received on this Exposure Draft, the Board proposes to establish an advisory committee to assume responsibility for advising on financial reporting in smaller entities and thus for the FRSSE. The committee is likely to meet regularly and to report as necessary to the Board. It would be committed to review the FRSSE after two years of operation and to propose revisions to the FRSSE as necessary to reflect developments in financial reporting. Any proposed changes (unless minor or inconsequential) to the FRSSE would be the subject of public consultation. The FRSSE would be formally approved, issued and revised by the Board.

The Board has received legal advice that smaller entities can properly be allowed exemptions or differing treatments from the requirements of other accounting standards provided that such differences are justified on rational grounds. The Board will have regard to the criteria listed below in determining whether such rational grounds exist. These criteria are based on those recommended by the CCAB Working Party.

(a) Is the standard or requirement likely to be regarded as of general application and an essential element of generally accepted accounting practice for all entities?

(b) Would the standard or requirement be likely to lead to a transaction being treated in a way that would be readily recognised by the proprietor or manager of the business as corresponding to their understanding of the transaction?

(c) Is the standard or requirement likely to meet the information needs and legitimate expectations of a user of a small entity's accounts?

(d) Does the standard or requirement result in disclosures that are likely to be meaningful and comprehensive to such a user? Where disclosures are aimed at a particular group of users, will that group receive the information, given that they may have access only to abbreviated accounts?

(e) Do the requirements of the standard significantly augment the treatment prescribed by legislation?

(f) Is the treatment prescribed by the standard or requirement compatible with that already used, or expected to be used, by the Inland Revenue in computing taxable profits?

(g) Does the standard or requirement provide the least cumbersome method of achieving the desired accounting treatment and/or disclosure for an entity that is not complex?

(h) Does the standard provide guidance that might be expected to be widely relevant to the transactions of small entities and is it written in terms that can be understood by such businesses?

(i) Are the measurement methods prescribed in the standard likely to be reasonably practical for small entities?

A preponderance of negative answers would suggest that exemption, or differing treatment, from the standard, or a specific requirement within that standard, would be appropriate.

Particular issues on which comments are invited

Comments are invited on any of the proposals in the Exposure Draft, and in particular on the following.

1 A number of commentators responding to 'Designed to fit' asked that the FRSSE should be capable of application to small groups. To cater for this, new sections have been added, to deal for example with foreign exchange

issues relating to group accounts, and other standards and UITF Abstracts are imported in paragraph 140.

Should the proposed FRSSE be capable of application to groups? If so, do you agree that the mechanism of applying those accounting standards and UITF Abstracts relevant to consolidated accounts is appropriate (paragraph 140)?

2   Do you support the deletion of the requirements for cash flow information that were contained in 'Designed to fit' or support the simplified version referred to above?

3   Do you support the inclusion of the related party disclosures (paragraphs 135–139)?

4   Do you agree that the provisions on debt factoring arrangements (paragraphs 89–91) should be included in the proposed FRSSE?

5   Are there other topics in FRS 5 (eg consignment stock) that should be covered in the FRSSE?

6   The 'Illustrative Examples and Practical Considerations' section (Appendix III) has been extended to give guidance relating to debt factoring and stocks and long-term contracts.

Do you believe it is necessary to include such an appendix? Are there illustrative examples in other accounting standards that should be added to this appendix?

7   In response to comments on earlier drafts, the length of the [draft] FRSSE has been increased to make it more self-contained and to give more guidance. For example, material has been included on topics that may not be relevant for most smaller entities. Do you think that the right balance has been achieved between brevity and completeness? If not, what would you omit or add?

8   Do you have any comments on the proposals for maintaining and updating the FRSSE as set out in the Preface? Do you agree with the criteria above for determining whether requirements of standards are appropriate for small entities? Are there any further criteria you regard as relevant?

Status of the [draft] FRSSE

General
The [draft] Financial Reporting Standard for Smaller Entities (FRSSE) prescribes the basis, for those entities within its scope that have chosen to adopt the FRSSE, for preparing and presenting their financial statements. The definitions and accounting treatments are consistent with the requirements

of companies legislation and, for the generality of small entities, are the same as those required by existing accounting standards or a simplified version of those requirements. The disclosure requirements of the [draft] FRSSE exclude a number of requirements stipulated in other accounting standards. In deciding to exclude these the Board has had regard to the criteria for justifying different treatment for small entities as set out in the [Preface].

Scope

The [draft] FRSSE may be applied to all financial statements intended to give a true and fair view of the financial position and profit or loss (or income and expenditure) of all entities* that are:

(a)   small companies or groups as defined in companies legislation; or
(b)   entities that would also qualify under (a) if they had been incorporated under companies legislation.

Accordingly, the [draft] FRSSE does not apply to:

(i)   large or medium–sized companies, groups and other entities;
(ii)   public companies;
(iii) banks or insurance companies; or
(iv) authorised persons under the Financial Services Act 1986 (in the UK) or the Investment Intermediaries Act 1995 (in the Republic of Ireland).

[Draft] Financial Reporting Standard for Smaller Entities

Objective

1   The objective of this [draft] Financial Reporting Standard for Smaller Entities (FRSSE) is to ensure that reporting entities falling within its scope provide in their financial statements information about the financial position, performance and financial adaptability of the entity that is useful to users in assessing the stewardship of management and for making economic decisions, recognising that the balance between users' needs in respect of stewardship and economic decision-making in respect of smaller entities is different from that for other reporting entities.

* *Some older accounting standards are drafted in terms of application to companies. References to companies and associated terms, such as board of directors and shareholders, in the [draft] FRSSE should therefore be taken to apply also to unincorporated entities.*

Statement of Standard Accounting Practice

Scope

2   The [draft] FRSSE applies to all financial statements intended to give a true and fair view of the financial position and profit or loss (or income and expenditure) of all entities that are:

(a)   companies incorporated under **companies legislation***** and entitled to the exemptions available in the legislation for small companies when filing accounts with the Registrar of Companies and stating, as required by the legislation, that advantage has been taken of those exemptions; or

(b)   entities that would have come into category (a) above had they been companies incorporated under **companies legislation**. Such entities should have regard to the **accounting principles,** presentation and disclosure requirements in **companies legislation** (or other equivalent legislation) that, taking into account the FRSSE, are necessary to present a true and fair view.

General

True and fair view

3   The financial statements should present a true and fair view of the results for the period and of the state of affairs at the end of the period. To achieve such a view, regard should be had to the substance of any arrangement or transaction, or series of such, into which the entity has entered. Where there is any doubt as to whether applying any provisions of the [draft] FRSSE would be sufficient to give a true and fair view, adequate explanation should be given in the notes to the accounts of the transaction or arrangement concerned and the treatment adopted.

Accounting principles and policies

4   The financial statements should state that they have been prepared in accordance with the [draft] FRSSE.**

5   If the financial statements are prepared on the basis of assumptions that differ in material respects from any of the **accounting principles,** the facts

---

***** *Terms appearing in* **bold** *in the text are explained in the Definitions set out in paragraphs 144-217.*
** *This statement may be included with that required by companies legislation to be given after the balance sheet. For example, in Great Britain the combined statement could read as follows 'In preparing the accounts, the directors have taken advantage of the special exemptions provided by Part I of Schedule 8 to the Companies Act 1985 applicable to small companies on the grounds that, in their opinion, the company is small and is therefore entitled to those exemptions. In addition, the accounts have been prepared in accordance with the Financial Reporting Standard for Smaller Entities.'*

should be explained. In the absence of a clear statement to the contrary, there is a presumption that the **accounting principles** have been observed.

6   The **accounting policies** followed for dealing with items that are judged material or critical in determining profit or loss for the year and in stating the financial position should be disclosed by way of note to the accounts. The explanations should be clear, fair and as brief as possible.

True and fair override disclosures

7   In cases where a true and fair view override is being invoked this should be stated clearly and unambiguously. To this end the following should be given:

(a)   a statement of the treatment that would normally be required in the circumstances and a description of the treatment actually adopted;

(b)   a statement as to why the treatment prescribed would not give a true and fair view; and

(c)   a description of how the position shown in the financial statements is different as a result of the departure, normally with quantification, except (i) where quantification is already evident in the financial statements themselves or (ii) whenever the effect cannot be reasonably quantified, in which case the **directors** should explain the circumstances.

8   Where a departure continues in subsequent financial statements, the disclosures should be made in all subsequent statements and should include corresponding amounts for the previous year.

Profit and loss account

General

9   All gains and losses recognised in the financial statements for the period should be included in the profit and loss account or the statement of **total recognised gains and losses**. Gains and losses may be excluded from the profit and loss account only if they are specifically permitted or required to be taken direct to reserves by this standard or by **companies legislation**.

Exceptional items

10   All **exceptional items**, other than those included in the items listed in the next paragraph, should be credited or charged in arriving at the profit or loss on **ordinary activities** by inclusion under the statutory format headings to which they relate. The amount of each exceptional item, either individually or as an aggregate of items of a similar type, should be disclosed separately by way of note, or on the face of the profit and loss account if that degree of

prominence is necessary in order to give a true and fair view. An adequate description of each exceptional item should be given to enable its nature to be understood.

11 The following items, including provisions in respect of such items, should be shown separately on the face of the profit and loss account after operating profit and before interest:

(a) profits or losses on the sale or termination of an operation;

(b) costs of a fundamental reorganisation or restructuring having a material effect on the nature and focus of the reporting entity's operations; and

(c) profits or losses on the disposal of fixed assets.

Profit or loss on disposal

12 The profit or loss on the disposal of an asset should be accounted for in the profit and loss account of the period in which the disposal occurs as the difference between the net sale proceeds and the net carrying amount, whether carried at historical cost (less any provisions made) or at a valuation. Profit or loss on disposal of a previously acquired business should include the attributable amount of purchased goodwill where it has previously been eliminated against reserves as a matter of accounting policy and has not previously been charged in the profit and loss account.

Extraordinary items

13 Any extraordinary profit or loss should be shown separately on the face of the profit and loss account, after the profit or loss on **ordinary activities** after taxation but before deducting any appropriations such as dividends paid or payable and, in the case of consolidated financial statements, after the figure for minority interests. The amount of each **extraordinary item** should be shown individually, either on the face of the profit and loss account or in a note, and an adequate description of each **extraordinary item** should be given to enable its nature to be understood. The tax on extraordinary profit or loss and, in the case of consolidated financial statements, the extraordinary profit or loss attributable to minority shareholders should be shown separately as a part of the **extraordinary item**, either on the face of the profit and loss account or in a note. Any subsequent adjustments to the tax on the extraordinary profit or loss in future periods should be shown as an **extraordinary item**.

Prior period adjustments

14 **Prior period adjustments** should be accounted for by restating the comparative figures for the preceding period in the primary statements and notes and adjusting the opening balance of reserves for the cumulative effect. The cumulative effect of the adjustments should also be noted at the foot of the statement of **total recognised gains and losses** of the current period. The effect of **prior period adjustments** on the results for the preceding period should be disclosed where practicable.

Disclosure of changes in accounting policy

15 Following a change in accounting policy, the amounts for the current and corresponding periods should be restated on the basis of the new policies. The disclosures necessary when a change of accounting policy is made should include, in addition to those for **prior period adjustments**, an indication of the effect on the current year's results. In those cases where the effect on the current year is immaterial, or similar to the quantified effect on the prior year, a simple statement saying this suffices. Where it is not practicable to give the effect on the current year, that fact, together with the reasons, should be stated.

Statement of total recognised gains and losses

16 A primary statement should be presented, with the same prominence as the profit and loss account, showing the **total** of **recognised gains and losses** and its components. The components should be the gains and losses that are **recognised** in the period insofar as they are attributable to shareholders.* Where the only **recognised** gains and losses are the results included in the profit and loss account no separate statement to this effect need be made.

Foreign currency translation

17 Subject to the provisions of paragraphs 19 and 21 each asset, liability, revenue or cost arising from a transaction denominated in a foreign currency should be translated into the **local currency** at the **exchange rate** in operation on the date on which the transaction occurred; if the rates do not fluctuate significantly, an average rate for a period may be used as an approximation. Where the transaction is to be settled at a contracted rate, that rate should be used. Where a trading transaction is covered by a related or matching **forward contract**, the rate of exchange specified in that contract may be used.

18 Subject to the special provisions of paragraph 21, which relate to the treatment of foreign equity investments financed by foreign currency borrowings, no subsequent **translations** should normally be made once non-monetary assets have been translated and recorded.

19 At each balance sheet date, monetary assets and liabilities denominated in a foreign currency should be translated by using the **closing rate** or, where appropriate, the rates of exchange fixed under the terms of the relevant transactions. Where there are related or matching **forward contracts** in

---

* *An illustration of a statement of total recognised gains and losses is given in Appendix III.*

respect of trading transactions, the rates of exchange specified in those contracts may be used.

20 All exchange gains or losses on settled transactions and unsettled **monetary items** should be reported as part of the profit or loss for the year from **ordinary activities** (unless they result from transactions which themselves would fall to be treated as **extraordinary items,** in which case the exchange gains or losses should be included as part of such items).

21 Where a company has used foreign currency borrowings to finance, or to provide a hedge against, its foreign equity investments and the conditions set out in this paragraph apply, the equity investments may be denominated in the appropriate foreign currencies and the carrying amounts translated at the end of each accounting period at **closing rates** for inclusion in the investing company's financial statements. Where investments are treated in this way, any exchange differences arising should be taken to reserves and the exchange gains or losses on the foreign currency borrowings should then be offset, as a reserve movement, against these exchange differences. The conditions that must apply are as follows:

(a) in any accounting period, exchange gains or losses arising on the borrowings may be offset only to the extent of exchange differences arising on the equity investments;

(b) the foreign currency borrowings, whose exchange gains or losses are used in the offset process, should not exceed, in the aggregate, the total amount of cash that the investments are expected to be able to generate, whether from profits or otherwise; and

(c) the accounting treatment adopted should be applied consistently from period to period.

22 When preparing group accounts for a company and its **foreign enterprises** (which includes the incorporation of the results of associated companies or foreign branches into those of an investing company) the **closing rate/net investment** method of translating the local current financial statements should normally be used.

23 Exchange differences arising from the retranslation of the opening **net investment** in a **foreign enterprise** at the **closing rate** should be recorded as a movement on reserves.

24 The profit and loss account of a **foreign enterprise** accounted for under the **closing rate/net investment** method should be translated at the **closing rate** or at an average rate for the period. Where an average rate is used, the difference between the profit and loss account translated at an average rate and at the **closing rate** should be recorded as a movement on reserves. The average rate used should be calculated by the method considered most appropriate for the circumstances of the **foreign enterprise.**

25   In those circumstances where the trade of the **foreign enterprise** is more dependent on the economic environment of the investing company's currency than that of its own reporting currency, the transactions of the foreign operation should be reported as though all of its transactions had been entered into by the investing company itself in its own currency, as stated in paragraphs 17–20.

26   The method used for translating the financial statements of each **foreign enterprise** should be applied consistently from period to period unless its financial and other operational relationships with the investing company change.

27   Where foreign currency borrowings have been used to finance, or provide a hedge against, group equity investments in **foreign enterprises**, exchange gains or losses on the borrowings, which would otherwise have been taken to the profit and loss account, may be offset as reserve movements against exchange differences arising on the retranslation of the **net investments** provided that:

(a)   the relationships between the investing company and the **foreign enterprises** concerned justify the use of the **closing rate** method for consolidation purposes;

(b)   in any accounting period, the exchange gains and losses arising on foreign currency borrowings are offset only to the extent of the exchange differences arising on the **net investments** in **foreign enterprises**;

(c)   the foreign currency borrowings, whose exchange gains or losses are used in the offset process, should not exceed, in the aggregate, the total amount of cash that the **net investments** are expected to be able to generate, whether from profits or otherwise; and

(d)   the accounting treatment is applied consistently from period to period.

Where the provisions of paragraph 21 have been applied in the investing company's financial statements to a foreign equity investment that is neither a subsidiary nor an associated company, the same offset procedure may be applied in the consolidated financial statements.

Taxation

General

28   For companies subject to taxation in the UK,* the following items should be included in the taxation charge in the profit and loss account and, where material, should be separately disclosed:

The equivalent requirements for companies subject to taxation in the Republic of Ireland are given in Appendix II.

(a) the amount of UK corporation tax specifying:
    (i) the charge for corporation tax on the income of the year;
    (ii) tax attributable to franked investment income;
    (iii) **irrecoverable advance corporation tax;**
    (iv) relief for overseas taxation;
(b) the total overseas taxation, relieved and unrelieved, specifying that part of the unrelieved overseas taxation which arises from the payment or proposed payment of dividends.

29 Any special circumstances that affect the overall tax charge or credit for the period, or may affect those of future periods, should be disclosed by way of note to the profit and loss account and their individual effects quantified. The effects of a fundamental change in the basis of taxation should be included in the tax charge or credit for the period and separately disclosed on the face of the profit and loss account.

Deferred tax*

30 **Deferred tax** should be computed under the **liability method.**

31 Tax deferred or accelerated by the effect of **timing differences** should be accounted for to the extent that it is probable that a liability or asset will crystallise.

32 The assessment of whether **deferred tax** liabilities or assets will or will not crystallise should be based upon reasonable assumptions.

33 The assumptions should take into account all relevant information available up to the date on which the financial statements are approved by the board of **directors,** and also the intentions of management. Ideally this information will include financial plans or projections covering a period of years sufficient to enable an assessment to be made of the likely pattern of future tax liabilities. A prudent view should be taken in the assessment of whether a tax liability will crystallise, particularly where the financial plans or projections are susceptible to a high degree of uncertainty or are not fully developed for the appropriate period.

34 The provision for **deferred tax** liabilities should be reduced by any **deferred tax** debit balances arising from separate categories of **timing differences** and any advance corporation tax that is available for offset against those liabilities.

35 **Deferred tax** net debit balances should not be carried forward as assets, except to the extent that they are expected to be recoverable without replacement by equivalent debit balances.

* *Guidance for the Republic of Ireland is given in Appendix II.*

36 Debit balances arising in respect of advance corporation tax on dividends payable or proposed at the balance sheet date should be carried forward to the extent that it is foreseen that sufficient corporation tax will be assessed on the profits or income of the succeeding accounting period, against which the advance corporation tax is available for offset.

37 Adjustments to **deferred tax** arising from changes in tax rates and tax allowances should normally be disclosed separately as part of the tax charge for the period.

38 The **deferred tax** balance, and its major components, should be disclosed in the balance sheet or notes.

39 Transfers to and from **deferred tax** should be disclosed in a note.

40 Where amounts of **deferred tax** arise that relate to movements on reserves (eg resulting from the expected disposal of revalued assets) the amounts transferred to or from **deferred tax** should be shown separately as part of such movements.

41 The total accumulated amount of any **deferred tax** unprovided for at the balance sheet date should be disclosed in a note, analysed into its major components.

42 The amount of any **deferred tax** unprovided for in respect of the period should be disclosed in a note, analysed into its major components.

43 Where a company is a member of a group, it should, in accounting for **deferred tax**, take account of any group relief that, on reasonable evidence, is expected to be available and any charge that will be made for such relief. Assumptions made as to the availability of group relief and payment therefor should be stated.

44 Notwithstanding the other requirements of paragraphs 30–43, either the full provision basis or the partial provision basis may be used in accounting for the **deferred tax** implications of pensions and other post-retirement benefits accounted for in accordance with paragraphs 108–117.

Advance corporation tax (for companies subject to taxation in the UK)*

45 Outgoing dividends should not include either the related advance corporation tax (ACT) or the attributable tax credit.

---

* *The equivalent requirements for companies subject to taxation in the Republic of Ireland are given in Appendix II.*

46 Incoming dividends from UK resident companies should be included at the amount of cash received or receivable plus the tax credit.

47 Dividends proposed (or declared and not yet payable) should be included in current liabilities, without the addition of the related ACT. The ACT on proposed dividends (whether recoverable or irrecoverable) should be included as a current tax liability.

Goodwill

48 No amount should be attributed to **non-purchased goodwill** in the balance sheets of companies or groups.

49 The amount to be attributed to **purchased goodwill** should be the difference between the **fair value** of the consideration given and the aggregate of the **fair values** of the **separable net assets** acquired.

50 The amount attributed to **purchased goodwill** should not include any value for separable intangibles. The amount of these, if material, should be included under the appropriate heading within intangible fixed assets in the balance sheet.

51 **Purchased goodwill** should not be carried in the balance sheet of a company or group as a permanent item.

52 **Purchased goodwill** (other than negative goodwill) should normally be eliminated from the accounts immediately on acquisition against reserves ('immediate write-off').*

53 Any excess of the aggregate of the **fair values** of the **separable net assets** acquired over the **fair value** of the consideration given (negative goodwill) should be credited direct to reserves.

54 **Purchased goodwill** (other than negative goodwill) may be eliminated from the accounts by amortisation through the profit and loss account in arriving at profit or loss on **ordinary activities** on a systematic basis over its **useful economic life** ('amortisation'). When this treatment is selected, the following points apply:

(a) **purchased goodwill** should not be revalued. If there is a permanent diminution in value of **purchased goodwill,** it should be written down immediately through the profit and loss account to its estimated recoverable amount.

(b) the **useful economic life** should be estimated at the time of acquisition. It should not include any allowance for the effects of subsequent

---

* *The treatment of such amounts on disposal of a business is set out in paragraph 12.*

expenditure or other circumstances subsequently affecting the company since these would have the effect of creating **non-purchased goodwill**.

(c) the estimated **useful economic life** over which **purchased goodwill** is being amortised may be shortened but may not be increased.

55 Nothing in this standard precludes a company from using both the immediate write-off treatment and the amortisation treatment in respect of the **goodwill** that relates to different acquisitions, so long as the accounting policies provide for the elimination of **goodwill** on a basis consistent with the standard.

Investment properties

56 **Investment properties** should not be subject to periodic charges for **depreciation** except for properties held on lease, which should be depreciated at least over the period when the unexpired term is 20 years or less.

57 **Investment properties** should be included in the balance sheet at their open market value.

58 The names of the persons making the valuation, or particulars of their qualifications, should be disclosed together with the bases of valuation used by them. If a person making a valuation is an employee or officer of the company or group that owns the property this fact should be disclosed.

59 Changes in the market value of **investment properties** should not be taken to the profit and loss account but should be taken to the statement of **total recognised gains and losses** (being a movement on an investment revaluation reserve), unless a deficit (or its reversal) on an individual **investment property** is expected to be permanent, in which case it should be charged (or credited) in the profit and loss account of the period.

60 Paragraphs 56–59 do not apply to **investment properties** owned by charities.

Depreciation

61 Paragraphs 62–73 apply to all fixed assets other than:

(a) **investment properties**;
(b) **goodwill**;
(c) **development** costs; and
(d) investments.

62 Provision for **depreciation** of fixed assets having a finite **useful economic life** should be made by allocating the cost (or revalued amount) less estimated **residual value** of the assets as fairly as possible to the periods expected to benefit from their use. The **depreciation** methods used should be the ones that are the most appropriate having regard to the types of asset and their use in the business.

63 The accounting treatment in the profit and loss account should be consistent with that used in the balance sheet. Hence, the **depreciation** charge in the profit and loss account for the period should be based on the carrying amount of the asset in the balance sheet, whether historical cost or revalued amount. The whole of the **depreciation** charge should be reflected in the profit and loss account. No part of the **depreciation** charge should be set directly against reserves.

64 It is essential that asset lives are estimated on a realistic basis. Identical asset lives should be used for the calculation of **depreciation** both on a historical cost basis and on any bases that reflect the effects of changing prices.

65 The **useful economic lives** of assets should be reviewed regularly and, when necessary, revised. The allocation of **depreciation** to accounting periods involves the exercise of judgement by management in the light of technical, commercial and accounting considerations and, accordingly, requires regular review. When, as a result of experience or of changed circumstances, it is considered that the original estimate of the economic useful life of an asset requires revision, the effect of the change in estimate on the results and financial position needs to be considered. Usually, when asset lives are reviewed regularly, there will be no material distortion of future results or financial position if the net book amount is written off over the revised remaining **useful economic life**. Where, however, future results would be materially distorted, the adjustment to accumulated **depreciation** should be recognised in the financial statements as an **exceptional item** included under the same statutory format heading as the ongoing **depreciation** charge. The nature and amount of the adjustment should be disclosed.

66 If at any time there is a permanent diminution in the value of an asset and the net book amount is considered not to be recoverable in full (perhaps as a result of obsolescence or a fall in demand for a product), the net book amount should be written down immediately to the estimated **recoverable amount,** which should then be written off over the remaining **useful economic life** of the asset. If at any time the reasons for making such a provision cease to apply, the provision should be written back to the extent that it is no longer necessary.

67 In the case of an asset that has not been revalued, provision for permanent diminution in value of an asset (and any reversals) should be charged (or credited) in the profit and loss account for the period.

68 A change from one method of providing **depreciation** to another is permissible only on the grounds that the new method will give a fairer presentation of the results and of the financial position. Such a change does not, however, constitute a change of accounting policy; the net book amount should be written off over the remaining **useful economic life**, commencing with the period in which the change is made.

69 Freehold land does not normally require a provision for **depreciation**, unless it is subject to depletion by, for example, the extraction of minerals. However, the value of freehold land may be adversely affected by considerations such as changes in the desirability of its location and in these circumstances it should be written down.

70 Buildings are no different from other fixed assets in that they have a limited **useful economic life**, albeit usually significantly longer than that of other types of assets. They should, therefore, be depreciated having regard to the same criteria.

71 The following should be disclosed in the financial statements for each major class of depreciable asset:
(a) the **depreciation** methods used;
(b) the **useful economic lives** or the **depreciation** rates used;
(c) total **depreciation** charged for the period; and
(d) the gross amount of depreciable assets and the related accumulated **depreciation**.

72 Where there has been a change in the **depreciation** method used, the effect, if material, should be disclosed in the period of change. The reason for the change should also be disclosed.

73 Where assets have been revalued, the effect of the revaluation on the **depreciation** charge should, if material, be disclosed in the year of revaluation.

Government grants*
74 Subject to paragraph 75, **government grants** should be recognised in the profit and loss account so as to match them with the expenditure towards which they are intended to contribute. To the extent that the grant is made as a contribution towards expenditure on a fixed asset, in principle it may be deducted from the purchase price or production cost of that asset. However, the option to deduct **government grants** from the purchase price or production costs of fixed assets is not available to companies governed by the accounting and reporting requirements of UK companies legislation. In such cases, the amount so deferred should be treated as deferred income.

* *Notes on the legal requirements for the Republic of Ireland are included in Appendix I.*

75 A **government grant** should not be recognised in the profit and loss account until the conditions for its receipt have been complied with and there is reasonable assurance that the grant will be received.

76 Potential liabilities to repay grants either in whole or in part in specified circumstances should be provided for only to the extent that repayment is probable. The repayment of a **government grant** should be accounted for by setting off the repayment against any unamortised deferred income relating to the grant. Any excess should be charged immediately to the profit and loss account.

77 The following information should be disclosed in the financial statements:
(a) the effects of **government grants** on the results for the period and/or the financial position of the entity; and
(b) where the results of the period are affected materially by the receipt of forms of **government** assistance other than grants, the nature of that assistance and, to the extent that the effects on the financial statements can be measured, an estimate of those effects.

Research and development
78 The cost of fixed assets acquired or constructed in order to provide facilities for **research and development** activities over a number of accounting periods should be capitalised and written off over their useful lives through the profit and loss account.

79 Expenditure on **pure** and **applied research** should be written off in the year of expenditure through the profit and loss account.

80 **Development** expenditure should be written off in the year of expenditure except in the following circumstances when it may be deferred to future periods:
(a) there is a clearly defined project; and
(b) the related expenditure is separately identifiable; and
(c) the outcome of such a project has been assessed with reasonable certainty as to:
  (i) its technical feasibility; and
  (ii) its ultimate commercial viability considered in the light of factors such as likely market conditions (including competing products), public opinion, consumer and environmental legislation; and
(d) the aggregate of the deferred **development** costs, any further **development** costs, and related production, selling and administration costs is reasonably expected to be exceeded by related future sales or other revenues; and

(e)   adequate resources exist, or are reasonably expected to be available, to enable the project to be completed and to provide any consequential increases in working capital.

81   In the foregoing circumstances **development** expenditure may be deferred to the extent that its recovery can be reasonably regarded as assured.

82   If an accounting policy of deferral of **development** expenditure is adopted, it should be applied to all development projects that meet the criteria in paragraph 80.

83   If **development** costs are deferred to future periods, they should be amortised. The amortisation should commence with the commercial production or application of the product, service, process or system and should be allocated on a systematic basis to each accounting period, by reference to either the sale or use of the product, service, process or system or the period over which these are expected to be sold or used.

84   Deferred **development** expenditure for each product should be reviewed at the end of each accounting period and where the circumstances that justified the deferral of expenditure no longer apply, or are considered doubtful, the expenditure, to the extent to which it is considered to be irrecoverable, should be written off immediately project by project.

Stocks and long-term contracts*
85   The amount at which stocks are stated in the financial statements should be the total of the lower of cost and **net realisable value** of the separate items of stock or of groups of similar items.

86   **Long-term contracts** should be assessed on a contract-by-contract basis and reflected in the profit and loss account by recording turnover and related costs as contract activity progresses. Turnover is ascertained in a manner appropriate to the stage of completion of the contract, the business and the industry in which it operates.

87   Where it is considered that the outcome of a **long-term contract** can be assessed with reasonable certainty before its conclusion, the prudently calculated **attributable profit** should be recognised in the profit and loss account as the difference between the reported turnover and related costs for that contract.

88   **Long-term contracts** should be disclosed in the balance sheet as follows:

* *Guidance on the practical considerations of arriving at amounts at which stocks and long-term contracts are stated in financial statements is given in Appendix III.*

(a) The amount by which recorded turnover is in excess of payments on account should be classified as 'amounts recoverable on contracts' and separately disclosed within debtors.

(b) The balance of payments on account (in excess of the amounts (i) matched with turnover and (ii) offset against **long-term contract** balances) should be classified as payments on account and separately disclosed within creditors.

(c) The amount of **long-term contracts**, at costs incurred, net of amounts transferred to cost of sales, after deducting **foreseeable losses** and payments on account not matched with turnover, should be classified as '**long-term contract** balances' and separately disclosed within the balance sheet heading 'stocks'. The balance sheet note should disclose separately the balances of:
(i)   net cost less **foreseeable losses**; and
(ii) applicable payments on account.

(d) The amount by which the provision or accrual for **foreseeable losses** exceeds the costs incurred (after transfers to cost of sales) should be included within either provisions for liabilities and charges or creditors as appropriate.

Debt factoring*

89 Where the entity has transferred to the factor all significant benefits (ie the future cash flows from payment by the debtors) and all significant risks (i.e., slow payment risk and the risk of bad debts) relating to the debts, and has no obligation to repay the factor, the debts should be removed from the entity's balance sheet and no liability should be shown in respect of the proceeds received from the factor. A profit or loss should be **recognised**, calculated as the difference between the carrying amount of the debts and the proceeds received.

90 Where the entity has retained significant benefits and risks relating to factored debts, but all the following conditions are met:

• there is absolutely no doubt that the entity's exposure to loss is limited to a fixed monetary amount (e.g., because there is no recourse or such recourse has a fixed monetary ceiling);

• amounts received from the factor are secured only on the debts factored;

• the debts factored are capable of separate identification;

• the debt factor has no recourse to other debts or assets;

• the entity has no right to reacquire the debts in the future;

• the factor has no right to return the debts even in the event of the cessation of the factoring agreement,

* *A table illustrating the considerations affecting the treatment of debt factoring is given in Appendix III.*

then the factored debts should be shown gross (after providing for bad debts, credit protection charges and any accrued interest) separately on the face of the balance sheet. Any amounts received from the factor in respect of those debts, to the extent that they are not returnable, should be shown as deductions therefrom on the face of the balance sheet. The financial statements should include a note stating that the company is not required to support bad debts in respect of factored debts and that the factors have stated in writing that they will not seek recourse other than out of factored debts. The interest element of the factor's charges should be recognised as it accrues and included in the profit and loss account with other interest charges.

91   In all other cases a separate presentation should be adopted. A gross asset (equivalent in amount to the gross amount of the debts) should be shown on the balance sheet of the entity within assets and a corresponding liability in respect of the proceeds received from the factor should be shown within liabilities. The interest element of the factor's charges and other factoring costs should be recognised as they accrue and included in the profit and loss account with other interest charges.

Leases

Hire purchase and leasing

92   Those **hire purchase contracts** which are of a financing nature should be accounted for on a basis similar to that set out below for **finance leases**. Conversely, other **hire purchase contracts** should be accounted for on a basis similar to that set out below for **operating leases**.

Accounting by lessees

93   A **finance lease** should be recorded in the balance sheet of a lessee as an asset and as an obligation to pay future rentals. At the **inception** of the lease the sum to be recorded both as an asset and as a liability should normally be the **fair value** of the asset.

94   In those cases where the **fair value** of the asset does not give a realistic estimate of the cost to the lessee of the asset and of the obligation entered into, a better estimate should be used. For example, the combined benefit to a lessor of any grants received, together with capital allowances that affect tax liabilities, may enable the **minimum lease payments** under a **finance lease** to be adjusted to a total that is less than the **fair value** of the asset. A negative finance charge should not be shown.

95   Rentals payable under **operating leases** and **finance charges** payable under **finance leases** should be charged on a straight-line basis over the **lease**

term even if the payments are not made on such a basis, unless another systematic and rational basis is more appropriate.

96 Incentives to sign a lease, in whatever form they may take, should be spread by the lessee on a straight-line basis over the lease term or, if shorter than the full lease term, over the period to the review date on which the rent is first expected to be adjusted to the prevailing market rate.

97 An asset leased under a **finance lease** should be depreciated over the shorter of the **lease term** or its useful life. However, in the case of a **hire purchase contract** that has the characteristics of a **finance lease** the asset should be depreciated over its useful life.

Accounting by lessors

98 The amount due from the lessee under a **finance lease** should be recorded in the balance sheet of a lessor as a debtor at the amount of the **net investment** in the lease after making provisions for items such as bad and doubtful rentals receivable.

99 The total **gross earnings** under **finance leases** and rental income from **operating leases** should be recognised on a systematic and rational basis. This will normally be a constant periodic rate of return on the lessor's **net investment**.

100 An asset held for use in **operating leases** by a lessor should be recorded as a fixed asset and depreciated over its useful life.

Manufacturer/dealer lessor

101 A manufacturer or dealer lessor should not recognise a selling profit under an **operating lease**. The selling profit under a **finance lease** should be restricted to the excess of the **fair value** of the asset over the manufacturer's or dealer's cost less any grants receivable by the manufacturer or dealer towards the purchase, construction or use of the asset.

Sale and leaseback transactions – accounting by the seller/lessee

102 In a sale and leaseback transaction that results in a **finance lease**, any apparent profit or loss (i.e., the difference between the sale price and the previous carrying value) should be deferred and amortised in the financial statements of the seller/lessee over the shorter of the **lease term** or the useful life of the asset.

103 If the leaseback is an **operating lease**:
(a) any profit or loss should be recognised immediately provided it is clear that the transaction is established at **fair value**;
(b) if the sale price is below **fair value** any profit or loss should be recognised

immediately, except that if the apparent loss is compensated for by future rentals at below market price it should to that extent be deferred and amortised over the remainder of the **lease term** (or, if shorter, the period during which the reduced rentals are chargeable);

(c) if the sale price is above **fair value,** the excess over **fair value** should be deferred and amortised over the shorter of the remainder of the **lease term** and the period to the next rent review (if any).

Sale and leaseback transactions – accounting by the buyer/lessor

104 A buyer/lessor should account for a sale and leaseback in the same way as other leases are accounted for, i.e., using the methods set out in paragraphs 98–100.

Disclosure by lessees

105 Disclosure should be made of:

(a) either:
   (i) the gross amounts of assets that are held under **finance leases** together with the related accumulated **depreciation** by each major class of asset; or
   (ii) alternatively to being shown separately from that in respect of owned fixed assets, the information in (i) above may be integrated with it, such that the totals of gross amount, accumulated **depreciation**, net amount and **depreciation** allocated for the period for each major class of asset for assets held under **finance leases** are included with similar amounts for owned fixed assets. Where this alternative treatment is adopted, the net amount of assets held under **finance leases** and the amount of **depreciation** allocated for the period in respect of assets under **finance leases** included in the overall total should be disclosed separately;

(b) the amounts of obligations related to **finance leases** (net of finance charges allocated to future periods). These should be disclosed separately from other obligations and liabilities, either on the face of the balance sheet or in the notes to the accounts;

(c) the amount of any commitments existing at the balance sheet date in respect of **finance leases** that have been entered into but whose **inception** occurs after the year-end.

106 In respect of **operating leases,** the lessee should disclose the payments that it is committed to make.

Disclosure by lessors

107 Disclosure should be made of:

(a) the gross amounts of assets held for use in **operating leases** and the related accumulated **depreciation** charges;

(b) the cost of assets acquired, whether by purchase or **finance lease**, for the purpose of letting under **finance leases;**

(c) the **net investment** in (i) **finance leases** and (ii) **hire purchase contracts** at each balance sheet date.

Pensions

108 The accounting objective is that the employer should recognise the expected cost of providing pensions and other post-retirement benefits on a systematic and rational basis over the period during which it derives benefit from the employees' services.

109 For a **defined contribution scheme,** the charge against profits should be the amount of contributions payable to the pension scheme in respect of the accounting period.

110 The following disclosures* should be made in respect of a **defined contribution scheme:**

(a) the nature of the scheme (i.e., defined contribution);
(b) the pension cost charge for the period; and
(c) any outstanding or prepaid contributions at the balance sheet date.

111 For **defined benefit schemes** the pension cost should be calculated using actuarial valuation methods. The actuarial assumptions and method, taken as a whole, should be compatible and should lead to the actuary's best estimate of the cost of providing the pension benefits promised. The method of providing for expected pension costs over the service life of employees in the scheme should be such that the regular pension cost is a substantially level percentage of the current and expected future pensionable payroll in the light of the current actuarial assumptions.

112 Variations from **regular cost** should be allocated over the expected remaining service lives of current employees in the scheme. A period representing the **average remaining service lives** may be used if desired.

113 Where *ex gratia* pensions are granted the capital cost, to the extent not covered by a surplus, should be recognised in the profit and loss account in the accounting period in which they are granted.

114 Where allowance for discretionary or *ex gratia* increases in pensions is not made in the actuarial assumptions, the capital cost of such increases should, to the extent not covered by a surplus, be recognised in the profit and loss account in the accounting period in which they are initially granted.

* *An illustration of disclosures for a defined contribution scheme is given in Appendix III.*

115   If the cumulative pension cost recognised in the profit and loss account has not been completely discharged by payment of contributions or directly paid pensions, the excess should be shown as a net pension provision. Similarly, any excess of contributions paid or directly paid pensions over the cumulative pension cost should be shown as a prepayment.

116   A subsidiary company which is a member of a group scheme should disclose this fact in its financial statements and disclose the nature of the group scheme indicating, where appropriate, that the contributions are based on pension costs across the group as a whole. Such a company is exempt from the disclosure requirements of paragraph 117(f) and (g) and should instead state the name of the holding company in whose financial statements particulars of the actuarial valuation of the group scheme are contained. This exemption applies only if the holding company is registered in the UK or the Republic of Ireland.

117   The following disclosures* should be made in respect of a **defined benefit scheme:**
(a)   the nature of the scheme (i.e., defined benefit);
(b)   whether it is **funded** or unfunded;
(c)   whether the pension cost and provision (or asset) are assessed in accordance with the advice of a professionally qualified actuary and, if so, the date of the most recent formal actuarial valuation or later formal review used for this purpose;
(d)   the pension cost charge for the period;
(e)   any provisions or prepayments in the balance sheet resulting from a difference between the amounts recognised as cost and the amounts funded or paid directly;
(f)   the amount of any deficiency on a **current funding level** basis, indicating the action, if any, being taken to deal with it in the current and future accounting periods;
(g)   an outline of the results of the most recent formal actuarial valuation or later formal review of the scheme on an ongoing basis;
(h)   any commitment to make additional payments over a limited number of years; and
(i)   details of the expected effects on future costs of any material changes in the group's and/or company's pension arrangements.

Capital instruments
118   **Capital instruments** other than shares should be classified as liabilities if they contain an obligation to transfer economic benefits (including a contingent obligation to transfer economic benefits). **Capital instruments** that do not contain an obligation to transfer economic benefits should be reported within shareholders' funds.

* *An illustration of disclosures for a defined benefit scheme is given in Appendix III.*

119 The **finance costs** of **debt** should be allocated to periods over the **term** of the **debt** at a constant rate on the carrying amount. All **finance costs** should be charged in the profit and loss account.

120 Where an **arrangement fee** is such as to represent a significant additional cost of finance when compared with the interest payable on the instrument, the treatment set out in paragraph 119 should be followed. Where this is not the case it should be charged in the profit and loss account immediately it is incurred.

121 Where the entitlement to dividends in respect of shares is calculated by reference to time, the dividends should be accounted for on an accruals basis except in those circumstances (for example where profits are insufficient to justify a dividend and dividend rights are non-cumulative) where ultimate payment is remote. All dividends should be reported as appropriations of profit in the profit and loss account.

Contingencies

122 In addition to amounts accrued under the accounting principle of prudence, a material contingent loss should be accrued in financial statements where it is probable that a future event will confirm a loss that can be estimated with reasonable accuracy at the date on which the financial statements are approved by the board of **directors**.

123 A material contingent loss not accrued under paragraph 122 should be disclosed except where the possibility of loss is remote.

124 Contingent gains should not be accrued in financial statements. A material contingent gain should be disclosed in financial statements only if it is probable that the gain will be realised.

125 In respect of each **contingency** that is required to be disclosed, the following information should be stated by way of note to the financial statements:
(a) the nature of the **contingency**;
(b) the uncertainties that are expected to affect the ultimate outcome; and
(c) a prudent estimate of the financial effect, made at the date on which the financial statements are approved by the board of **directors**, or a statement that it is not practicable to make such an estimate.

126 Where there is disclosure of an estimate of the financial effect of a **contingency**, the amount disclosed should be the potential financial effect. In the case of a contingent loss, this should be reduced by:
(a) any amount accrued; and
(b) the amount of any components where the possibility of loss is remote.

Only the net amount need be disclosed.

127 The estimate of the financial effect should be disclosed before taking account of taxation, and the taxation implications of a **contingency** crystallising should be explained where necessary for a proper understanding of the financial position.

128 Where both the nature of, and the uncertainties that affect, a **contingency** in respect of an individual transaction are common to a large number of similar transactions, the financial effect of the **contingency** need not be individually estimated but may be based on a group of similar transactions. In these circumstances the separate contingencies need not be individually disclosed.

Post balance sheet events

129 Financial statements should be prepared on the basis of conditions existing at the balance sheet date.

130 A material **post balance sheet event** requires changes in the amounts to be included in financial statements where:

(a) it is an **adjusting event**; or
(b) it indicates that application of the going concern concept to the whole or a material part of the entity is not appropriate.

131 A material **post balance sheet event** should be disclosed where:

(a) it is a **non-adjusting event** of such materiality that its non-disclosure would affect the ability of the users of financial statements to reach a proper understanding of the financial position; or
(b) it is the reversal or maturity after the year-end of a transaction entered into before the year-end, the substance of which was primarily to alter the appearance of the entity's balance sheet.

132 In respect of each **post balance sheet event** that is required to be disclosed, the following information should be stated by way of notes in the financial statements:

(a) the nature of the event; and
(b) an estimate of the financial effect, or a statement that it is not practicable to make such an estimate.

133 The estimate of the financial effect should be disclosed before taking account of taxation, and the taxation implications should be explained where necessary for a proper understanding of the financial position.

134 The date on which the financial statements are approved by the board of **directors** should be disclosed in the financial statements.

Related party disclosures

135 Financial statements should disclose material transactions undertaken by the reporting entity with a **related party**. Disclosure should be made irrespective of whether a price is charged. The disclosure should include:

(a) the names of the transacting **related parties;**
(b) a description of the relationship between the parties;
(c) a description of the transactions;
(d) the amounts involved;
(e) any other elements of the transactions necessary for an understanding of the financial statements;
(f) the amounts due to or from **related parties** at the balance sheet date and provisions for doubtful debts due from such parties at that date; and
(g) amounts written off in the period in respect of debts due to or from **related parties.**

The materiality of a **related party transaction** should be judged not only in terms of its significance to the reporting entity, but also in relation to the other **related party.**

136 Transactions with **related parties** may be disclosed on an aggregated basis (aggregation of similar transactions by type of **related party**) unless disclosure of an individual transaction, or connected transactions, is necessary for an understanding of the impact of the transactions on the financial statements of the reporting entity or is required by law.

137 Disclosure is not required of emoluments in respect of services as an employee of the reporting entity and of the relationship and transactions between the reporting entity and the parties listed below simply as a result of their role as:

(a) providers of finance in the course of their business in that regard;
(b) utility companies;
(c) **government** departments and their sponsored bodies,

even though they may circumscribe the freedom of action of an entity or participate in its decision-making process; and

(d) a customer, supplier, franchiser, distributor or general agent with whom an entity transacts a significant volume of business.

138 Personal guarantees given by **directors** in respect of borrowings by the reporting entity should be disclosed in the notes to the financial statements.

139 When the reporting entity is controlled by another party, there should be disclosure of the **related party** relationship and the name of that party and, if different, that of the ultimate controlling party. If the controlling party or ultimate controlling party of the reporting entity is not known, that fact should be disclosed. This information should be disclosed irrespective of whether any transactions have taken place between the controlling parties and the reporting entity.

Consolidated financial statements

140 Where the reporting entity is preparing **consolidated financial statements,** it should regard as standard the accounting practices and disclosure requirements set out in FRSs 2, 6, 7 and, as they apply in respect of consolidated financial statements, FRS 5, SSAPs 1 and 22, and UITF Abstract 3.

Date from which effective

141 The accounting practices set out in the [draft] FRSSE should be regarded as standard in respect of financial statements relating to accounting periods ending on or after [date]. Earlier adoption is encouraged but not required.

Amendment of SSAPs, FRSs and UITF Abstracts

142 The following (adjusted as appropriate) shall be inserted as a new paragraph:

(a) immediately following the 'scope' paragraph(s) or, if there is none, immediately preceding the 'date from which effective' paragraph of:
   (i)   the Standard Accounting Practice section in SSAPs 2–5, 8, 9, 12, 13, 15, 17–21, 24 and 25;
   (ii) the Statement of Standard Accounting Practice in FRSs 1(Revised 1996), 3, 4 and 8; and
(b) immediately before the UITF Consensus in UITF Abstracts 4–7 and 9–15:

   '*Application to smaller entities*

   Reporting entities applying the Financial Reporting Standard for Smaller Entities are exempt from this [accounting standard]/[Abstract].'

143 The following (adjusted as appropriate, consistently with paragraph 140) shall be inserted as a new paragraph:

(a) immediately following the 'scope' paragraph(s) or, if there is none, immediately preceding the 'date from which effective' paragraph of:
   (i)   the Standard Accounting Practice section in SSAPs 1 and 22;
   (ii) the Statement of Standard Accounting Practice in FRSs 2 and 5–7; and
(b) immediately before the UITF Consensus in UITF Abstract 3:

'Application to smaller entities

Reporting entities applying the Financial Reporting Standard for Smaller Entities are exempt from this [accounting standard]/[Abstract] unless preparing consolidated financial statements, when such entities should regard as standard the accounting practices and disclosure requirements set out in this [accounting standard]/[Abstract][as it applies in respect of such statements].'

Definitions

144 The following definitions shall apply in the [draft] FRSSE and in particular in the Statement of Standard Accounting Practice set out in paragraphs 2–143.

145 *Accounting policies:*
Accounting policies are the specific accounting bases selected and consistently followed by an entity as being, in the opinion of the management, appropriate to its circumstances and best suited to present fairly its results and financial position.

146 *Accounting principles:*
Accounting principles are the fundamental accounting concepts that underlie the periodic financial statements of entities. These accounting principles are set out in companies legislation and are reproduced in Appendix I, paragraph 5.

147 *Adjusting events:*
Adjusting events are post balance sheet events that provide additional evidence of conditions existing at the balance sheet date. They include events that because of statutory or conventional requirements are reflected in financial statements.

148 *Applied research:*
Original or critical investigation undertaken in order to gain new scientific or technical knowledge and directed towards a specific practical aim or objective.

149 *Arrangement fees:*
The costs that are incurred directly in connection with the issue of a **capital instrument,** i.e., those costs that would not have been incurred if the specific instrument in question had not been issued.

150 *Attributable profit:*
That part of the total profit currently estimated to arise over the duration of

the contract, after allowing for estimated remedial and maintenance costs and increases in costs so far as not recoverable under the terms of the contract, that fairly reflects the profit attributable to that part of the work performed at the accounting date. (There can be no attributable profit until the profitable outcome of the contract can be assessed with reasonable certainty.)

151 *Average remaining service life:*
A weighted average of the expected future service of the current members of the pension scheme up to their normal retirement dates or expected dates of earlier withdrawal or death in service.

152 *Capital instruments:*
All instruments that are issued (or arrangements entered into) by reporting entities as a means of raising finance, including shares, debentures, loans and debt instruments, options and warrants that give the holder the right to subscribe for or obtain capital instruments. In the case of **consolidated financial statements** the term includes capital instruments issued by subsidiaries except those that are held by another member of the group that is included in the consolidation.

153 *Close family:*
Close members of the family of an individual are those family members, or members of the same household, who may be expected to influence, or be influenced by, that person in their dealings with the reporting entity.

154 *Closing rate:*
The closing rate is the **exchange rate** for spot transactions ruling at the balance sheet date and is the mean of the buying and selling rates at the close of business on the day for which the rate is to be ascertained.

155 *Companies legislation:*
(a)   in Great Britain, the Companies Act 1985;
(b)   in Northern Ireland, the Companies (Northern Ireland) Order 1986; and
(c)   in the Republic of Ireland, the Companies Acts 1963–1990 and the European Communities (Companies: Group Accounts) Regulations 1992.

156 *Consolidated financial statements:*
The financial statements of a group prepared by consolidation. A group is a parent undertaking and its subsidiary undertakings. Consolidation is the process of adjusting and combining financial information from the

individual financial statements of a parent undertaking and its subsidiary undertakings to prepare consolidated financial statements that present financial information for the group as a single economic entity.

157 *Contingency:*
Contingency is a condition that exists at the balance sheet date, where the outcome will be confirmed only on the occurrence or non-occurrence of one or more uncertain future events. A contingent gain or loss is a gain or loss dependent on a contingency.

158 *Current funding level (of a pension scheme):*
A current funding level valuation considers whether the assets would have been sufficient at the valuation date to cover liabilities arising in respect of pensions in payment, preserved benefits for members whose pensionable service has ceased and accrued benefits for members in pensionable service, based on pensionable service to and pensionable earnings at, the date of valuation including revaluation on the statutory basis or such higher basis as has been promised.

159 *Debt:*
Capital instruments that are classified as liabilities.

160 *Deferred tax:*
Deferred tax is the tax attributable to **timing differences**.

161 *Defined benefit scheme:*
A **pension scheme** in which the rules specify the benefits to be paid and the scheme is financed accordingly.

162 *Defined contribution scheme:*
A **pension scheme** in which the benefits are directly determined by the value of contributions paid in respect of each member.

163 *Depreciation:*
Depreciation is the measure of the wearing out, consumption or other reduction in the **useful economic life** of a fixed asset whether arising from use, effluxion of time or obsolescence through technological or market changes. The assessment of depreciation, and its allocation to accounting periods, involves the consideration of three factors:
(a)   the carrying amount of the asset (whether cost or valuation);
(b)   the length of the asset's expected **useful economic life** to the business of the enterprise, having due regard to the incidence of obsolescence; and
(c)   the estimated **residual value** of the asset at the end of its **useful economic life** in the business of the enterprise.

164 *Development:*
Use of scientific or technical knowledge in order to produce new or substantially improved materials, devices, products or services, to install new processes or systems before the commencement of commercial production or commercial applications, or to improve substantially those already produced or installed.

165 *Directors:*
The directors of a company or other body, the partners, proprietors, committee of management or trustees of other forms of entity, or equivalent persons responsible for directing the entity's affairs and preparing its financial statements.

166 *Ex gratia pension:*
A pension that the employer has no legal, contractual or implied commitment to provide.

167 *Exceptional items:*
Material items that derive from events or transactions that fall within the **ordinary activities** of the reporting entity and individually or, if of a similar type, in aggregate, need to be disclosed by virtue of their size or incidence if the financial statements are to give a true and fair view.

168 *Exchange rate:*
An exchange rate is a rate at which two currencies may be exchanged for each other at a particular point in time; different rates apply for spot and forward transactions.

169 *Extraordinary items:*
Material items possessing a high degree of abnormality that arise from events or transactions that fall outside the **ordinary activities** of the reporting entity and are not expected to recur. They do not include **exceptional items** nor do they include prior period items merely because they relate to a prior period.

170 *Fair value:*
Fair value is the price at which an asset could be exchanged in an arm's length transaction less, where applicable, any grants receivable towards the purchase or use of the asset.

171 *Finance charge (on a lease):*
The finance charge is the amount borne by the lessee over the lease term, representing the difference between the total of the **minimum lease payments** (including any residual amounts guaranteed by it) and the amount at which it records the leased asset at the inception of the lease.

172 *Finance costs (of a capital instrument):*
The difference between the net proceeds of a **capital instrument** and the total amount of the payments (or other transfer of economic benefits) that the issuer may be required to make in respect of the instrument other than **arrangement fees**.

173 *Finance lease:*
A finance lease is a lease that transfers substantially all the risks and rewards of ownership of an asset to the lessee. It should be presumed that such a transfer of risks and rewards occurs if at the **inception** of a lease the present value of the **minimum lease payments,** including any initial payment, amounts to substantially all (normally 90 per cent or more) of the **fair value** of the leased asset. If the **fair value** of the asset is not determinable an estimate thereof should be used. The present value should be calculated by using the interest rate implicit in the lease.

174 *Foreign enterprise:*
A foreign enterprise is a subsidiary, associated company or branch whose operations are based in a country other than that of the investing company or whose assets and liabilities are denominated mainly in a foreign currency.

175 *Foreseeable losses (on a long-term contract):*
Losses that are currently estimated to arise over the duration of the contract (after allowing for estimated remedial and maintenance costs and increases in costs so far as not recoverable under the terms of the contract). This estimate is required irrespective of:

(a)   whether work has yet commenced on such contracts;
(b)   the proportion of work carried out at the accounting date; or
(c)   the amount of profits expected to arise on other contracts.

176 *Forward contract:*
A forward contract is an agreement to exchange different currencies at a specified future date and at a specified rate. The difference between the specified rate and the spot rate ruling on the date the contract was entered into is the discount or premium on the forward contract.

177 *Funded scheme:*
A **pension scheme** where the future liabilities for benefits are provided for by the accumulation of assets held externally to the employing entity's business.

178 *Goodwill:*
Goodwill is the difference between the value of a business as a whole and the aggregate of the **fair values** of its **separable net assets**.

179 *Government:*
Government includes government and inter-governmental agencies and similar bodies whether local, national or international.

180 *Government grants:*
Government grants are assistance by **government** in the form of cash or transfers of assets to an entity in return for past or future compliance with certain conditions relating to the operating activities of the entity.

181 *Gross earnings (from a lease):*
Gross earnings comprise the lessor's gross finance income over the **lease term**, representing the difference between its gross investment in the lease and the cost of the leased asset less any grants receivable towards the purchase or use of the asset.

182 *Hire purchase contract:*
A hire purchase contract is a contract for the hire of an asset that contains a provision giving the hirer an option to acquire legal title to the asset upon the fulfilment of certain conditions stated in the contract.

183 *Inception:*
The inception of a lease is the earlier of the time the asset is brought into use and the date from which rentals first accrue.

184 *Investment property:*
An investment property is an interest in land and/or buildings:
(a) in respect of which construction work and development have been completed; and
(b) which is held for its investment potential, any rental income being negotiated at arm's length,

but excluding:
(c) a property that is owned and occupied by a company for its own purposes; and
(d) a property let to and occupied by another group company.

185 *Irrecoverable ACT:*
Advance corporation tax (ACT) paid or payable on outgoing dividends paid and proposed other than **recoverable ACT**.

186 *Lease term:*
The lease term is the period for which the lessee has contracted to lease the asset and any further terms for which the lessee has the option to continue to lease the asset with or without further payment, which option it is reasonably certain at the **inception** of the lease that the lessee will exercise.

187 *Liability method:*
The liability method is a method of computing **deferred tax** by calculating it at the rate of tax that it is estimated will apply when the **timing differences** reverse. Under the liability method **deferred tax** not provided for is calculated at the expected long-term tax rate.

188 *Local currency:*
An entity's local currency is the currency of the primary economic environment in which it operates and generates net cash flows.

189 *Long-term contract:*
A contract entered into for the design, manufacture or construction of a single substantial asset or the provision of a service (or of a combination of assets or services that together constitute a single project) where the time taken substantially to complete the contract is such that the contract activity falls into different accounting periods. A contract that is required to be accounted for as long-term by the [draft] FRSSE will usually extend for a period exceeding one year. However, a duration exceeding one year is not an essential feature of a long-term contract. Some contracts with a shorter duration than one year should be accounted for as long-term contracts if they are sufficiently material to the activity of the period that not to record turnover and attributable profit would lead to distortion of the period's turnover and results such that the financial statements would not give a true and fair view, provided that the policy is applied consistently within the reporting entity and from year to year.

190 *Minimum lease payments:*
The minimum lease payments are the minimum payments over the remaining part of the **lease term** (excluding charges for services and taxes to be paid by the lessor) and:
(a)   in the case of the lessee any residual amounts guaranteed by it or by a party related to it; or
(b)   in the case of the lessor any residual amounts guaranteed by the lessee or by an independent third party.

191 *Monetary items:*
Monetary items are money held and amounts to be received or paid in money and should be categorised as either short-term or long-term. Short-term monetary items are those that fall due within one year of the balance sheet date.

192 *Net investment (in a foreign enterprise):*
The net investment that a company has in a **foreign enterprise** is its effective equity stake and comprises its proportion of such **foreign enterprise's** net assets; in appropriate circumstances, intragroup loans and other deferred balances may be regarded as part of the effective equity stake.

193 *Net investment (in a lease):*
The net investment in a lease at a point in time comprises:

(a) the gross investment in a lease (i.e., the total of the **minimum lease payments** and that portion of the **residual value** of the leased asset, the realisation of which by the lessor is not assured or is guaranteed solely by a party related to the lessor); less

(b) **gross earnings** allocated to future periods.

194 *Net realisable value:*
The actual or estimated selling price (net of trade but before settlement discounts) less:

(a) all further costs to completion; and

(b) all costs to be incurred in marketing, selling and distributing.

195 *Non-adjusting events:*
Non-adjusting events are **post balance sheet events** that concern conditions that did not exist at the balance sheet date.

196 *Non-purchased goodwill:*
Non-purchased goodwill is any **goodwill** other than **purchased goodwill**.

197 *Operating lease:*
An operating lease is a lease other than a **finance lease**.

198 *Ordinary activities:*
Any activities that are undertaken by a reporting entity as part of its business and such related activities in which the reporting entity engages in furtherance of, incidental to, or arising from, these activities. Ordinary activities include the effects on the reporting entity of any event in the various environments in which it operates, including the political, regulatory, economic and geographical environments, irrespective of the frequency or unusual nature of the events.

199 *Pension schemes:*
A pension scheme is an arrangement (other than accident insurance) to provide pension and/or other benefits for members on leaving service or retiring and, after a member's death, for his/her dependants.

200 *Post balance sheet events:*
Post balance sheet events are those events, both favourable and unfavourable, that occur between the balance sheet date and the date on which the financial statements are approved by the board of **directors**.

201 *Prior period adjustments:*
Material adjustments applicable to prior periods arising from changes in **accounting policies** or from the correction of fundamental errors. They do

not include normal recurring adjustments or corrections of accounting estimates made in prior periods.

202 *Purchased goodwill:*
Purchased goodwill is **goodwill** that is established as a result of the purchase of a business accounted for as an acquisition. **Goodwill** arising on consolidation is one form of purchased goodwill.

203 *Pure (or basic) research:*
Experimental or theoretical work undertaken primarily to acquire new scientific or technological knowledge for its own sake rather than directed towards any specific aim or application.

204 *Recognised:*
Recognition is the process of incorporating an item into the primary financial statements under the appropriate heading. It involves depiction of the item in words and by a monetary amount and inclusion of that amount in the statement totals.

205 *Recoverable ACT:*
The amount of advance corporation tax (ACT) paid or payable on outgoing dividends paid and proposed that can be:
(a) set off against a corporation tax liability on the profits of the period under review or of previous periods; or
(b) properly set off against a credit balance on **deferred tax** account; or
(c) expected to be recoverable taking into account expected profits and dividends – normally those of the next accounting period only.

206 *Recoverable amount:*
Recoverable amount is the greater of the **net realisable value** of an asset and, where appropriate, the amount recoverable from its further use.

207 *Regular (pension) cost:*
The consistent ongoing cost recognised under the actuarial method used.

208 *Related parties:*
(a) Two or more parties are related parties when at any time during the financial period:
   (i) one party has direct or indirect control of the other party; or
   (ii) the parties are subject to common control from the same source; or
   (iii) one party has influence over the financial and operating policies of the other party to an extent that that other party might be inhibited from pursuing at all times its own separate interests; or
   (iv) the parties, in entering a transaction, are subject to influence from

the same source to such an extent that one of the parties to the transaction has subordinated its own separate interests.

(b) For the avoidance of doubt, the following are related parties of the reporting entity:

   (i) its ultimate and intermediate parent undertakings, subsidiary undertakings, and fellow subsidiary undertakings;

   (ii) its associates and joint ventures;

   (iii) the investor or venturer in respect of which the reporting entity is an associate or a joint venture;

   (iv) **directors** of the reporting entity and the **directors** of its ultimate and intermediate parent undertakings. **Directors** include shadow directors, which are defined in **companies legislation** as persons in accordance with whose directions or instructions the **directors** of the company are accustomed to act; and

   (v) pension funds for the benefit of employees of the reporting entity or of any entity that is a related party of the reporting entity;

(c) and the following are presumed to be related parties of the reporting entity unless it can be demonstrated that neither party has influenced the financial and operating policies of the other in such a way as to inhibit the pursuit of separate interests:

   (i) the key management of the reporting entity and the key management of its parent undertaking or undertakings;

   (ii) a person owning or able to exercise control over 20 per cent or more of the voting rights of the reporting entity, whether directly or through nominees;

   (iii) each person acting in concert in such a way as to be able to exercise control or influence over the reporting entity in terms of (a)(iii) above; and

   (iv) an entity managing or managed by the reporting entity under a management contract.

(d) Additionally, because of their relationship with certain parties that are, or are presumed to be, related parties of the reporting entity, the following are also presumed to be related parties of the reporting entity:

   (i) members of the **close family** of any individual falling under parties mentioned in (a)–(c) above; and

   (ii) partnerships, companies, trusts or other entities in which any individual or member of the close family in (a)–(c) above has a controlling interest.

Sub-paragraphs (b), (c) and (d) are not intended to be an exhaustive list of related parties.

209 *Related party transaction:*

The transfer of assets or liabilities or the performance of services by, to or for a **related party** irrespective of whether a price is charged.

210   *Research and development expenditure:*

Research and development expenditure means expenditure falling into one or more of the broad categories of **pure (or basic) research, applied research** and **development** (except to the extent that it relates to locating or exploiting oil, gas or mineral deposits or is reimbursable by third parties either directly or under the terms of a firm contract to develop and manufacture at an agreed price calculated to reimburse both elements of expenditure).

211   *Residual value:*

Residual value is the realisable value of the asset at the end of its **useful economic life,** based on prices prevailing at the date of acquisition or revaluation, where this has taken place. Realisation costs should be deducted in arriving at the residual value.

212   *Separable net assets:*

Separable net assets are assets and liabilities of the acquired entity that are capable of being disposed of or settled separately, without disposing of a business of the entity.

213   *Term (of a capital instrument):*

The period from the date of issue of the **capital instrument** to the date at which it will expire, be redeemed, or be cancelled. If either party has the option to require the instrument to be redeemed or cancelled and, under the terms of the instrument, it is uncertain whether such an option will be exercised, the term should be taken to end on the earliest date at which the instrument would be redeemed or cancelled on exercise of such an option. If either party has the right to extend the period of an instrument, the term should not include the period of the extension if there is a genuine commercial possibility that the period will not be extended.

214   *Timing differences:*

Timing differences are differences between profits or losses as computed for tax purposes and results as stated in financial statements, which arise from the inclusion of items of income and expenditure in tax computations in periods different from those in which they are included in financial statements. Timing differences originate in one period and are capable of reversal in one or more subsequent periods.

215   *Total recognised gains and losses:*

The total of all gains and losses of the reporting entity that are **recognised** in a period and are attributable to the shareholders.

216   *Translation:*

Translation is the process whereby financial data denominated in one currency are expressed in terms of another currency. It includes both the expression of individual transactions in terms of another currency and the expression of a complete set of financial statements prepared in one currency in terms of another currency.

217   *Useful economic life:*

The useful economic life of an asset is the period over which the present owner will derive economic benefits from its use.

Appendix I – Note on legal requirements

Great Britain

Companies Act 1985, sections 246-249

1   The definition of a small company is contained in sections 246 and 247 of the Companies Act 1985. The qualifying conditions are met by a company in a year in which it does not exceed two or more of the following criteria:

Turnover	£2,800,000
Balance sheet total	£1,400,000
Average number of employees	50

For any company, other than a newly incorporated company, the conditions must have been satisfied in two of the last three years.

2   Certain companies are excluded by section 246 from the 'small company' criteria for reasons of public interest. These are any entity that is, or is in a group that includes:
- a public company;
- a banking or insurance company;
- a body corporate that (not being a company) has the power to offer its shares or debentures to the public and may lawfully exercise that power;
- an authorised institution under the Banking Act 1987;
- an insurance company to which Part II of the Insurance Companies Act 1982 applies; or
- an authorised person under the Financial Services Act 1986.

3   A parent company shall not be treated as qualifying as a small company in relation to a financial year unless the group headed by it qualifies as a small group.

4   The definition of a small group is contained in section 249. The qualifying conditions are met by a group in a year in which it does not exceed two or more of the following criteria:

Aggregate turnover	£2,800,000 net (or £3,360,000 gross)
Aggregate balance sheet total	£1,400,000 net (or £1,680,000 gross)
Aggregate number of employees	50

'Net' means after the set-offs and other adjustments required by Schedule 4A in the case of group accounts, and 'gross' means without those set-offs and adjustments. A company may satisfy the relevant requirements on the basis of either the net or the gross figure.

Companies Act 1985, Schedule 4, paragraphs 10–14

5   Schedule 4 sets out the accounting principles in the following terms:

'10.   The company shall be presumed to be carrying on business as a going concern.

11.   Accounting policies shall be applied consistently within the same accounts and from one financial year to the next.

12.   The amount of any item shall be determined on a prudent basis, and in particular
   (a) only profits realised at the balance sheet date shall be included in the profit and loss account; and
   (b) all liabilities and losses which have arisen or are likely to arise in respect of the financial year to which the accounts relate or a previous financial year shall be taken into account, including those which only become apparent between the balance sheet date and the date on which it is signed on behalf of the board of directors in pursuance of section 233 of this Act.

13.   All income and charges relating to the financial year to which the accounts relate shall be taken into account, without regard to the date of receipt or payment.

14.   In determining the aggregate amount of any item the amount of each individual asset or liability that falls to be taken into account shall be determined separately.'

Northern Ireland

6   The legal requirements in Northern Ireland are very similar to those in Great Britain. The following table shows the references to the Companies (Northern Ireland) Order 1986 that correspond to the legal references in paragraphs 1–5 above.

GREAT BRITAIN	NORTHERN IRELAND
Sections 246–249	Articles 254–257
Schedule 4, paragraphs 10–14	Schedule 4, paragraphs 10–14

Republic of Ireland

7   The following table shows the references in companies legislation in the Republic of Ireland that correspond to the legal references in paragraphs 1–5 above.

GREAT BRITAIN	REPUBLIC OF IRELAND
Sections 246 and 247	Companies (Amendment) Act 1986, sections 8 and 9
Sections 248 and 249	European Communities (Companies Group Accounts) Regulations 1992, Regulations 6 and 7
Schedule 4, paragraphs 10–14	Companies (Amendment) Act 1986, section 5

Government grants – legal requirements in the Republic of Ireland

8   References below are to the Companies (Amendment) Act 1986 and the Schedule to that Act unless otherwise stated.

9   Note 8 to the balance sheet formats in the Schedule provides that government grants included in the item 'Accruals and deferred income' must be shown separately in a note to the accounts if not shown separately in the balance sheet. However, Note 8 does not impose an obligation to include government grants under 'Accruals and deferred income' and such grants may, therefore, be placed under a separate heading. This separate heading is often placed between liabilities and share/capital reserves. If a new heading is adopted (using section 4(12)), the requirement under Note 8 to have a separate mention of the amount is not applicable.

10   Paragraph 36(2) of the Schedule provides that 'The following information shall be given with respect to any other contingent liability not provided for –
(a)   the amount or estimated amount of that liability,
(b)   its legal nature, and
(c)   whether any valuable security has been provided by the company in connection with that liability and, if so, what.'

11   Section 40 of the Companies (Amendment) Act 1983 requires the convening of an extraordinary general meeting not later than 28 days from the earliest day on which it is known to a director of the company that its net assets have fallen to half or less of the company's called-up share capital (that a 'financial situation' exists). The Act also extends the reporting duties of auditors by requiring auditors to state whether in their opinion there existed at the balance sheet date a 'financial situation' in the context of section 40 that would require the convening of an extraordinary general meeting. For the purpose of calculating the net assets of the company, the term 'liability' should be taken to include not only creditors, but also provisions for liabilities and charges, accruals and deferred income. Government grants treated as deferred income should, therefore, be regarded as a liability for the purposes of calculating net assets under section 40.

Appendix II – Requirements for companies subject to taxation in the Republic of Ireland

1   Paragraphs 2–10 below contain the statement of standard accounting practice for application to companies subject to taxation in the Republic of Ireland. Paragraphs 11–13 below give guidance on the treatment of deferred tax for companies subject to taxation in the Republic of Ireland.

Taxation under the imputation system in the Republic of Ireland

Profit and loss account

2   The following items should be included in the taxation charge or credit in the profit and loss account and, where material, should be separately disclosed:

(a)   the amount of corporation tax specifying:
  (i)   the charge or credit for corporation tax on the income of the year;
  (ii)   transfers between the deferred taxation account and the profit and loss account; and
  (iii) the relief for overseas taxation;
(b)   the total overseas taxation relieved and unrelieved;
(c)   tax attributable to franked investment income;
(d)   irrecoverable advance corporation tax (ACT) (specifying the basis of the charge);
(e)   ACT previously written off as irrecoverable now recovered or regarded as recoverable (specifying the basis of the credit).

3   Material adjustments in respect of previous periods should be disclosed. Where a company benefits from export sales relief, manufacturing relief or Shannon exemption this should be disclosed together with the dates of expiry of the relief. Where the tax charge is materially affected by timing differences not provided for, this should be disclosed.

4   The rate of corporation tax used should be disclosed. If the rate of corporation tax is not known for the whole or part of the period covered by the accounts the latest known rate should be used.

5   Outgoing dividends should not include either the related ACT or the attributable tax credit. However, the tax credit attaching to dividends paid or proposed should be disclosed in the notes to the accounts.

6   Incoming dividends from Republic of Ireland resident companies should be included in profit before taxation at the amount of cash received or receivable plus the tax credit.

Balance sheet

7   Dividends proposed (or declared and not yet payable) should be included in current liabilities, without the addition of the related ACT.

8   Where ACT on dividends paid in the accounting period under review is exceeded by provisions for corporation tax on the income of the accounting period under review and/or the preceding accounting period(s) (against which that ACT can be set), no separate liability for this ACT should be recorded, as ACT would not result in any increase in the overall tax liability. To the extent that this ACT exceeds such provisions it should be provided for as a separate current liability.

9   Where ACT on both dividends paid and dividends proposed in the account period under review is exceeded by the provision for corporation tax on the income of that period no separate liability needs to be recorded for ACT on the proposed dividends. This is because the current period's corporation tax is available to discharge the subsequent period's ACT, ensuring that the ACT on the proposed dividends will not result in any increase in the overall tax liability. To the extent that ACT on dividends proposed exceeds the corporation tax provision, as reduced by ACT on dividends paid, it should be provided for as a separate non-current liability.

10   If a separate liability for ACT has to be provided for under paragraphs 8 and/or 9 above, the corresponding asset that arises if this ACT is regarded as recoverable should be deducted from any provision for deferred taxation on income in the balance sheet. To the extent that such provision is inadequate to cover it, the recoverable ACT should be shown as a current or non-current asset as appropriate. At each subsequent balance sheet date, the recoverability of this asset should be reassessed. If the ACT for which a separate liability has to be provided for under paragraphs 7 and/or 8 above is not regarded as recoverable, the provision for the liability should be created by a charge to the profit and loss account for irrecoverable ACT.

Deferred tax – guidance notes for companies subject to taxation in the Republic of Ireland

11   Differences exist between UK law and Republic of Ireland law on ACT. Deferred tax is affected by ACT in the following respects: (a) the offset of ACT against a deferred tax liability; and (b) the carry-forward of a net debit balance on the deferred tax account represented by ACT. The general provisions of the statement in regard to these two matters will be applicable to Republic of Ireland companies with one exception. Because ACT is payable six months from the end of the accounting period in which the dividend is paid, it will be necessary to consider the possibility of offsetting an ACT liability against the asset representing ACT recoverable. If such an

offset were probable the ACT recoverable would not be deducted from a deferred tax credit balance under paragraph 34 of the [draft] FRSSE or recognised as a deferred tax debit balance under paragraph 36 of the [draft] FRSSE.

12   Certain Republic of Ireland companies and branches of foreign companies are totally relieved of corporation tax or are subject to tax at reduced rates on profits arising from the export of manufactured goods and services (export sales relief and Shannon relief). Where such companies have timing differences originating during the period of total relief or of reduced relief and it is probable that these differences will reverse after expiry of the relief period – or when the reduced rates no longer apply – and that a tax liability will crystallise, then provision should be made for taxation deferred. The amount of tax to be deferred in respect of such timing differences should be calculated by reference to the effective rate estimated to be applicable in the years of reversal.

13   A reduced rate of corporation tax applies to companies in regard to income arising from the sale of goods manufactured in the Republic of Ireland. Under present legislation the relief is for sales made in periods up to 31 December 2000. In calculating deferred tax provisions where a reduced rate applies, similar considerations to those given in the preceding paragraphs should be taken into account.

Appendix III – Illustrative examples and practical considerations

The following is for general guidance and does not form part of the [draft] Financial Reporting Standard. The best form of the disclosure will depend on individual circumstances.

Example: Statement of total recognised gains and losses

	1996	1995 as restated
	£	£
Profit for the financial year	29,000	7,000
Unrealised surplus on revaluation of property	4,000	6,000
Unrealised (loss)/gain on trade investment	(3,000)	7,000
Total recognised gains and losses relating to the year	30,000	20,000
Prior year adjustment (as explained in note x)	(10,000)	
Total gains and losses recognised since last annual report	20,000	

Example: Disclosure – defined contribution pension scheme

The company operates a defined contribution pension scheme. The assets of the scheme are held separately from those of the company in an independently administered fund. The pension cost charge represents contributions payable by the company to the fund and amounted to £50,000 (1995 £45,000). Contributions totalling £2,500 (1995 £1,500) were payable to the fund at the year-end and are included in creditors.

Example: Disclosure – defined benefit pension scheme

The company operates a pension scheme providing benefits based on final pensionable pay. The assets of the scheme are held separately from those of the company, being invested with insurance companies. Contributions to the scheme are charged to the profit and loss account so as to spread the cost of pensions over employees' working lives with the company. The contributions are determined by a qualified actuary on the basis of triennial valuations using the projected unit method. The most recent valuation was as at 31 December 1995. The assumptions that have the most significant effect on the results of the valuation are those relating to the rate of return on investments and the rate of increase in salaries and pensions. It was assumed that the investment returns would be 8 per cent per annum, that salary increases would average 6 per cent per annum and that present and future pensions would increase at the rate of 3 per cent per annum.

The pension charge for the year was £50,000 (1995 £48,000). This included £5,200 (1995 £5,000) in respect of the amortisation of experience surpluses that are being recognised over ten years, the average remaining service lives of employees.

The most recent actuarial valuation showed that the market value of the scheme's assets were £1,200,000 and that the actuarial value of those assets represented 104 per cent of the benefits that had accrued to members, after allowing for expected future increases in earnings. The contributions of the company and employees will remain at 10 per cent and 5 per cent of earnings respectively.

Practical considerations: Stocks and long-term contracts

Many of the problems involved in arriving at the amount at which stocks and long-term contracts are stated in financial statements are of a practical nature rather than resulting from matters of principle. The following paragraphs discuss some particular areas in which difficulty may be encountered.

The allocation of overheads

1   Production overheads are included in the cost of conversion together with direct labour, direct expenses and subcontracted work. This inclusion is a necessary corollary of the principle that expenditure should be included to the extent to which it has been incurred in bringing the product 'to its present location and condition'. However, all abnormal conversion costs (such as exceptional spoilage, idle capacity and other losses) that are avoidable under normal operating conditions need, for the same reason, to be excluded.

2   Where firm sales contracts have been entered into for the provision of goods or services to customer's specification, overheads relating to design, and marketing and selling costs incurred before manufacture, may be included in arriving at cost.

3   The costing methods adopted by a business are usually designed to ensure that all direct material, direct labour, direct expenses and subcontracted work are identified and charged on a reasonable and consistent basis, but problems arise on the allocation of overheads, which must usually involve the exercise of personal judgement in the selection of an appropriate convention.

4   The classification of overheads necessary to achieve this allocation takes the function of the overhead as its distinguishing characteristic (e.g., whether

it is a function of production, marketing, selling or administration), rather than whether the overhead tends to vary with time or with volume.

5 The costs of general management, as distinct from functional management, are not directly related to current production and are, therefore, excluded from the cost of conversion and, hence, from the cost of stocks and long-term contracts.

6 In the case of smaller organisations whose management may be involved in the daily administration of each of the various functions, particular problems may arise in practice in distinguishing these general management overheads. In such organisations the costs of management may fairly be allocated on suitable bases to the functions of production, marketing, selling and administration.

7 Problems may also arise in allocating the costs of central service departments, the allocation of which should depend on the function or functions that the department is serving. For example, the accounts department will normally support the following functions:

(a) production – by paying direct and indirect production wages and salaries, by controlling purchases and by preparing periodic financial statements for the production units;
(b) marketing and distribution – by analysing sales and by controlling the sales ledger;
(c) general administration – by preparing management accounts and annual financial statements and budgets, by controlling cash resources and by planning investments.

Only those costs of the accounts department that can reasonably be allocated to the production function fall to be included in the cost of conversion.

8 The allocation of overheads included in the valuation of stocks and long-term contracts needs to be based on the company's normal level of activity, taking one year with another.

The governing factor is that the cost of unused capacity should be written off in the current year. In determining what constitutes 'normal' the following factors need to be considered:

• the volume of production that the production facilities are intended by their designers and by management to produce under the working conditions (e.g., single or double shift) prevailing during the year;
• the budgeted level of activity for the year under review and for the ensuing year;
• the level of activity achieved both in the year under review and in previous years.

Although temporary changes in the load of activity may be ignored, persistent variation should lead to revision of the previous norm.

9   Where management accounts are prepared on a marginal cost basis, it will be necessary to add to the figure of stocks so arrived at the appropriate proportion of those production overheads not already included in the marginal cost.

10   The adoption of a conservative approach to the valuation of stocks and long-term contracts has sometimes been used as one of the reasons for omitting selected production overheads. In so far as the circumstances of the business require an element of prudence in determining the amount at which stocks and long-term contracts are stated, this needs to be taken into account in the determination of net realisable value and not by the exclusion from cost of selected overheads.

Methods of costing

11   It is frequently not practicable to relate expenditure to specific units of stocks and long-term contracts. The ascertainment of the nearest approximation to cost gives rise to two problems:

(a)   the selection of an appropriate method for relating costs to stocks and long-term contracts (e.g., job costing, batch costing, process costing, standard costing);

(b)   the selection of an appropriate method for calculating the related costs where a number of identical items have been purchased or made at different times (e.g., unit cost, average cost or 'first in, first out' (FIFO)).

12   In selecting the methods referred to in paragraphs 11(a) and (b) above, management must exercise judgement to ensure that the methods chosen provide the fairest practicable approximation to cost. Furthermore, where standard costs are used they need to be reviewed frequently to ensure that they bear a reasonable relationship to actual costs obtaining during the period. Methods such as base stock and 'last in, first out' (LIFO) are not usually appropriate methods of stock valuation because they often result in stocks being stated in the balance sheet at amounts that bear little relationship to recent cost levels. When this happens, not only is the presentation of current assets misleading, but there is potential distortion of subsequent results if stock levels reduce and out-of-date costs are drawn into the profit and loss account.

13   The method of arriving at cost by applying the latest purchase price to the total number of units in stock is unacceptable in principle because it is not necessarily the same as actual cost and, in times of rising prices, will result in the taking of a profit that has not been realised.

14   One method of arriving at cost, in the absence of a satisfactory costing system, is the use of selling price less an estimated profit margin. This is acceptable only if it can be demonstrated that the method gives a reasonable approximation of the actual cost.

15   In industries where the cost of minor by-products is not separable from the cost of the principal products, stocks of such by-products may be stated in accounts at their net realisable value. In this case the costs of the main products are calculated after deducting the net realisable value of the by-products.

The determination of net realisable value

16   The initial calculation of provisions to reduce stocks from cost to net realisable value may often be made by the use of formulae based on predetermined criteria. The formulae normally take account of the age, movements in the past, expected future movements and estimated scrap values of the stock, as appropriate. Whilst the use of such formulae establishes a basis for making a provision that can be consistently applied, it is still necessary for the results to be reviewed in the light of any special circumstances that cannot be anticipated in the formulae, such as changes in the state of the order book.

17   Where a provision is required to reduce the value of finished goods below cost, the stocks of the parts and sub-assemblies held for the purpose of the manufacture of such products, together with stocks on order, need to be reviewed to determine if provision is also required against such items.

18   Where stocks of spares are held for sale, special consideration of the factors in paragraph 16 will be required in the context of:

(a)   the number of units sold to which they are applicable;
(b)   the estimated frequency with which a replacement spare is required;
(c)   the expected useful life of the unit to which they are applicable.

19   Events occurring between the balance sheet date and the date of completion of the financial statements need to be considered in arriving at the net realisable value at the balance sheet date (e.g., a subsequent reduction in selling prices). However, no reduction falls to be made when the realisable value of material stocks is less than the purchase price, provided that the goods into which the materials are to be incorporated can still be sold at a profit after incorporating the materials at cost price.

The application of net realisable value

20   The principal situations in which net realisable value is likely to be less than cost are where there has been:

(a) an increase in costs or a fall in selling price;

(b) physical deterioration of stocks;

(c) obsolescence of products;

(d) a decision as part of a company's marketing strategy to manufacture and sell products at a loss;

(e) errors in production or purchasing.

Furthermore, when stocks are held that are unlikely to be sold within the turnover period normal in that company (i.e., excess stocks), the impending delay in realisation increases the risk that the situations outlined in (a)–(c) above may occur before the stocks are sold and needs to be taken into account in assessing net realisable value.

Long-term contracts

21 In ascertaining costs of long-term contracts it is not normally appropriate to include interest payable on borrowed money. However, in circumstances where sums borrowed can be identified as financing specific long-term contracts, it may be appropriate to include such related interest in cost, in which circumstances the inclusion of interest and the amount of interest so included should be disclosed in a note to the financial statements.

22 In some businesses, long-term contracts for the supply of services or manufacture and supply of goods exist where the prices are determined and invoiced according to separate parts of the contract. In these businesses the most appropriate method of reflecting profits on each contract is usually to match costs against performance of the separable parts of the contract, treating each such separable part as a separate contract. In such instances, however, future revenues from the contract need to be compared with future estimated costs and provision made for any foreseen loss.

23 Turnover (ascertained in a matter appropriate to the industry, the nature of the contracts concerned and the contractual relationship with the customer) and related costs should be recorded in the profit and loss account as contract activity progresses. Turnover may sometimes be ascertained by reference to valuation of the work carried out to date. In other cases, there may be specific points during a contract at which individual elements of work done with separately ascertainable sales and values and costs can be identified and appropriately recorded as turnover (e.g., because delivery or customer acceptance has taken place). The [draft] FRSSE does not provide a definition of turnover in view of the different methods of ascertaining it as outlined above.

24 In determining whether the stage has been reached at which it is appropriate to recognise profit, account should be taken of the nature of the business concerned. It is necessary to define the earliest point for each particular contract before which no profit is taken up, the overriding principle being that there can be no attributable profit until the outcome of a contract can reasonably be foreseen. Of the profit that in the light of all the circumstances can be foreseen with a reasonable degree of certainty to arise on completion of the contract, there should be regarded as earned to date only that part which prudently reflects the amount of work performed to date. The method used for taking up such profit needs to be consistently applied.

25 In calculating the total estimated profit on the contract, it is necessary to take into account not only the total costs to date and the total estimated further costs to completion (calculated by reference to the same principles as were applied to cost to date) but also the estimated future costs of rectification and guarantee work, and any other future work to be undertaken under the terms of the contract. These are then compared with the total sales value of the contract. In considering future costs, it is necessary to have regard to likely increases in wages and salaries, to likely increases in the price of raw materials and to rises in general overheads, so far as these items are not recoverable from the customer under the terms of the contract.

26 Where approved variations have been made to a contract in the course of it and the amount to be received in respect of these variations has not yet been settled and is likely to be a material factor in the outcome, it is necessary to make a conservative estimate of the amount likely to be received and this is then treated as part of the total sales value. On the other hand, allowance needs to be made for foreseen claims or penalties payable arising out of delays in completion or from other causes.

27 The settlement of claims arising from circumstances not envisaged in the contract or arising as an indirect consequence of approved variations is subject to a high level of uncertainty relating to the outcome of future negotiations. In view of this, it is generally prudent to recognise receipts in respect of such claims only when negotiations have reached an advanced stage and there is sufficient evidence of the acceptability of the claim in principle to the purchaser, with an indication of the amount involved also being available.

28 The amounts to be included in the year's profit and loss account will be both the appropriate amount of turnover and the associated costs of achieving that turnover, to the extent that these amounts exceed corresponding amounts recognised in previous years. The estimated outcome of a contract that extends over several accounting years will nearly always vary in the light of changes in circumstances and for this reason the result of the year will not necessarily represent the proportion of the total profit on the contract that is appropriate to the amount of work carried out in the period; it may also reflect the effect of changes in circumstances during the year that affect the total profit estimated to accrue on completion.

Practical considerations – Debt factoring

29   To assist in using paragraphs 89–91 of the [draft] FRSSE, the following table is provided.

Indications that derecognition is appropriate (debts are not an asset of the seller)	Indications that a linked presentation is appropriate	Indications that a separate presentation is appropriate (debts are an asset of the seller)
Transfer is for a single, non-returnable fixed sum.	Some non-returnable proceeds received, but seller has rights to further sums from the factor (or vice versa) whose amount depends on whether or when debtors pay.	Finance cost varies with speed of collection of debts, e.g.: – by adjustment to consideration for original transfer; or – subsequent transfers priced to recover costs of earlier transfers.
There is no recourse to the seller for losses.	There is either no recourse for losses, or such recourse has a fixed monetary ceiling.	There is full recourse to the seller for losses.
Factor is paid all amounts received from the factored debts (and no more). Seller has no rights to further sums from the factor.	Factor is paid only out of amounts collected from the factored debts, and seller has no right or obligation to repurchase debts.	Seller is required to repay amounts received from the factor on or before a set date, regardless of timing or amounts of collections from debtors.

Appendix IV – Compliance with International Accounting Standards

1   The International Accounting Standards Committee (IASC) recognises in its Framework document that 'the objective of financial statements is to provide information about the financial position, performance and changes in financial position of an enterprise that is useful to a wide range of users in making economic decisions'.

2   This objective is shared by the Board, which has a similar objective for financial statements in Chapter 1 of its draft Statement of Principles for Financial Reporting.

3   Furthermore, as part of the Board's support for IASC, each FRS contains a section explaining how it relates to the International Accounting Standard dealing with the same topic.

4   There is no international equivalent for this [draft] FRSSE. Therefore no comparison has been provided.

Appendix V – The development of the Exposure Draft

History

1 For many years there has been different reporting by different types of company: the requirements for public companies have been more onerous than for private companies and those for larger companies more onerous than for smaller companies. In particular, the provisions of the EC Fourth and Seventh Company Law Directives have been adopted in the UK, through which the disclosure requirements for large, medium-sized and small companies have been varied, allowing small companies more extensive exemptions both in the abbreviated accounts to be filed with the Registrar of Companies and in the statutory accounts for shareholders.

2 The application of accounting standards for smaller companies has also been an issue for standard-setters. The Board's predecessor, the Accounting Standards Committee (ASC), set up a Working Party in 1986 to consider the issue. Its findings, which were reported in Technical Release 690 issued in 1988, were that 'there is no evidence to suggest that, in general, small companies find compliance with accounting standards unduly burdensome'. This Technical Release was followed up with TR706 from the ASC which accepted that in specific circumstances it was appropriate to exempt small entities from certain provisions of accounting standards. Where exemption was merited, the ASC proposed a relaxation for all entities other than:

- public limited companies;
- companies that had public limited companies as subsidiaries; and
- other reporting entities that were required to prepare true and fair accounts and exceeded ten times the qualifying conditions for a company to be treated as medium-sized under section 247 of the Companies Act 1985.

The effect of this third condition would have been potentially widespread, as it caught companies with turnover in excess of £112 million. As events turned out, such differentiation was used only in SSAP 13 (as revised in 1989) on research and development and SSAP 25 on segmental reporting.

3 In the 1990s, the momentum to reduce the burdens on business has continued. The Board, prompted by this consideration, asked the Consultative Committee of Accountancy Bodies (CCAB) to establish a Working Party to examine the issue and to undertake wide consultation thereon. This recognised that:

- the debate on the application of accounting standards to smaller entities has never been satisfactorily resolved and that exemptions could continue to be made available on a piecemeal basis;
- the law in this area was developing and, in particular, the Companies Act 1985 (Accounts of Small and Medium-Sized Enterprises and Publication

253

of Accounts in ECUs) Regulations 1992 (SI 1992/2452) were issued in 1992; and

● FRSs were likely to continue to be relatively lengthy documents to cope with the business complexities associated with larger entities.

4   The CCAB Working Party issued a Consultative Document in November 1994. This proposed that, with the exception of the accounting standards and UITF Abstracts noted below, the Board should exempt from compliance with accounting standards and Abstracts all entities that met the Companies Act definition of a small company. The accounting standards and UITF Abstracts that would continue to apply would have been:

SSAP 4	'Accounting for government grants'
SSAP 9	'Stocks and long-term contracts'
SSAP 13	'Accounting for research and development'
SSAP 17	'Accounting for post balance sheet events'
SSAP 18	'Accounting for contingencies'
UITF Abstract 7	'True and fair view override disclosures'.

5   In response to that Consultative Document 112 letters of comment were received. While the comments indicated support for the use of the small companies threshold and for some change to the present system whereby small entities were required to comply with almost all accounting standards, there was no clear support for the proposal of piecemeal application of a limited number of standards. In examining the comments, a number of recurrent themes were noted, including the need for guidance on measurement issues and the suggestion that a codification of all standards should be undertaken as well as a comprehensive review of those standards that were perceived as needing revision or updating, particularly in the context of their application to smaller entities. On the latter point, the amount of time needed for this codification and review was recognised, as was the observation that it might not provide a complete solution for the issues faced by smaller entities.

6   Prompted by the comments received, the proposals in the DTI's Consultative Document 'Accounting Simplifications' issued in May 1995 and the wish to focus on the needs of smaller entities, the CCAB Working Party proposed in its Paper 'Designed to fit', published in December 1995, that there should be a specific Financial Reporting Standard for Smaller Entities (the FRSSE). To demonstrate that this approach was feasible, practical and capable of delivering benefits to those involved with financial statements for smaller entities, a draft FRSSE was included in 'Designed to fit'.

7   Over 100 letters of comment were received in response to 'Designed to fit'. These responses indicated general support for the promulgation of a FRSSE that might be applied by small companies and groups, as defined in companies legislation. Accordingly, the CCAB Working Party recommended to the Board that it should issue, as part of its due process, an Exposure Draft containing the proposed FRSSE, amended as appropriate to incorporate comments made on the draft contained in 'Designed to fit'.

Link with companies legislation

8   The proposal to link use of the FRSSE with accounts drawn up in Great Britain under Schedule 8 to the Companies Act 1985* is continued in the Exposure Draft for the following reasons:

- it would allow the establishment of a clearly distinguishable regime, i.e., the relevant statutory Schedule and the FRSSE. This point is of increasing relevance as, in July 1996, the DTI issued a Consultative Document on a redrafted Schedule 8, which will contain all of the provisions applying to small companies;
- it would create the link with the current Schedule 8 provisions on a true and fair view, which may be of assistance to standard-setters and others in justifying different disclosure and any simplified measurement regime; and
- if the words 'true and fair view … as applicable to small companies' currently adopted by some auditors were to be adopted more widely, it would limit the 'expectation gap' as readers would be on notice that these were Schedule 8 and FRSSE financial statements. On this point, the Exposure Draft suggests that the directors highlight the use of the FRSSE in the note appearing after the balance sheet, which explains that the directors have taken advantage of these special exemptions provided by companies legislation applicable to small companies.

Application to small groups

9   Commentators on 'Designed to fit' asked that the FRSSE should be capable of application to small groups. Although those commentators were in a minority, the CCAB Working Party considered how the FRSSE could be made capable of application to groups. To repeat all provisions applicable to groups within the FRSSE would have virtually doubled its length. Accordingly, the Working Party preferred to extend the FRSSE in certain areas and then require small groups to follow those accounting standards and UITF Abstracts that deal with consolidated financial statements.

10   The Exposure Draft is drafted to be capable of application to small groups. However, the Working Party took the view that the FRSSE should

---

* *The equivalent legislation in Northern Ireland is Schedule 8 to the Companies (Northern Ireland) Order 1986 and in the Republic of Ireland is sections 10–12 of the Companies (Amendment) Act 1986.*

not be made capable of application to groups, on the grounds that such entities in practice rarely prepare statutory group accounts, and that to cater for the few who did would complicate the FRSSE unnecessarily. Potentially such complexities could hinder the development of the FRSSE as a document providing clear guidance on the financial statements of small companies. Therefore, the Working Party agreed that the views of commentators on this issue should be sought. The Board does not have a strong view on this issue and would therefore welcome respondents' views.

Cash flow statements

11   The draft FRSSE in 'Designed to fit' proposed that a simplified cash flow statement should be required for smaller entities. While the Working Party's membership was split on the issue, the proposal was included to obtain commentators' views. A clear majority of commentators favoured continuing the exemption from preparation of a cash flow statement granted to small entities by FRS 1, although some commentators, representing main users of financial statements, were strongly opposed. Some commentators also noted that a summary cash flow statement would be of extremely limited use and suggested that if such a statement were to be required then it should be done comprehensively. Consistently with the views of the majority of commentators, the Exposure Draft does not propose any cash flow disclosures but the Board would welcome comment on this issue.

Related party disclosures

12   When FRS 8 'Related Party Disclosures' was published in October 1995, the Board noted that it was aware of the work of the CCAB Working Party. Concern had been expressed that if small companies were to be exempt from the requirements of FRS 8 in advance of the outcome of this work, some transactions that would normally be disclosed could be hidden, using the exemption as justification. Accordingly, the Board decided that the FRS should apply to all financial statements that are intended to give a true and fair view, with no exemption for small companies.

13   In reaching this conclusion, the Board noted that Parts II and III of Schedule 6 to the Companies Act 1985 apply equally to companies of all sizes and are concerned mainly with dealings in favour of directors and connected persons. These provisions overlapped in many respects with the disclosure requirements of FRS 8; however, the FRS was broader in scope and, in particular, expressed more clearly than the statute the spirit of Schedule 6. It also clarified, to the benefit of both preparers and auditors, the disclosures necessary to meet the fundamental requirement that accounts should give a true and fair view.

14   Accordingly, the CCAB Working Party, whose members were evenly divided on the issue, agreed to reflect the main requirements of FRS 8 in its

draft FRSSE published in December 1995. In response, a clear majority of commentators argued that these provisions on related party disclosures were unnecessary given that the statute would already pick up dealings in favour of directors and connected persons. Furthermore, if there was a material transaction with a related party, possibly executed at a value other than fair value, then reference might be made to paragraph 3 of the Exposure Draft and in particular its provision that if there was any doubt as to whether applying any provision of the FRSSE would be sufficient to give a true and fair view, then adequate explanation should be given in the notes to the accounts of the transaction or arrangement concerned and the treatment adopted. Accordingly, the CCAB Working Party recommended to the Board that there should be no explicit related party disclosures in the Exposure Draft. However, the Board, having noted particular views that application of specific related party disclosures is often more important in respect of smaller entities than others has concluded at this time that the main provisions extracted from FRS 8 should continue to be reflected in the FRSSE. Comment on this issue is invited. For the avoidance of doubt, it should however be noted that until FRS 8 is amended it continues to apply to all financial statements intended to give a true and fair view.

Debt factoring and FRS 5

15   The [draft] FRSSE requires that regard should be had to the substance of any arrangement or transaction, or series of such, into which an entity has entered. But it does not contain the extensive discussion in FRS 5 'Reporting the Substance of Transactions' on reflecting the substance of transactions. This is because small entities generally do not enter into complex transactions. However, debt factoring is a common feature of such entities and accordingly the provisions, principally in FRS 5's Application Notes, are likely to be of value to small entities in treating factored debts. Accordingly, the necessary guidance in FRS 5 has been included in the Exposure Draft.

Relationship with other ASB documents

16   In 'Designed to fit' it was made clear that the proposed FRSSE should be read in the context of the Board's Foreword to Accounting Standards. That paper also dealt with the question of the relationship between the FRSSE and other accounting standards and UITF Abstracts. In particular, it considered the question of whether, in the absence of guidance within the FRSSE, preparers and auditors would be required to follow all other SSAPs, FRSs and UITF Abstracts to the extent that they provided guidance on transactions of relevance to the smaller entity. The Working Party's view, formulated after consultation with legal advisers and others involved in the standard-setting process, was that users' expectation was that financial statements would be prepared using accepted practice. If a practice was clearly established and accepted, it should be followed unless there were

good reasons to depart from it. Accordingly, preparers and auditors would have regard to SSAPs, FRSs and UITF Abstracts, not as mandatory documents, but as a means of establishing current practice.

17   Some commentators asked that there should be specific cross-references to other SSAPs, FRSs and UITF Abstracts within the FRSSE. The CCAB Working Party and the Board have rejected this request because such cross-references would mean that preparers and auditors would have to consider those standards in all cases, as well as the FRSSE, thereby lengthening checklists and adding to the burden. Furthermore, it is recognised that as new FRSs are issued that amend generally accepted accounting practice as it applies to larger entities it may not be appropriate for such rules to apply to smaller entities. An example that has been frequently cited, but on which the Board has not established a firm position at this time, is that some of the likely proposals on marking to market fixed interest instruments, while appropriate for larger entities, would not be appropriate for smaller entities. Because generally accepted accounting practice had not been established for all in this area then there would not be an expectation that smaller entities should have regard to such a new rule.

18   The Board accepts that the [draft] FRSSE is not comprehensive and that there may be issues of general application on which guidance will be sought. Accordingly, it will be a responsibility of the advisory committee to be established by the Board to consider the needs of preparers and users and to propose amendments to the FRSSE as appropriate in the future.

Index

References are to chapters 1–8 and are to paragraph